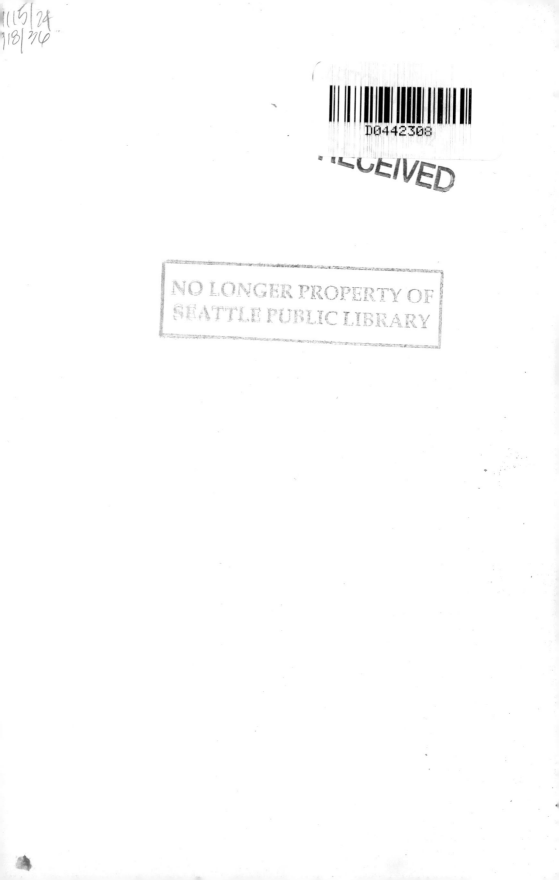

JUDY GARLAND

Other Books by Michael Freedland

JUDY GARLAND

The Other Side of the Rainbow

Michael Freedland

NOTE! THE WRITER OF THIS BOOK IS
'ENGLISH

BOOKS

Picture credits
page 1: Bettman /Corbis
page 2: top: Rex Features, bottom: Bettman /Corbis
page 3: top: Bettman /Corbis, bottom: Pictorial Press/Alamy
page 4: top: bottom: Bettman /Corbis, bottom: Bettman /Corbis
page 5: Hulton Archive/Getty Images
page 6: top: Pictorial Press /Alamy, bottom: Popperfoto/Getty Images
page 7: top: AF Archive /Alamy, bottom: Rex Features
Page 8: top: Bettman /Corbis, bottom: Hulton Archive/Getty Images

First published in Great Britain in 2010 by
JR Books, 10 Greenland Street, London NW1 0ND
www.jrbooks.com

Copyright © 2010 Michael Freedland

A catalogue record for this book is available from the British Library.

ISBN 978-1-907532-09-2

3 5 7 9 10 8 6 4 2

Printed by the MPG Books Group

FOR FIONA
Whose courage is matched only by her love
and wonderful personality

Contents

Acknowledgements

L et me start with an explanation: this is not a conventional biography of a great star. Most star biographies, unless put together with the aid of Google and/or a pair of scissors and a pot of paste (which was the only way some people used to write books about other people), feature interviews with famous personalities. There have been a number of Judy Garland biographies, so there seemed little point in writing another one that was just rehashing what readers knew already.

This book will, naturally enough, outline the events of her life in between its personal stories – which explains how this book is different. It concentrates on people whose names mean little or nothing to the average person walking into a bookshop. But these were the people who knew Judy best. Not mainly the other stars, although a few names do crop up occasionally, but the ones who worked with her, loved her, were exasperated by her, the folks who grew up with her in Grand Rapids, Minnesota, and then in Lancaster, California, as well as in Hollywood, London and on Broadway. Even, in one memorable case, an elderly lady who remembered Judy's parents better than she did the girl born Frances Ethel Gumm, who from the age of two was determined to sing.

That is the thing about small-town USA. The people living there, some for generations, remember the little details. They recall the buildings that once stood where a supermarket now sells the necessities of a life the Gumm family couldn't even dream of one day needing. They have memories of little Frances Ethel's first performances in public as though they were describing a show they had seen at a local playhouse just a few days before. Of course, when one of their own becomes a star as big as Judy, it is easy for memories to go into exaggeration mode. I might have made allowances for that – except that I treated this project rather like a trial. What I did, in fact, was to call witnesses and then sum up the evidence. No jury would convict on the basis of some of the stories, stories which might surprise you, but I am content to publish them. It is clear from the people who went into my metaphorical witness box that even the most remarkable tales fit in with the personality I am discussing.

So that was how I called my evidence. But what of the charge? Judy Garland is on trial to answer the claim that she was one of the greatest entertainers of the 20th century. On the following pages, the prosecuting counsel and the judge sum up the case that will be put before you.

It is presented with the help of the following, who submitted to my cross-examination – some of them originally in the BBC radio series *The Judy Garland Trail*, which followed similar rules as to whose evidence was to be sought and accepted. There were no star names then either. As for this book, I didn't want the glamour and the conceits of stardom to colour the final picture. Or the final verdict.

Therefore, allow me to thank the people who gave of their time to make these projects work as well as I wanted them to. Let me begin with the name of Neil Rosser, my producer on the Radio Two Garland show as on many more broadcast programmes. Then, Barbara Paskin, who set up most of the interviews. Her help was more than merely invaluable; it was essential and I remain grateful. The people who were interviewed by me, specifically for the radio show and this book and on other occasions, include: Ray Aghayan; the late Fred Astaire; the late Irving Berlin; the late Betsy Blair; Buddy Bregman; the late Sammy Cahn; Lilah Crowe; Maureen Davis; Jean Denzil; Peri Fleischman; Joe Franklin; Brian Glanvill; Frank de Gregoria; Norma Gurber; Bill Harbach; Howard Hirsch; Sam Irvine; the late George Jessel; John Kelsch; the late Gene Kelly; the late Alan King; the late Burton Lane;

Vernon Larson; Lorna Luft; the late Sid Luft; Martin McQuade; Ian Maksik; Jerry Maren; Daphne Myron; the late Donald O'Connor; Stevie Phillips; Al Poland; Meredith Ponedel; Paul Rabwin; the late Ginger Rogers; the late David Rose; George Schlatter; Ken Sefton; Glen Settle; Irma Storey; George Sunga; Irene Swanson; Dennis Sykes; the late Sophie Tucker; Judy Van Herfen; Charles Walters; Margaret Whiting; Chris Woodward; and Bob Wynn.

INTRODUCTION

A Girl, a Woman and a Rainbow

The real truth dawned on Brian Glanvill with a call from a London florist. What, the caller asked, did he want to do with the bouquet he had ordered to be sent to Judy Garland? He had intended the flowers as a good-luck wish to go to his idol, the one for whom he had forgone meals and sleep and because of whom he had walked miles in the middle of the night – and never regretted a moment of it.

Now, the bouquet would travel with Judy from Heathrow Airport to New York. Along with her coffin. It was June 1969.

The news had come over the radio the day before. Brian, a highly articulate actor in children's plays, cried. The call from the florist underlined his sorrow.

It was a scenario enacted all over the world. Judy wasn't only a great star, she was, to those who proudly call themselves fans, part of their very existence. In show business itself, she was an icon. As George Jessel, the actor and public speaker who rejoiced in the title of America's Toastmaster General and the man who actually gave her the name that put her at the top of the world of entertainment, put it: 'This little girl is a combination of Nora Bayes [a big star of the Ziegfeld Follies], Danny Kaye and Al Jolson.'

The joining of her name with that of Al Jolson was something that constantly occurred both in her lifetime and afterwards. Jolson called himself The World's Greatest Entertainer and never heard anyone argue with him. Yet Alan King, the comedian who shared the bill with Judy on countless live engagements, not only knew how apt the comparison was, he thought she would have won any

1

competition between them. He himself had seen Jolson at work and knew that Enrico Caruso refused to follow the then blackface singer at a concert (hardly surprising, for when Al went on after him at a Metropolitan Opera war bonds benefit in 1917, he threw out his arms and declared, 'You ain't heard nothing yet'). Judy would have had no qualms. 'Jolson would have opened for Judy,' King said.

Just days after Garland's death in London, fans lined the pavements around the Frank E. Campbell funeral home in New York's East 81st Street. Inside, her fellow artists wept as much as Brian Glanvill did 3,000 miles away. Mickey Rooney, her co-star in all those 'Let's make a show' black-and-white movies, threw himself on to her white casket – painted white on the instructions of Judy's mentor Kay Thompson, who said: 'We're from MGM. Just do it.'

To this day, people in the business still talk about Judy Garland in the present sense. As Bob Wynn, who was creative consultant for her television shows, put it to me: 'The lady is a performer beyond belief.'

Nevertheless, this was a woman with problems. Stevie Phillips, who acted as Judy's minder when she first went on the road, did not hold back when I asked her to sum up the woman she knew so well. 'Off stage,' she said, 'Judy was a car wreck.' A car wreck who could summon up support from a rescue team comprising some of the most famous names in her industry.

But, to extend the metaphor further, eventually the ambulances came too late for Brian Glanvill's flowers to reach her in time.

It is not easy to explain the complications of being Judy Garland. Obviously, some people see her as merely an example of the problems we read about each day that come with perhaps too much fame, too much money, too much adulation. Judy had all that, but her story was, despite all the apparent similarities, unique. Unlike other stars she was not always arrogant in pushing her ever-changing weight around, rather it is obvious she laboured under an intense inferiority complex. Unlike other singers, the quality of her voice varied as frequently as her performances.

Unlike other women with drink and drug problems, she showed extreme kindness along with amazingly precise cries for help.

This then is the story of Judy Garland, a.k.a. Frances Ethel Gumm, told mainly through the memories of men and women who actually knew her.

CHAPTER ONE

Grand Rapids

It's a charming little place, Grand Rapids. Grand Rapids, Minnesota, that is, not the one in Michigan, where the word 'Grand' is perhaps a little more appropriate. There is little grand about this miniature town, which still likes to think about the days when it was even tinier. There are no big, impressive buildings, no boulevards with fashionable shops. The place of government there still has the words 'Village Hall' inscribed over its portals and if you talk to the older citizens round and about, that was the way it should be. To them, Grand Rapids should still be a village, and the days when it was a village is the place that they remember most affectionately.

That was when Frank Gumm ran the local movie-cum-variety theatre where his wife Ethel played the piano in the pit, providing fast runs along the keyboard for a chase around the prairie or soft, smoochy love tunes for when Rudolph Valentino made love to Gloria Swanson. The really exciting days at the New Grand theatre was when it was able to offer live entertainment, with Ethel herself dancing, or singing duets with her husband. As Lilah Crowe, who runs one of the two museums in Grand Rapids – an achievement in itself – put it to me: 'For a little town like Grand Rapids to have a theatre at all, let alone a variety theatre, it was impressive.'

They had ambitions, these Gumms; at first they took their act on the road. But somehow the performances of Jack and Virginia Lee, Sweet Southern Singers, didn't ring too many bells with the people who paid ten cents or so over a box-office counter – even if Frank at least lived up to his billing. He had a much-praised voice and

4

was a Southerner, born in Tennessee, which years later would be known as the birthplace of rock'n'roll.

Ethel could only have called herself a southerner by association. She had been born in Michigan but had gone with her family to live in Superior, Wisconsin. It was there that Frank met her, after a time working in theatres and performing his own vaudeville singing act whenever he could get a job. When he met Ethel, he concluded that they had it made as a double act both privately and professionally. Neither would work out quite according to plan. They were good, but not brilliant enough to be noticed by others in the business, although the people who went to their shows probably didn't know that. The chances of seeing and hearing professional acts at all in such a small village were rare and so, when they went on stage, they were received enthusiastically.

What they sang, tunes like Stephen Foster's 'Beautiful Dreamer' or the sedate 'Come into the Garden, Maude', couldn't have been further away from the numbers people like Elvis Presley would be introducing in Frank's home state 40 years later. They had the sense to realise that they weren't going to cut any ice on the national scene and concentrated their talents on the village where they had made their home soon after their wedding in January 1914.

Not that they only performed in the New Grand. An advertisement of the time proudly announced: 'Mr. and Mrs. F. Gumm are to sing at an entertainment at State University in Minneapolis next Friday evening.' It was a big hall and at that time they might possibly have concluded that, despite all, they were on their way. They weren't. Entertaining at local masonic lodges was probably enough.

When their children arrived, there was little doubt that the kids would follow in their voice prints. As soon as they were old enough to produce tunes, their daughters Mary Jane (who became known as Suzie, born a year after the Gumms' wedding) and Virginia (two years younger, and who for reasons nobody has ever been able to explain would always be known as Jimmy, or Jimmie) joined them on the stage of the New Grand.

It didn't surprise anyone living in Grand Rapids who knew anything about the Gumms – and it was the sort of place where everybody knew everybody and everybody's business, too – when the smallest and youngest of the family of entertainers, Frances Ethel, aged two, became part of the act as well. Early on in her career, she would tell an interviewer: 'Everything I remember about Grand Rapids has charm and gaiety.' It was, she said, 'a beautiful town'.

But it might never have happened had it not been for a young doctor called Marcus (always known as Marc) Rabwin. In fact, if it hadn't been for him, there might never have been anyone at all called either Frances Ethel Gumm – or Judy Garland.

Rabwin had a relationship with Judy that was rather like that of a fairy godfather. For both of them that was almost an understatement. He was younger than Frank, but was actually *his* godfather – which would have made him Judy's god-grandfather (it was plainly not a 'godparenthood' that would have been approved by his church – but the reverse of the generations seems to sum up how each felt for the other). They first met in the midst of a business deal that other, older, more cynical men would have considered something to avoid. How a medical student and a man running a movie theatre would find anything in common is not all that obvious. Until, that is, you get to realise that Frank needed what Marc had to offer. Just how much so would become evident in the years that followed their initial meeting – which happened simply because Marc was hungry. For the moment, this had nothing to do with either sickness or medicine. But before long, it certainly would involve just that – while also helping Frank Gumm develop his business.

The young student had to divide his time between anatomy lessons and elementary surgical procedures and a part-time job he hoped would bring him enough money for subsistence while he was attending lectures. He was selling and renting films – a commodity that was essential in the movie theatre business. Frank was a willing buyer. But others in the trade were finding Gumm a very difficult customer indeed to deal with.

Marc's son, Paul Rabwin, told me about it, sitting in the Hollywood studio where he was producing the TV series *The X Files* and the US version of *Life on Mars*. According to him, it started like this: 'Dad was in his early years in medical school. He worked for the Hutchinson Company, delivering films, taking a train and going to various movie houses in Minnesota. He was warned about this crotchety guy named Gumm who had a theatre and wouldn't buy anything. He was a pain in the rear end. My father went to him just the same. I think [the other salesmen] had been put off because [Frank] was ill and didn't know it. They hit it off.'

And that was partly because this so-far unqualified medical man did a bit of on-the-spot diagnosis while in the process of discussing the merits of the current Western or Charlie Chaplin comedy. 'My father goes to sell him the one-reelers or whatever it was he was selling and he diagnosed that Frank Gumm had thyroid disease,' said Paul.

He realised before long that Grand Rapids was the centre of what was known as 'goitre country'. As Paul told me: 'I don't know if they knew about dangers from nearby chemical plants or if it had something to do with the water there. It's possible that the immigrants who moved into the area had a genetic marker.'

Whatever the reason, Frank Gumm had a goitre on his neck removed as a result of Marc Rabwin's intervention – 'by this young doctor [who was not yet a doctor] making this discovery. He was treated for thyroid disease which nobody else had ever suggested. So suddenly, he has got a friend. This relationship continued.' Paul added: 'I've never heard an unkind word about my father. He gave off an aura of kindness, gentleness and goodness, and that was why the entire Gumm family embraced him.' It was the perfect story of the country doctor and his patients, the kind who knew not only all their illnesses, but their likes and dislikes, their joys and their tragedies.

But Marc himself couldn't have known that when he knocked on the 'crotchety' man's door. When he discovered Frank wasn't really crotchety at all, but ill, it was the start of a beautiful friendship

– even though it was one that surprised a lot of people who knew of Frank's personality.

As Paul said: 'For some reason, they hit it off.'

As a result, the Rabwin–Gumm friendship involved more than merely treating his goitre and selling a few films on the side. Rabwin qualified and became Frank's first stop when he needed advice on a more professional basis. It really proved its value when Ethel, already mother of two daughters from whom she expected so much, fell pregnant again. Could the young doctor help?

According to Paul: 'Frank and Ethel came to my father [to say] they couldn't afford to have another child. My father, very vehemently, insisted that if Ethel went through with an abortion, she would not survive it. He said: "As a doctor, I don't recommend it and I'm telling you that if you have this other child, you will be grateful." That was how Judy was born.'

Rabwin wasn't the doctor at the birth. That honour went to a certain Dr J.H. Burnett, who assisted in the delivery at the local hospital.

The date was 10 June 1922. It was one that Dr Marc Rabwin had no need to inscribe in his diary. 'Judy always felt that, through my father, she was alive. Judy was just devoted to him.'

The fans of Judy Garland throughout the world have their own reasons for being devoted to him, too, not least those old folks in Grand Rapids who experienced the first of those Frances Ethel Gumm shows.

They were events that people today in their late eighties and nineties in Grand Rapids remember with the kind of affection usually reserved for moments from their own family histories, events most would have long forgotten, but which come back to mind with a nudge and a push, prompting the phrase, 'Oh yeah!'

There are a lot of 'Oh yeah!' moments in Grand Rapids as people walk along the wide roads or shelter in the parks under the trees, mostly white pine, which give the city/town/village its special character. It's trees that made Grand Rapids – apart, that is, from Frances Ethel Gumm. They provided the raw material for the logging industry, which benefited from its closeness to the source of the Mississippi River, just 100 miles away to the north. This is the great Mississippi about which the Southern Singers crooned. Not that you would think it if you walked by its banks near Grand Rapids. There it is barely a stream, a stream people walk across, using the pebbles on the riverbed to try to keep their feet dry.

In American terms those 100 miles mean the river source is virtually round the corner. It was the dampness in the air and the white pine trees that made Grand Rapids so suitable a site for Blandin's paper mill, which since 1916 had provided much of the employment in the area. Old Mr Blandin left his fortune to Grand Rapids rather than give it to his son, whom he considered far too concerned about the frivolous things in life.

The town loves to claim Judy Garland as its favourite daughter. The museum put up by the local historical society includes pictures of Judy, not just when she lived in Grand Rapids but in her career as a star. The brightly lit museum − not at all like a conventional home of historical artefacts − has a replica pair of red shoes, copies of the ones she wore in *The Wizard of Oz*. 'There were four original pairs,' said John Kelsch, who runs the main Judy Garland Museum. 'Two are in private collections, one is in the Smithsonian museum − and we ourselves had the fourth pair, which had been loaned to us by a private collector and was then stolen. It was a terrible experience.'

The *Wizard* film is undoubtedly the most obvious of Judy Garland's career milestones on view at the museum today − a giant cut out of the Wizard himself (played by Frank Morgan), the tin man (Jack Haley), the cowardly lion (Bert Lahr), the scarecrow (Ray Bolger) and little Dorothy Gale (Judy) in her gingham dress dominates the outer corridor. The most expensive item is the ebony open carriage used in the movie, which had originally been made for Abraham Lincoln and also featured in 200 Civil War films.

Strictly speaking, you don't need to go further than this and one other centre to know how Judy Garland spent her early childhood. But it helps to talk to the people still around in Grand Rapids who recall her.

Lilah Crowe's museum is in the old yellow-fronted Central

School, which has been converted into a big collection of local memorabilia – not least a room devoted to what they call Garlandia. It has Frank's golf clubs in a frayed leather case alongside a picture of him wearing traditional golfing plus fours, and Frances Ethel's cradle. The women of Grand Rapids knew all about that cradle – it was shared around the mothers of the village. 'It was a basic cradle, not an ornate one with lots of lace around it,' said Lilah Crowe. She is perhaps proudest of all of the yellow brick road outside – Judy fans are invited to buy bricks ($59 for two lines; $69 for three) on which they can inscribe the names of Garland films or songs, or merely those of the people who paid for them.

Inside the museum library is a real rarity – a picture of Judy Garland in the nude, completely naked from head to foot. She was a year old at the time.

Another picture of a slightly older Judy appeared in newspapers a few years later: 'Here's Judy Garland, Young and Lovely and here's the beauty soap she uses every day – Lux.' There's almost every commercial record Judy Garland ever made and tapes of radio shows. But the really interesting items are the older ones. There's a review published in the local *Itaska Independent* (Grand Rapids is in Itaska County) of a play called *Don't Park Here*. The part of Mrs O'Terry was played by 'Mrs. F.A. Gumm'.

The Gumms lived in a white two-storey clapboard house with a black door, three big windows downstairs and a balcony surrounding the top floor with two big windows behind the balcony rails. It had been built in 1892 by a retired sea captain called Shuck (Frances Ethel's best friend was one of his descendants, Maggy Shuck). The house has twice been moved from its original site, but it stands today on a spacious lawn, with as many trees as could be planted without disturbing the view of the home. It was a complicated business, moving that house. 'It was slowly jacked up,' John Kelsch remembers (not something that could have been done with a brick-built house, but for this one holes were drilled in the foundations).

The house has now been furnished in conjunction with the Judy

Garland Museum next door, just as they imagined it would have been when the Gumms lived there. Actually, it is more than just a matter of imagination. There were enough photographs of the house from the time when the family were in residence to avoid the necessity of guesswork.

Go into the living room and you are instantly transported to the home where Frances Ethel crawled around the furniture and toddled her way up and down the stairs, a glass of malted milk in her sticky hands (she was addicted to marmalade). On the staircase is a framed message: 'Baby Gumm and her sisters rehearsed on this landing.' Not far away is the first known photograph of Judy, a babe in arms.

This is the background to Judy's early life and, more significantly, typical 1920s Middle America – from the specially commissioned flowered wallpaper, just like the one the Gumms had, to the Victrola gramophone, complete with a disc of the Duncan Sisters, generally regarded as the idols of the sisters living in this house. Frank Gumm's rocking chair has pride of place, and nearby is a baby grand piano. As an example of how much in tune they really were with everything new and bright and beautiful, they had a radio set with a detachable horn speaker, a real rarity since a radio tower serving Grand Rapids only went up in 1922, the year Frances Ethel Gumm was born.

In the window of the living room is a sewing machine. Ethel made all her children's stage clothes, which was considered part of her work.

It's the dining room that gives evidence of Frank's own business life – an adding machine (also state of the art technology in the 1920s) sits next to a typewriter. He used to write articles for the local *Independent*, in which he featured his family 700 times in the course of a nine-year period. He only wrote pleasant things – which distinctly did not say anything about his daughters' real failings: their hysterical fear of thunderstorms or the parts of the house they would choose to hide in when the lightning turned the sky outside an eerie orange.

You can see a toilet and a tiny bath in a room adjoining the

Gumm seniors' bedroom, but a fascinating aspect of the house is its summer kitchen – the wood-burning stove used in the winter scullery would have made the home far too hot in which to live from June to August – that was re-created from an old insurance map found at the local courthouse. It is there that the icebox stands or, rather, the ice chest. What was actually called the icebox stood outside the house – with a number placed by the side of it. This told the iceman how many blocks he should deliver on his daily trips, just as the milkman would bring bottles to the door (or, in the early days of the Gumms' residence, how many ladles of milk from his churns).

The Gumms plainly believed in buying the best they could. The porch has the kind of toys that Frances Ethel would have played with – when not sleeping there on a hot summer's evening.

That all this can still be seen in the 21st century, almost 90 years after 'Baby' Gumm was born, is due to the last person living in the house, Pat Casey. He offered it to the historical society and a benefactor living in Minneapolis paid the $50,000 bill as a tribute to the only star anyone knows to have been born in their town (Bob Dylan came from Hibbing, 30 miles away in the Duluth area, to which the whole Gumm family would travel for occasional shows).

If by some miracle Judy Garland could be transported back to the town, there are few sights there that she would recognise. The hospital where she was born, built in 1917, the year America entered World War One, has long been replaced, although the structure is still standing, all its windows smashed. She might point out the steeple of one of the churches to which her family never went, she might recognise the remaining hotel still standing. What she would surely appreciate is what John Kelsch says is almost the logo of what he still likes to think of as his village, the blue lake surrounded by . . . yes, more trees.

The Gumm family loved going there on Sunday afternoons, almost as much as they would enjoy the county fair, with its animal shows, vegetable growing contests and, most exciting of all, its horseback demonstrations, a sort of local rodeo in miniature.

The trees still give Grand Rapids its charm. You see them everywhere, but never more clearly than when you take a trip by car along the town's roads, which were still rough and unmade when the Gumms lived there. Along with the trees, there is the ever-present smell of wood, the fine aroma of pine to be enjoyed much as visitors to the coast revel in that first snatch of ocean breeze.

Plainly, trees bring joy in Grand Rapids. No one ever takes them for granted, not even those who have lived long lives in the town like Jean Denzil. Jean was in her nineties when we met, a spare but sparkling woman with a slight sight problem, although that didn't matter since she could look back into the past as if the years were days. It was in her small living room at the Pleasant Living retirement home, sheltered from the summer heat by yet more trees, that we talked. Yes, to her, it's always been pleasant living in Grand Rapids. 'It's a great town,' she told me. 'Always has been.'

When she was young, the Gumm sisters were too. It was a time when there were just 'two thousand souls' – as Jean put it – who lived in her own birthplace. That 2,000 was a figure enhanced only when visitors came into Grand Rapids by train, arriving like the Gumms' relatives from nearby Duluth at the railroad station that still reverberates with that iconically American whistle-cum-siren that announces an engine's arrival.

Even now, there are only about 8,000 people living in the town. But four times as big is . . . four times as big. That is not the only difference. The two-lane road along which I drove with John Kelsch is now a main highway. In Judy's day, there weren't even traffic signals. Farms abounded close to where now stands the ubiquitous local McDonalds. The string of Grand Rapids motels takes up space where there was once open countryside. Only the one hotel and the Romanesque-style yellow-brick school, where Jimmy and Mary Jane went and where Frances Ethel would visit them, now remain from those days.

John Kelsch explained those visits to her sisters' school: 'It was all so close to home, and was only two blocks away from their father's theatre and she roamed the halls with her sisters many times.' With them, she would go to McAlpin's drug store. A soda while sitting at the bar of the store, barely able to see the top of the counter, was the big treat, and one that must have come back to her when she did just that dozens of times as the teenage girl next door to Mickey Rooney in the Andy Hardy movies and the other boy-and-girl films they made together.

Her parents seemed to take the things Frances Ethel did as a matter of course, although Frank got annoyed when she opened the bags of pennies he had brought home from the theatre and threw them downstairs – joyously watching them roll on to the floor below.

That was the nice part of Grand Rapids. But life could be hard too – for the labourers who were in the town in order to make a living.

'Most men worked in the paper mill, of course,' Jean Denzil remembered. That was true in much of Grand Rapids itself, yet there were iron ore mines nearby and they brought in a huge number of immigrants to Minnesota, mainly from Europe, particularly from Scandinavia. The mines supplied most of the iron ore for the war efforts of both 1917–18 and 1941–45.

The cold winter climate – for around 30 days from late December through January the temperature can go from 20 degrees Fahrenheit below freezing point to ten above at the most (-30 to -12 Celsius) – made the area feel like a home from home for the newcomers from Finland who came to live in the village when they got jobs in the logging industry.

Climate and geography dictated everything in Grand Rapids. Certainly, winter cold made the warmth of the theatre enticing. But when snows came in from Lake Superior, which the locals called The Lake Effect, there were no customers and on really bitter days nothing stayed open.

But that was the only life anyone knew, grown men and women who had never gone over the state line and not a few who hadn't ever taken a step outside Grand Rapids itself. As Jean Denzil said: 'Everybody knew everybody. Now, there's an awful lot of people I don't know, but a lot of them are children, grandchildren, great-grandchildren of people I did know.' Alas, not of the Gumms. The three girls are long dead. The stories about this family who brought show business to Grand Rapids are stored in the memories of people like Jean, whose sister June was at school with the two older sisters, Jimmy and Mary Jane.

They were a family who seem to have made a big impression on the Grand Rapids of the 1920s, partly because of their theatrical associations. But only partly. Ethel belonged to the women's club and Frank was a volunteer fireman, who also played golf.

'My mom and dad,' recalled the nonagenarian Jean Denzil, 'and Mr and Mrs Gumm belonged to a group that had plays up at the High School auditorium. They were friends. They would get together to play cards, that sort of thing.' The girls themselves took part in plays at the elementary school in the village. 'They were just a regular family, just like the rest of us.'

And then there was the church. They were pillars of the local Episcopalian house of worship. Frank Gumm was the organist and sang in the choir, which he also conducted. Having a real professional singer among them was something to be boasted of – and the church took advantage of that. And Frank used his enhanced status there to show how important he thought he was. As John Kelsch put it: 'Frank was a showman. He would come into church three or four minutes late, walk down the aisle and then it would start.'

The family were expected to go there every Sunday – at least. The church has long ago been rebuilt on the same site, but there are pictures in the present building of Frank with members of his choir and, most significantly a framed certificate that says: 'We do certify that, according to the ordinance of our Lord, Jesus Christ, we did administer to Frances Ethel Gumm, who was born at Grand Rapids, Minnesota, on June 10, 1922, the sacrament of Holy Baptism with water.'

The time would come when some people would have reason to wonder about the association of Frank Gumm with the religious life of Grand Rapids, but not when that certificate was presented to what was then a very pious family.

Jean Denzil's memories go back to when she baby-sat little Frances Ethel, an appropriate term for looking after the girl known for ever after by her mother as 'Baby' or, in her more relaxed moments (and, in truth, there were not may of those), simply as 'Babe'.

'We would be out there playing and Mrs Gumm told the girls, Mary Jane and Jimmy, to go in and practise.' And before long it was Baby Gumm, too, who was made to suffer the shouted instructions of the woman who was fast developing into a typical stage mother. Even so Jean has only the fondest memories of her.

'I always liked the Gumms,' she told me. 'Mrs Gumm was clever.' And she didn't think being that stage mother altered people's opinion of her: '. . . if she were one; we do hear about that, but I never saw it. I wouldn't know.

'They were so happy. When she called the girls in to practise the little skits that they did, she would ask my sister June and me to go in and we would sit on the floor and watch. They had a platform in their living room and they would do their little thing there. I remember one birthday party we were at − I didn't go to all the nice things that others did − and she was just a great person. All the kids went to the party. She would have a string outside the house and you'd pick your string and get a gift. I thought that was great. It was nice. There was music. It was wonderful.'

Yes, it was a simple time and the Gumms lived an equally simple life. The youngest daughter was, as Jean recalls, 'a little doll, a real cutie'.

There are still plenty who can recall Judy Garland on screen as a 'little doll', but not many who, like Jean Denzil, knew her in real life when she was that young. 'She was the greatest performer Grand Rapids ever produced,' she insisted, not to emphasise the obvious, but to stress the pride that she and the dwindling band of men and women who still remember feel.

Hearing the stories this veteran citizen of the town tells brings to life one of the great songs that the grown-up Judy sang in what was probably the best of all her films, *A Star Is Born*. Performing that, she sat on the apron of a stage and told how she was 'Born in a Trunk' in a small town called Pocatello, Idaho. Judy wasn't quite born in a trunk in Grand Rapids, Minnesota. But to hear Jean Denzil tell it, that was merely a matter of detail.

The big treat for the kids in the area had always been to go to Frank Gumm's theatre. The most popular night was Friday when the admission price was a standard ten cents. This was not a particularly beautiful place, but when the house lights were turned down it was a hall of magic. The films seem mainly to have been Westerns, perhaps because that was what Marc Rabwin's employers specialised in. It didn't matter. Anything flashed on to the screen took these Northerners, living in virtually the centre of the top of the map of the United States, to a part of their own country that they had never seen or could ever hope to see. As for the odd chance to view a romantic drama set in Paris or Venice or London, the girls swooned at the handsome men in their powdered wigs and the women in fashions they couldn't believe ever existed.

But it was the stage shows that really excited them – even if they did know Mr and Mrs Gumm and their two older daughters as their neighbours.

The two older girls were very much part of the stage scene in Grand Rapids. The enthusiasm shown by the youngest of the three sisters was evident – and it was obvious, too, that little Frances Ethel would join the act.

It was 26 December 1924 when it first happened and when the older duet sang 'When My Sugar Walks down the Street'. The two-and-a-half-year-old Baby Gumm's debut solo was 'Jingle Bells', accompanied by the ringing of a bell that seemed almost as big as she was. It was a highly appropriate Christmas number. Certainly, Frances Ethel thought so. She went on with the song and when it finished sang it again – and kept on singing it, jingling all the way, loving every moment of it. The audience first started laughing and then cheered till they were hoarse. Little Frances Ethel, even at that age, discovered that she loved the sound of applause almost as much as she did the ice cream she was given at the end of a performance.

Her mother made her a little white dress for the next time she would sing 'Jingle Bells'.

'The first time I saw her,' said Jean Denzil, 'she was just three. She would come out on to the stage and do her little tap dance. Judy was obviously the one with the talent. People know about the sister act, but I don't think they ever amounted to much.

'Pictures were silent in those days and there was a pit in the theatre and Mrs Gumm would play the piano for any entertainment there was and the girls would be dancing. But when Frances Ethel came on, you couldn't get her off the stage. You could hear her dad call from the wings: "Hey, Babe, get off the stage." She just wouldn't get off that stage. And the whole theatre was just laughing. I was just laughing. The theatre was just roaring. And Mrs Gumm was just ahead of me in the pit and I looked out to see what she was doing. She was laughing, too.'

Ethel really fostered her youngest daughter's career even from that early on. And so would Frank.

Judy herself would remember how she and a two-year-old 'little girl friend' would practise. Her father taught her and her friend to sing 'My Country, 'Tis of Thee' while he pounded the piano in their house. 'Then,' she later recalled, 'he conned my mother and sisters into listening to me – and I was terribly proud because they said I was good.' So good, that it was he who said that 'Baby' Gumm could join the act.

As she said in a radio interview: 'I'd run in a little circle and everybody started to applaud. I just stayed there and stayed there.'

It happened every time. On that first occasion, Frances Ethel's grandmother, Eva Milne, Ethel's mother, had pushed her on to the stage, but didn't know what she was letting herself in for. While the 'Babe' was performing, Eva was watching with the other members of the family from the wings. When it became obvious that she'd been on too long, she rushed up to the footlights, scooped up the child in her arms and took her into what served as a dressing room, while the audience clapped and cheered and the little girl protested, 'I want to sing some more'. No matter how difficult she might make producers' lives in future years, that was how it was always going to be. The woman who made a movie called *I Could Go On Singing* had established a mantra for herself.

She always wanted to sing some more. She may not have actually been born in a trunk, but the smell of greasepaint was all around her.

There was another smell that wasn't quite so pleasant. There were stories that Frank Gumm was a little too fond of boys and young men. That part of the tale is pretty well accepted by all who have bothered to find out about the family. Other points are in contention – particularly those that suggest he was chased out of town as a result of his predilection. The stories settled once the family had left Grand Rapids for the West – going first to Los Angeles and then to another small town where everyone knew everyone else, called Lancaster.

Paul Rabwin says: 'My mother used to talk about the relationship that Frank and Ethel had. Frank was open about his homosexuality. She wasn't going to leave him.' Not yet, she wasn't.

The future would see a different story. Lilah Crowe says that, even today, people don't like talking about their departure. But Lilah was now willing to tell me. 'There was,' she told me, 'a family with a fifteen-year-old son who said that Frank Gumm abused him. Local researchers found that out.' But not the man who does more researching about the Gumms than anyone else, John Kelsch.

The unsavoury stories, he conceded, '. . . well, could be true. It seems he had some relationships.'

The diferent aspects of the story divide when it comes to telling about the repercussions of Frank's sexual tastes. 'I don't believe,' he said, 'that he was kicked out of town, like they say. That is totally false. For God's sake, the church gave a huge going-away party for him. And for the family, there were other parties. They printed Frank's letters from California in the local paper for years after they moved away. I can't see that happening if he had that kind of reputation here.' But he accepts that not everybody liked what they heard about him. Grand Rapids, after all, was a very prim and proper place. 'He may have been a bisexual and had relationships. There have been stories in Lancaster.'

But then he added: 'The stories really only appeared after Frank was dead and Ethel was dead and there was no way of checking them. It doesn't matter to us.'

It certainly has no effect on the associations between Judy Garland and her birthplace. Jean Denzil confirmed that for me. 'I was working at the historical society as a volunteer when they had their first celebration for Judy Garland. And people came from Australia and lots from England. I've never been a fan, as such, like these people. But they are just crazy about her. As a matter of fact, I was sitting at a desk outside, giving people a cheery welcome, that sort of thing, and a lady stopped and said, "You knew Judy Garland?" And I said, "Yes". She said, "Can I touch you?"'

CHAPTER TWO

Lancaster

Whether Frank *had* to leave Grand Rapids in the summer of 1926 or just chose to do so, the undeniable fact is that he and Ethel and their three daughters picked up their sticks fairly quickly and moved about as far away from the Minnesota town as could be imagined: Lancaster in California was some 90 miles north of Los Angeles.

The family troupe had gone to California for what they claimed was a holiday. On the way, they took a few engagements in small-time theatres and did the now usual round of masonic functions in other towns which they passed through on their journey. 'Gratifying results,' Frank reported to his home town. He was referring to the latest – and last – performances from Jack and Virginia Lee and among the first by the Gumm Sisters, with 'Baby' Gumm showing what she could do with the Charleston. Again, audiences laughed and gave the smallest and youngest entertainer they had ever seen a standing ovation.

At first the sisters were delighted to have Judy in their act. After all, she had given it new life and new audiences. But as time wore on, there were perhaps the seeds of jealousy being planted. Judy became conceited in their eyes and they let her know it. The fights between them were not yet part of the currency of local conversations, but before long people knew about them.

Like most other 'immigrants' to California, they first made for Los Angeles. They loved the weather. They liked the people. They liked the houses – and they probably also liked the trees, 'Down Among the Sheltering Palms' as the 'Lees' sang.

They booked into a nondescript hotel, the St Moritz (also the name of one of the plushest hostelries in New York, opposite Central Park). This St Moritz wasn't situated in the fashionable part of the long, long Sunset Boulevard. It was a nice family establishment in the 1920s. Today, it's in a run-down section of the street from which most people would like to think they could soon escape. The hotel still exists, much more shabby than it was when the Gumms' friend Marc Rabwin recommended it to them.

Rabwin, who had moved to the Sunshine State himself, was the one who suggested they think about settling in California – possibly to escape what everyone, apart from John Kelsch, thinks was the opprobrium of the ever-circulating stories of the scandal in which Frank was involved.

Gumm had no doubt he was going to stay in the movie theatre business. But he wasn't going to be satisfied with merely managing a theatre. He was going to buy one. First, he thought of West Hollywood. He plainly was tickled with the idea of showing films so close to where they were shot. Then he switched his attention to Glendale. But it was Marc Rabwin who suggested that he, his wife and children might be happier in a small town like the one where they still had their home.

He told them about Lancaster. There was a theatre there that he could buy on a mortgage.

The family returned to Grand Rapids, packed their bags, sold their little house and the ice chest, said goodbye to people like Jean Denzil and were on their way. Frank had a new theatre and the family had a new life.

Lancaster is in cowboy country – or at least the rest of the Antelope Valley in which it is situated is. Lancaster is its main town. Drive through the valley on the journey from Los Angeles – which the locals, only slightly deprecatingly, call 'Down Below' – and you see the mountains and landscape featured in only a few thousand Westerns. It is not difficult to imagine a tribe of Apaches rounding one of the magnificent hills. Come across an area of desert and, surely, the wagons of the Gold Rush settlers can only be just over the horizon. When it came to re-enacting Custer's last stand, this was the place for it.

That is an image that becomes clear from a glance at any list of some of Lancaster's most famous citizens. One records not only the name Frances Gumm ('also known as Judy Garland') but that of John Wayne, too.

Wayne once wrote that he was registered at Lancaster Grammar School – the equivalent of the primary classes in Britain – under the name of Marion M. Morrison. It was the same school that Frances Ethel attended a few years later. His method of travelling to school gives a perfect idea of what a Western town really was like. He may not have worn a ten-gallon hat as a child, but he went to school on horseback. He said his mount was called Skinny 'because I rode an old switchback nag to school which was so old, we couldn't fatten him up'.

At that school, the Gumm girl, as some locals remember her, was selected for the lead in the kindergarten play – *Goldilocks and the Three Bears*. As she said later, thinking about that, it was quite a move by the teacher Miss DuVal – because 'my hair was neither golden nor curly'.

Hollywood's connection with the area was established early. Harold Lloyd apparently worked in the Antelope Valley before becoming a star. He was one of the workers building an aqueduct. The story is that Hal Roach, Laurel and Hardy's principal producer, was the foreman of that team building the aqueduct and left when he read in the Lancaster local paper that a studio was looking for cowboys. Buster Keaton filmed one of his first talkies, about baseball, there. In more recent years, Frank Zappa lived in the area. It was never really part of the lawless Wild West, although it had its first jail in 1909 and, to this day, there are huge advertisement billboards bearing legends like: 'The Herman family will provide you with bail bonds.'

The Antelope Valley is in the heart of the Mojave Desert, yet still part of Los Angeles County. Lancaster is today a city with a population of about 145,000 and is the eighth biggest in the county. In fact, the story is that this is the fastest-growing town in the whole country. It is the home of the Edwards Air Force base and a leading centre for the aviation and space industry. In 2000, it had a population of 118,000 – in 1977, when the city was incorporated, there were only 37,000 people living there. When the Gumms moved to Lancaster, it was less than a quarter of the size of Grand Rapids, with a population hovering around the 500 mark, which suited the family perfectly well. They settled in there and did the same things as they had in their old home town, making friends with the same sort of people.

The older people still talk about the Gumms. They are the ones who saw Frances Ethel grow up. One or two of them remember when this was *Grapes of Wrath* territory, the place to which some of the poorest people in the land came to avoid the dust bowl which epitomised so much of the Depression. That was the point about Lancaster history: almost every event that happened thereabouts was recorded in the movies. Cowboys and Indians not only looked their best in this desert, but even in all those fictional films, they were simply re-enacting what had really occurred in that very spot where the cameras turned. It also had a lot going for it. It was the place where, for some time, the Southern Pacific Railroad stopped. But prosperity was a long time coming, which was why Frank Gumm was able to buy the Lancaster Theater for a knockdown price.

It wasn't a great place for a gold rush, although some people tried. There was a gold mine at nearby Rosamond in Kern County, but silver was a much more likely treasure to dig from the ground. Between 1881 and 1924, some $26m-worth of the precious metal was produced. Antelope Valley folk thought there would be an oil rush, too. But although they started to drill in the area around Lancaster, no oil was ever found.

When the Gumms arrived and set up home at 44659 Cedar Avenue – then after a short time in the house next door – it only had two paved streets. There was no electricity in some houses and gas didn't come to Lancaster until 1930.

In a way, the growth of the town dictated the kind of people who chose to live there. Without doubt, the roller coaster of hopes that materialised and faded had its effect on the population of not only Lancaster itself but the other hamlets in the valley.

'There were [very few] people living here then,' recalled one of Judy Garland's childhood friends, Irma Storey. 'Now it's terrible.' It was so very different when the Gumm family first came to town. 'People were very prim and proper then.' But, being so prim and proper, it is a wonder that Frank's tastes in some of his extramural activities were tolerated there – which they were for 12 years. Most of the people living in Lancaster today, who vie with Grand Rapids in declaring this to be Judy Garland's home town, seem convinced that Frank brought his family to Lancaster mainly because of all the rumours about his sex life in Minnesota. There are even some who think that, like in Grand Rapids, he was eventually drummed out of town. Plainly, it didn't happen overnight – yet the residents, those with memories which they use to recall long-ago events more clearly than they remember yesterday's lunch menu, tend to think that Frank was not immune to the same kind of stories in Lancaster that had plagued him in Grand Rapids – or, as some see it, the same kind of evidence. But it would take some time to become evident.

For the moment, they were welcomed with the traditional small-town open arms. They were nice people. That was obvious – and if Frank were going to get the Lancaster Theater on to its very shaky feet that would be marvellous.

If Frank's life there was not to be perfect, his youngest daughter's was. Maybe, with the gift of hindsight, it was not obviously idyllic, but to her it seemed to offer all she could desire as a child who just wanted to sing. To her mother, it was the perfect setting-off point for her role as that stage mom. If there were clouds on the horizon of the child who, when she arrived, was still called Baby, they seemed to settle, as far as the family's social circle was concerned, on how her mother treated the little one, now just over four years old. An iron hand appeared to be the perfect description of Ethel's philosophy. That was the way she was going to live vicariously through her youngest child. She herself had dreamed of being a star and had ended up as a failed

'Southern' singer, playing piano in the pit of a theatre. What she herself had longed for but never managed to achieve, Frances Ethel was going to do for her.

The other girls, of course, suffered from her strictures too, but it is fairly obvious that Ethel realised that Baby, if any of them, was the one who was going to go places – and she was determined to go there with her.

The Lancaster Theater was one of the hopeful signs that things could improve in the town – which is perhaps why Frank was so popular there and why blind eyes were turned when it came to his peccadilloes. The building, on the west side of Antelope Avenue between 10th and 11th Streets, was in urgent need of attention. Frank was ready to give it the kiss of life. The kiss was to be a relevant part of that phrase, even though the life-saving process hadn't been invented yet. It was to be a love affair between him and his building. He lavished everything he could on what was, for miles around, this first ever purpose-built playhouse.

He knew the value of publicity and used it to sell what he wanted to market most – himself and his family. A notice appeared in the local newspapers headed: 'Extra Special'. After naming the venue and the date, it went on to explain: 'Mr. And Mrs. Frank Gumm and Daughters will present a cycle of songs and dances between shows each evening at 9 o'clock and also at the Sunday Matinee'.

It went on to egg the pudding further: 'Having purchased the theater, I am taking this method of introducing the family to the good people of Lancaster and Antelope Valley. It is my intention to continue presenting the high class picture program . . . and I cordially ask the support of the public in keeping the entertainment up to the highest possible standard. Your co-operation will be appreciated. Respectfully, Frank A. Gumm.'

How he thought that the starring appearances of the totally unknown 'Mr. and Mrs. Frank Gumm and Daughters' would drag the people of Lancaster into his new theatre is a question worth asking. They were hardly stars, but it was an age when any kind of live entertainment would have them banging on the doors of church halls, just to listen to a fat lady with a fan, advising them to make love by a silvery moon or telling audiences what would happen 'After the Ball'. The songs were old, but there was no radio in Lancaster yet and they were the ones the locals wanted to hear. They knew few others. The Gumms offered something very new.

And they had ready-made vaudeville bills without bothering professional agents or anyone else in the business. When the show didn't consist entirely of his family, Ethel made full use of pupils from the dancing school she had set up there.

People did come. As Glen Settle, a 91-year-old who has spent his entire life in Lancaster, told me: 'Everyone turned out because that was about the only entertainment we kids had in the valley. You could see even then that Francis Ethel had a lot of talent. Her voice would carry out over the others. She was also always the best dancer in the group. She was the one who would lead the group on the stage. On the other hand, the sisters were only average, I guess. Judy was always the leader. The sisters were nice girls. They got on great. My brother went with Virginia for several years. I used to see her a lot when she came to our house. And Mary Jane and my wife went to school together.' That was small-town America. It was almost, some thought, incestuous because every-one did know everyone else so very well.

Whether it was the attraction of the family entertainers or purely because the customers were inquisitive is a matter of guesswork, but the theatre was, from the off, a hit. Frank made his playhouse his mission as well as his passion – apart, that is, from young men. It was a new start for an old theatre and, he told everyone, for the town. So Frank decided it also needed a new name. He changed it to the Valley Theater and put in new seating as part of what was a wholesale reconstruction of the building. Of course, he had an ulterior motive: it was going to be the one place where the name 'The Gumm Sisters' could be seen on a marquee. The title of the film showing that week, which he almost regarded as an irrelevance, was advertised on the top line and the billing for his daughters ('On the Stage') was in the same size lettering underneath.

Judy herself would remember that after her parents had finished their own act, Ethel would run to the pit to play the honky-tonk piano and Frank would change the girls into their costumes – using a flashlight in the dark. As she later recalled: 'I did those horrible belly rolls in an Egyptian outfit with those big balloon pants and a lot of ankle bracelets and spangles.'

Her sisters had Spanish costumes to go with their principal number 'In a Little Spanish Town'. Her father, she said, 'usually managed to get both of my legs into one pant leg, so there would be a big ballooning pant leg left over. Then, he'd run to the wings and tell my sisters to do another chorus.' One night, they did 15 choruses of 'Spanish Town'! As Judy said, it was no wonder that they 'hated show business'. 'Baby' clearly did not – at least, not at that stage in her life. She was four years old and enjoying every moment of it.

When she wasn't 'on' herself, she didn't think the other girls ought to be able to do what she couldn't. She would creep up to them on stage and tickle their ribs. Certainly, she tickled the ribs of her fellow Lancastrians.

It happened at the theatre and also at the local high school where the music teacher, Miss Adeline Kinnerman, used to organise shows. When the Gumms arrived in town, news of their talents spread and Miss Kinnerman wasted very little time in knocking on their front door. As Norma Gurber, formerly the curator at the local museum and art gallery, which boasts a large 'Garlandia' collection, told me: 'Miss Kinnerman was beloved here. She would do a lot of musical entertainment at a local park. She was so pleased when she heard about the Gumm family and that they were a vaudeville family, but she thought that Frances Ethel had an operatic voice. She couldn't believe that she hadn't had operatic training.'

Today, sitting in the front room of what used to be the Gumms' home in Cedar Avenue, a group of women recalled for me the child who was their neighbour and playmate. And her parents.

Daphne Myron enjoyed reminiscing. 'I remember her very well. She came over to have a birthday party at my house and my mother made the sandwiches. I recall she didn't like mayonnaise on hers, so refused to eat them, but my mom didn't mind. She was a wonderful girl and she sang just beautifully.'

That, however, was not enough. 'We wanted her to come out to play, but she always had to practise. Her mother was very strict.'

Daphne, like the other women gathered in that room where Judy Garland probably ate her meals, was prepared to say what she thought of the Gumms. Frank, she maintained, was 'just a gentleman'. But Ethel . . . 'she was all right', which was damning her with faint praise. 'She was very hard on Judy. She made her practise, even during lunch times.' So we can be assured that lunch times were never idle times for the little child at this early stage in her life. Such memories go to make up the story and were confirmed by other now very elderly ladies talking to me.

Irma Storey enjoyed telling how she and the girl who was still called 'Baby' by her parents but was Frances Ethel to her friends would play baseball together. 'The Gumms had a bigger backyard than we did,' she explained. So that gave her a good idea of domestic matters in their household.

'We played together every day,' she told me. 'We went to the same church and her dad played the organ and she and I were choir partners. She could sing and I was the same size.' That was, apparently, as far as the similarities went. 'I didn't have the same voice. Not even "Johnny One Note",' she laughed, referring to a famous early Garland hit.

But they were good playmates. 'We played in the street and on the school grounds. We played baseball, we had a swing set. I played football with the boys and Mrs Gumm didn't like that.' It was as if she thought she was sullying her little lady with a tomboy – and everybody knew what happened to tomboys . . .

It was during those games that the precocious little girl would talk about her ambitions. 'Oh, she was a very good little friend and such a beautiful singer, actually – with lots and lots of talent,' Irma said. 'I remember that she was just five years old and was down at our house. My uncle was down there. He asked: "What do you want to be when you grow up?" And she said: "I'm going to be a movie actress and a dancer and a singer." That had been drilled into her by her mother, but she wanted that, too.'

Even at five, Irma thought that Ethel was 'too hard on Judy'. She was a woman who threw her weight around – and had no concern as to where it landed. In small towns like Lancaster, the local schoolteachers, like the doctors and clergymen, were people to look up to, not with whom you argued. That was of no concern to Mrs Gumm – although she wasn't beyond calling on a proxy to do her dirty work. Irma remembered: 'Like all the kids, Judy talked a lot in school and had to spend fifteen or twenty minutes [after everybody went home] before the teacher would let her out. If I got out before her after my own detention and Mrs Gumm would see me, she would lean out of her kitchen window and holler at me. "Where's Babe?" she'd call. And then she said: "You go and tell that teacher she has to come home and practise." She just wouldn't let up on her.'

Not that this 'Babe' was always cowed by her mother. This was a child who knew her own mind. And her father would almost always take her part. 'She and Mr Gumm got into some pretty good arguments. I heard them. He really wanted her to be able to play with us. I remember him saying, "There's plenty of time to practise dancing."'

Ethel would take no notice of that and, truth to tell, she was even harder on some of the other children she taught to dance – or to do acrobatics. Among them were Frances Ethel's friend 'Mugsy' Maine and another pal at the time, Irene Duzak.

Another of the group, Irene Swanson, whose father had what was generally agreed to be the best restaurant in Lancaster just a couple of doors away from the Valley Theater, loves to talk about their childhood together. These are jolly, immaculately dressed and made-up ladies who talk as though it is therapeutic to exercise their memories. Not just that, they thoroughly enjoy reminiscing and talking about shared moments. For Irene Swanson, like the others, these were also highly personal family occasions.

For her, there was one abiding memory: 'She would invite me to the movies, if I gave her hamburgers.' She, too, thinks kindly of

Frank Gumm who, just as he had in Grand Rapids, demonstrated his 'quite nice voice' in church. A lot happened at that church. Frank, once again at the keys of the pump organ, used to stand up and give a talk – about his daughter, the actress. 'When her mother was taking her Down Below, meeting studio people and suchlike, every Sunday, her father would give a report on how she was doing.' As for his singing, quite a nice voice, maybe, but not, to Irene Swanson, a notable one, certainly not like his daughter's.

The Gumm Sisters by now had a new name when they appeared on stage – The Gumm Drops, which probably sounded better in the late 1920s and early 1930s than the rather corny title sounds today. They sometimes even attracted other performers – like when they appeared at a local festival, with their own backcloth, and were joined by a barber who had come from Michigan to reprise an act he had done with the family before they moved to Lancaster.

Ms Swanson is convinced of that special relationship between Frank and Frances Ethel. But in Lancaster, too, he would have his problems. For the moment, he revelled in his children's success – and there were no thoughts at that moment of the Gumm Drops failing to stick together, even though the name was soon chewed over and abandoned. They were not only featuring at the Valley Theater, but were doing gigs elsewhere, too.

At some of them, they didn't quite gel as they would have liked. Things were generally much safer at the Valley Theater, although Daphne Myron remembered that sometimes the movies Frank showed there were 'too risqué'. But then she adds: 'Everyone was very happy in the town that we had a theatre. It was the first one here.'

What is more, in Lancaster, if you ask the elderly citizens about performances outside their own city borders – or limits as they call them in those parts – they remember one that towers above them all.

Frances Ethel was still at school in Lancaster when the news spread that she was going to appear at the Shrine Auditorium in Los Angeles. This was not just a big hall, it was one of the biggest in the United States. It was the sort of place in which Adolf Hitler would have loved to have held one of his infamous Nuremberg rallies, a fact that would not have pleased the Shriners movement who set it up, but it was a wonderful venue for massive Hollywood events when all that mattered was fostering the good works of people, mostly those in the movie business. In later years, it would be the centre chosen for the annual Oscar ceremonies. Forgotten films would be reborn and have their big showings there – not just films that had never been shown before but, as with Abel Gance's *Napoleon,* those that had remained dormant for generations. Above all, in those days – as now – they had marvellous concerts there, featuring artists guaranteed to get people paying up to a dollar for a balcony seat that could be so far from the stage you needed not so much opera glasses as field binoculars to see what was going on.

Frances Ethel was about five years old when she sang at the Shrine Auditorium. Those field glasses would have been needed with extra magnification, but hearing aids were not required. The tiny little girl in her little white dress wouldn't have been tall enough to reach a microphone, if there had been one. There wasn't. But, more significantly, she didn't need one. Irene Swanson remembered that well. 'I have been continually amazed at the thought of such a powerful voice coming from such a small person.'

It was literally the talk of the town. A couple of schoolteachers from Lancaster went 'Down Below' to hear Frances Ethel Gumm. 'I remember one of them telling my mother that her voice filled the whole auditorium,' Daphne Myron told me. The show place had great acoustics. 'She just blew the audience away. She had a tremendous ovation.'

When she came back to Lancaster, the prodigy singer, no more than four feet high, was wearing a white ermine coat.

The Shrine Auditorium evening was not just an important event in the life story of an important entertainer, but in the story of Lancaster, too. The locals knew just how talented she was. 'I was not in the least surprised that Frances Ethel Gumm became a big star,' said Daphne, 'she was destined for that.'

On the night of that concert, Irma Storey remembered, Frank

sent back an important message to his home town. He told them, she 'really brought the house down'.

It was a comparatively rare solo performance for the youngest of the Gumm Sisters. That group had not yet established itself as a recognisable entity. They were no longer being billed along with their parents as '. . . And Daughters'. This was the age when 'Sisters' acts were very popular. Not only were there the Duncan Sisters, who were such an inspiration for the Gumm girls, but the Boswell Sisters were just establishing themselves and, before long, the Andrews Sisters would be top of the pops. So the Gumm Drops had a comparatively short existence and the Gumm Sisters they again became.

'Baby' and her mother were now spending a lot of time in the big city. Sometimes her Lancaster friends went with her when she went to do 'gigs' with her dancing school. 'Usually,' said Daphne, 'they would go down on a Friday afternoon and Saturday. I only went with them once, because I got car-sick and I was afraid I'd get sick in Mrs Gumm's car. But I was glad I went on the day that I did. I met artists who had dressing rooms next to Judy's. One of them played the "Cradle Song" just for me.'

Essentially, Frances Ethel was 'Down Below' to have singing and dancing lessons at the Maurice Kussell Theatrical Dance Studio and the Lawlor Professional School. There was also the Ethel Meglin Dance School, which put on a week's show at Lowe's State Theatre in the big city, which was akin to going on stage at New York's Radio City Music Hall. It surprised no one that Frances Ethel, aged six, would get the solo spot in the Meglin Kiddies 1928 production.

Through the names of those establishments, it becomes very clear where Ethel Gumm was heading. These were no ordinary dance schools, the kind that little children are encouraged to attend so they learn to sing and dance 'well', like her own at Lancaster. They really were intended to train youngsters for professional show business in what was by the 1930s accepted as the capital of that business. 'This was a major commitment that Ethel Gumm was making,' Paul Rabwin declared. 'Yes, [Ethel] may have been a stage mother but certainly it was a very strong message to send to Judy.' On the other hand, he is convinced that she 'adored' her mother as much as people believed she loved Frank.

Paul's father, the doctor, not infrequently got messages about the child, too. Frances Ethel had always suffered badly from hay fever, which was particularly prevalent in Lancaster. She developed other allergies, which Ethel decided needed treatment in Los Angeles. So she would bundle up her daughter, make the three-hour car ride (no freeways in those days) while little 'Baby' Gumm would protest, 'Mom, I can't breathe.' They would then return home the following morning, when the child would be taken straight to bed.

After a difficult professional time on a Saturday in Los Angeles, she was allowed to skip church the next day, which disappointed her choir partners.

To Ethel there was never any doubt that 'Baby' was the target of her aspirations. The Lancastrians, certainly, knew that. They marvelled not so much at her voice – they had taken that for granted for as long as they had known her – but at the subtle change it was demonstrating. Her contemporary Irene Swanson remembered: 'She had always had this amazing voice, but at the beginning it wasn't well trained. It was mostly loud, but she soon learned pretty rapidly how to control that voice.'

As the young girl's voice got stronger and more emotional – not an easy thing for a child to achieve without being syrupy and mawkish – it was clear that her sisters were being relegated to the role of a mere backup group.

They were part of the Antelope Valley landscape and in a way they remain so – just like the railroad station where, every time the raucous whistle of a passing train echoes through the nearby streets, close to where the Valley Theater used to be, someone, somewhere finds him or herself singing about 'The Atchison, Topeka and the Santa Fe' from the Judy Garland film *The Harvey Girls*. Unfortunately, the Atchison, Topeka and Santa Fe never stopped at Lancaster (which did, though, boast that a train could travel to Los Angeles in two hours).

Frank Gumm occasionally took that train when he went 'Down Below' to watch his daughter's progress. Everybody in this then tiny town knew Frank. 'He did a lot for the kids. He had a beautiful voice,' Irma Storey said. 'In church, Judy sat where she could see him best.' They did a lot for that Episcopalian church. Frank not only led the choir and played the organ, he and Ethel made generous donations to the church.

'The Gumms contributed a lot to the church,' says Irene Storey. 'It was a very small congregation.'

The Gumms seem to have had an aura about them – fostered mainly by Ethel, although Frank had his part in establishing it. This led to a certain amount of jealousy and unease, particularly in their church. As Irma told me, the minister 'put them on a pedestal'. In fact, to this day, the locals talk about the 'respect' shown to the family by the minister, the Rev. Parker. Sometimes, it seemed more like intimidation of the other congregants. Irene Swanson told me: 'The Rev. Parker was very strait-laced, although he did a lot for the town. He told his daughter Dorothy that she had to be nice to Frances Ethel – which irritated her. Dorothy wasn't very nice to her.' And it was to remain like that for the rest of Dorothy's life. 'When people came to ask information about Judy, she would not talk to them.'

But, all things considered, in Lancaster it was Frank who was the star of the town if not of their act. Glen Settle, living in a local retirement home, told me that Frank was the one person in the town's life whom he remembered affectionately from those days. Glen is tall, thin and with a wonderfully strong voice – and memory. 'I remember he had a great sense of humour. Frank was a happy man. He was a lot of fun.' He knew that from experience – he played golf with Frank. He doesn't feel the same way about Mrs Gumm. 'I used to deliver groceries to their house and she was always in a hurry to get me out of the way. All she wanted to do was to take Judy to rehearsals in Los Angeles. Her whole life was built around Judy.'

The girls were very different from each other, Irene Swanson told me. 'The older sisters were both much taller and Judy was a very little girl.' Most of the people around at that time agree that the family would have settled in Lancaster as their permanent home had there not been the problem with Frank. As Irene Swanson put it: 'Her father had difficulties. He was, it appears, involved with young men in the town.

'There must have been some substance to some of this. He did move, eventually, Down Below.' For the second time – if those stories are to be believed – he was to be drummed out of town. But that would come later.

And Irma Storey had to agree. 'I believe it was true. I remember hearing about him from a local boy who was raised by his grandfather, and my brother told me it was true.' On the other hand, it has to be said that the slightest evidence of a citizen not following the established mores would in those days have had tongues wagging. It was, as I kept hearing, a very prim and proper place.

Judy had grown a bit by the time Glen Settle got to know her. She had now turned 10. 'The Gumm family were very popular, [Judy] was like any other ten-year-old girl, you know.' Any other 10-year-old with an enormous portion of talent, that is. 'You could see that she had a lot of talent and her mother, who used to give dancing lessons, knew that very well. The other girls didn't have a strong voice like Judy. She was always the one who would lead the group on to the stage.'

According to Glen: 'The three girls all got on great.' And he definitely *was* speaking from experience.

Just a short drive away from Glen Settle's retirement home stands probably the most imposing building in Lancaster – at least it will be when all the refurbishing that is being promised is completed. This is the school Judy never attended (by the time she would have been old enough she was away launching her career) but which she frequently visited with her sisters and where they frequently entertained. It stands, complete with Grecian pillars and pediment, near her home in Cedar Avenue. This is a testimonial not only to the Gumm family who had the foresight to choose it for their elder children, but also to the value and importance of education in Lancaster. Today, it serves as a repository for the equipment needed for all Lancaster's schools. When I went there, even the assembly hall, or auditorium, which in its day was as impressive as the exterior, was full of computer terminals, stationery and all the other things schoolchildren need. Now, there are people who are hoping it will serve as some kind of memorial to Judy Garland.

I had been told by the former editor of the local newspaper, Vernon Larson, that the town ought to do more to foster the memory of Judy Garland there. 'The city of Lancaster hasn't done much to promote Judy Garland the way Grand Rapids does,' he told me. 'I've written for years that we should. I've campaigned for that. That would be wonderful. But there is a plaque dedicated to Judy that tells people that when they come into town, they know this is a place where Judy lived.'

But if the school were preserved, it would go a long way to making sure that more people knew. Several would love the building to be turned into a school again – and, if not that, that the auditorium with all its promises could be turned into a playhouse named after Judy: a Judy Garland Theatre. We were standing next to the stage that very likely was the first one on which Judy Garland appeared in Lancaster. The locals are hoping that the family would approve them calling this the Judy Garland Theatre.

There are those who disagree that Lancaster doesn't honour Judy's memory and associations with the town adequately. There might not be any formal memorial but, for the moment, they do have the town's museum, which, like those in Grand Rapids, has a Judy Garland collection. Norma Gurber is very proud of Lancaster's association with the star.

The museum has scenes from Judy's films and other antiquities dating from her days in town. Like most of the centres of Garlandia, it makes a great deal of Frank's contribution. There is a panoramic view of the town in his day, with a picture of the Valley Theater at its centre. There is even a tip–up seat from the cinema, which is one of the treasures of the museum. Norma talked about the Valley's boast that it was 'the coolest place in town'. That slogan referred to the installation in summer of air conditioning there, not the kind of entertainment it offered. But Frank wouldn't have objected to that other use of the word – if anyone did at that time. As Norma said: 'When he came here, the show [the theatre] was falling apart a bit. It [became] the place in town where people went for the action. It really was cool.'

The museum is not content with merely having exhibits behind its doors. The one in Grand Rapids has its yellow brick road. Lancaster's has the local version of what used to be known as Grauman's Chinese Theater, 'Down Below' in Hollywood. Just a few feet away, literally – and you have to look carefully to find it – five-year-old Judy's footsteps and those of her friend, Ina Maine (the one who gloried in the name of Mugsy) are preserved in cement.

Not that the idea of a Lancaster Grauman's was the original intention. As Norma explained: 'She and her little friend Mugsy were kinda goofing around and saw some fresh cement being poured in the pavement. So they thought, "I think we'll be naughty". They ran across the wet cement and we have preserved the sidewalk for visitors to enjoy when they visit the museum.'

The cement takes a little finding, almost hidden near trees in the garden of the museum, which used to be the Western Hotel – they still call it the Western Hotel Museum to distinguish it from another building – and belongs to the woman who became Lancaster's oldest citizen, Ruby Webber. Mrs Webber, who used to sell doughnuts from her kitchen window, possibly saw the girls being 'naughty', but nobody talked about it for years.

What I found surprising was the prescience of a town that decided to keep the footprints of a couple of then totally unknown little girls. The answer was that no one wanted to go to the trouble and expense of moving the flagstones – and it was only many years later that Mugsy told the story. 'There are six cement sections and they were kinda heavy to remove and most people did not know about it. Just a kinda small-town thing.'

But a small-town thing that, when the story came out, this small town decided to make the most of – by removing the cement panels and placing them under the tree at the museum. 'Little footprints here, little toes there,' as Norma Gurber put it.

But why did this little 'naughty' episode take so long to be revealed? And was it really true?

'Oh, I know it was true. People at the time didn't spread stories like that and Mugsy had a very good reputation. She didn't go round telling lies.'

The wonder is that the footsteps were preserved at all. 'They are not so deep – because they had to get out real fast in case someone came along to yell at them.' But Norma and her colleagues have studied the footprints as though they were gathering forensic evidence.

'Mugsy decided not to tell anyone because she knew they would get into trouble. One footprint is with shoes, one without. We think the one with shoes is Judy Garland's. Mugsy said she had to take her shoes off because she would get into trouble if she spoiled her shoes. Judy's parents could probably afford a more expensive pair.'

At the time, the girls kept it to themselves, but later on Mugsy revealed the story. 'They didn't tell anyone for years, but then people found out about it.' Norma said she has no doubt it was 'Judy's show'. 'Mugsy had a very good reputation, but everyone had a story about Judy.' The footprints story is now regarded, one could say, as concrete evidence.

This was such a small community that the local newspaper would have loved to have heard about this story, even before she was a well-known name in Lancaster. The really interesting thing is that this says more about Lancaster than about Frances Ethel Gumm herself. That such a tiny event plays such an important part in the town's history is remarkable in its own way. Judy never went back to see those footprints herself, though she did return to the town briefly in 1962 – to pick up the daughter of her god-daughter on the way to take her to Paris.

But, just as in Grand Rapids, the people of Lancaster were constantly being fed a huge amount of information of their favourite citizen's activities and had been doing so since she was very small.

When she fell off a swing, the local paper recorded the fact. Today, people like the girls I met in Cedar Avenue still talk about her at the earliest opportunity. A local resident has a paper parasol that she proudly tells friends Judy Garland gave to her at a birthday party.

That party was covered in the local paper, too, as though recording a state banquet at the White House.

When Frances narrowly avoided being run down by a truck coming out of a side alley, that was published in the papers. 'She was almost killed by the truck, coming from a car repair workshop,' said Norma. 'She was with her friend Mugsy and a boy who was also with her was hit. He always said that Frank Gumm was appreciative that the youngster had saved his daughter's life. Afterwards, they closed off the road.' Norma happily shows visitors to Lancaster the exact spot of the accident. She regards it as a local landmark.

Later on, those newspapers printed stories about Frances going to the nearby ice-cream parlour and reported what she ordered. When she and the other teenagers in those Hollywood films did the same thing, the Lancaster populace might have thought the scenes were based on events in their own backyard. For, as Irma Storey told me, 'Absolutely everyone knew them. It was during the Depression and Lancaster wasn't very big. It was a pretty poor town.'

It is fairly obvious that while Ethel was more than merely strict with her youngest daughter – she supervised everything she did like a trainer with a racehorse on a winning streak – Frank was not just more indulgent, but there was a more obvious love between them. He was generous to her as any loving father would be. But not just to her.

Next to the Valley Theater was the Jazz candy store, run by Charlie Wakefield. Charlie would make every child in town a 'candy cane' – a sweet shaped in the form of a walking stick – each Christmas. Said Irene Storey: 'Mr Gumm would have free movies and they'd give us a candy cane during the movie. Even when I was in high school, once or twice a year, he would have some kind of matinee during the week and the whole school would get out and come to it. It cost ten cents to go to the movie on Saturdays, but if you didn't have the money, he'd still let you in.'

But it's the candy these octogenarian ladies remember, not the movies. Whenever Frank and his youngest daughter were together, he would make sure she had enough sweets and chocolates to keep her going. Frank would pick up Frances Ethel from school at the end of a morning and walk the one block to one of the neighbourhood restaurants where they had lunch together. If Ethel had been around, it would never have happened. She would have insisted that 'Baby' used the time to practise. With her father it was simply an altogether loving relationship.

Certainly, he was every bit as proud of her as was his wife. Customers lining up to put their ten cents over the box-office counter, waiting for their tickets to pop out of the brass slot that signified the money had been paid, regaled him with stories of hearing the voice of Frances Ethel singing until late at night at home with the windows open in the hot summer. They heard her, they would say, up to two or more blocks away. None of them complained. They loved the voice and those who knew her said they loved the singer just as much.

That being said, it can't be suggested that this little girl with the angelic voice and tiny, perfectly dressed frame was some kind of Goody Two Shoes. Said Norma: 'I've heard it said that at ten, she'd be walking around the main Lancaster Boulevard, smoking. So no one could tell, she'd hide the cigarette in the palm of her hand and kinda sneak a puff. It was kinda, what can I get away with today?'

That sort of story would not be published in the paper. It was a good-news paper, with nothing unsavoury like a child smoking allowed on to its pages. Nor, one would think, would it be 'published' to Mrs Gumm, who believed that any sullying of her child's reputation could only result in disaster for her career.

For much the same reason, nothing was published about what came to be known in town as 'Frank Gumm's problem'.

The young women in town were spared all knowledge of his

liking for young men until they were much older. Irma Storey said: 'I believe it's true because the boy who ran the projector was a Carter; the Carter family who owned the [surrounding] building. He was raised by his grandfather who one day came over to talk to my father.'

He wanted to tell him that his grandson had been assaulted. It was by way of warning, not gossip – because he knew that Irma's brother also worked with Gumm as a projectionist. 'He was in the projection room every day,' Irma told me. 'It was my brother who, I guess, was the one who finally told us. He was at our mother's house one day and we said we had heard the rumour and he said, "Well, it's true". It wasn't something you would talk to a little girl about. Now, it's hard to remember what it was like as a small town. I didn't get out and about very much. I was eleven years old before I ever saw the ocean.'

At school, Frances Ethel Gumm is remembered as being just a normal classmate – a schoolgirl called 'Gummy', which she seemed to prefer to her mother's insistence on still naming her 'Baby'. She was also less than pleased – as were her parents – when one of the bills advertising the family act listed them as 'The Glumm Sisters'. There was nothing glum about Frances Ethel. Her adventures were not those of a miserable child, except, always, there was the hope that she could be allowed not to have to spend so much time practising. The filly was desperate to sometimes leave the paddock.

What happened next would not have happened without the trainer's strict regime.

Assuming that nobody of any importance got to know that this was a naughty little girl, the career her mother was so very anxious to foster was growing apace. By the time she was getting away with rather more raucous adventures, she was a local celebrity. Her mother had started hawking her children around agents' offices and trying – with amazing success, considering how difficult it always was – to get the sisters jobs. There was now not the slightest doubt that of all the girls, 'Baby' was by miles the best. The best girl who needed the best name. The people of Lancaster were never surprised to know how much better the youngest of the three sisters was than her siblings. But it was through one of her father's Sunday morning reports in church that they heard the really big news. Frances Ethel wasn't Frances Ethel Gumm any more. She had, he told the Episcopalian church congregation, a new name.

How this came about is still subject to a degree of controversy. Some say there was a film starring the elegant Carol Lombard – Mrs Clark Gable – featuring a girl called Garland. The usually accepted story, though, was that the girls were on a vaudeville bill with George Jessel and he suggested that she call herself Frances Garland – 'because she is like a garland of flowers'.

Within days, and after a great deal of thought by her mother, Frances Garland became Judy Garland.

CHAPTER THREE

Out and About

It was the beginning of the life of Judy Garland. Soon afterwards, it was the end of what Paul Rabwin describes as the 'uncomfortable relationship' between the husband and wife, Judy's parents. Frank would die of meningitis. Ethel did better. She went on to to confirm her role as the epitome of the stage mother. But, for the moment, the family were still residents of Lancaster and still trying to consolidate the success of their youngest daughter. The fact that the older girls were by now little more than a chorus to Judy didn't appear to upset them – or surprise the locals.

Then in 1929 came the big opportunity. George Jessel, who was about to give Frances Ethel her new name, was not the only important, influential show-business figure to spot the little girl with the big – no, the huge – talent. There may be a few people around who remember Jessel. He had a new career in his later life, hosting television 'roasts', making rude speeches for people like Bob Hope or Jack Warner, head of the Warner Bros. studio. Most of all, they doubtless recall his love of totally phoney uniforms and medals with lots of gold braid and tassels that signified only his services to George Jessel. But these days, probably only old (very old) vaudevillians or entertainment historians could summon up the name Gus Edwards.

Yet Edwards was a very important figure indeed. He was vitally important in the life of Judy Garland before that is, she had her new name.

The man who had put on shows and discovered talents of all kinds was the one who took her career – and, at first, potentially those of her sisters – to undreamed of heights. He was a songwriter ('By the Light of the Silvery Moon' and 'In My Merry Oldsmobile' among others), a writer for the stage (including *The Ziegfeld Follies*) and a producer with his own variety shows that were among the most popular in the land. Above all, he was an influential discoverer of talent – not least, the same George Jessel. More significantly, there were Eddie Cantor, Walter Winchell and Eleanor Powell. Oh yes, and a little act called the Marx Brothers.

Edwards had a successful regular show called *Kids Kabaret*. If there were a market to be cornered in juvenile performers, he did it. Improbably, his *School Days* was among the most popular shows in America. He heard Judy Garland singing and suggested he could take her as far as any of those others had travelled. If he could do it with the strange-looking brothers called Marx, he could surely do so with the sisters named Gumm. He may not have actually said to the girls, 'I can get you into pictures', but that was his message. Edwards – born Gus Simon in Hohensalza in Prussia – agreed that he could find work for the sisters, but it was the girl he discovered called Judy Garland in whom he was most interested. As an impresario, he was important and influential enough for his words not to be taken lightly.

Ethel Gumm realised that as a discoverer of juvenile talent, he had the whole genre all to himself. After all, *Kids Kabaret* toured the United States year after year. When he went to see the Meglin Kiddies show, it was not because he was enamoured by the idea of child entertainers, it was in the course of his very successful business. As far as these sisters from Minnesota were concerned, it wasn't conventional vaudeville he had in mind. Less than two years earlier, the movie screen had learned how to talk. Edwards was going to get in on the act with a new group of singers not many people had ever heard of and put them on the screen. This was a new chance for him to run up a flag and say he had something big to offer.

He had been contracted by MGM – long before they deserved the soubriquet of Makers of Great Musicals – to provide what at the time was an essential part of a movie programme, a series of 'shorts'. Today, people go into a cinema and expect to see no more than a main film – with the addition, of course, of a series of trailers and an advertisement that tells people who had previously been encouraged to drink a Bacardi on a Caribbean beach to turn off their mobile phones. In 1929, there would have been a riot if just one part of the advertised offerings were missing. Audiences felt cheated if they didn't have, in addition to the 'main attraction' – as the business liked to call the big picture – a 'short', along with a newsreel, a trailer and the inevitable second feature.

The fact that audiences could come into the cinema any time they liked, just so long as they paid their ten cents (or sixpence in Britain) was beside the point. They wanted their money's worth. And they got it, trying to put together the story they had missed, which had begun sometimes an hour or more before. It was like reading a newspaper serial story for the first time weeks after it had begun – except there was no one to say, 'New readers begin here'. It didn't matter. They stayed till the continuous performance returned to 'where we came in'. That became a saying of the age, a defence invoked when men or women were charged with not listening to a whole story. Actually, there wouldn't be much of a story to worry about in the 'shorts'. Frequently, they were just vaudeville turns. Gus Edwards himself appeared in one the same year he was selling his idea to Louis B. Mayer. His was a comedy routine with two other now-forgotten entertainers, introduced by Jack Benny.

These were the kind of fodder to pad out cinema programmes as if they were fragile parcels. They were the brown paper around the package. But it was the cinematic equivalent of no ordinary package, but of a pass-the-parcel nursery game, one of the interminable wrappers around the gift itself.

Edwards was now planning to turn what he had done on the stage into a 'flicker', as they were called at the time. Since he was the recognised master of this art, the studio were happy to leave it all to him. But there was a routine meeting at the MGM Culver City studios first, number one in a catalogue of visits from a lady called Judy Garland. No one there was prescient enough to realise that that meeting was going to be the start of a relationship between the company and one of their most remarkable stars. Certainly, the kid who was still being billed as one of the Gumm sisters had no idea how significant it would be. If she had, she would have protested that she was just not up to it all. She had lost a front tooth, a problem every child had to face. But Judy was not going to be placated by a visit from the tooth fairy. Instead, there would be a contract – for the 'short'. Yet the empty space in her gum was only one difficulty. She had a stye in one of her eyes, which meant it was virtually shut most of the time. In addition, she would later say she could barely open her mouth because she had a cold sore. Reportedly, Gus Edwards said she should go ahead with her audition because she had such a wonderful ear – for music. As Judy later admitted, with the sense of humour that in later years would characterise even her saddest moments, saying she had a good ear was drawing attention to the only part of her face that looked normal.

Yet that was precisely what was going to be her biggest attraction to a film studio. For years, she always seemed normal, playing the girl next door – if a well-tailored, beautifully but lightly made-up girl next door who blossomed from puppy fat to curvy woman.

It is not possible to say if Judy, aged seven, thought about such things when she and the other girls appeared in the first of these mini pictures, *The Big Revue*. But the residents of Lancaster remembered what she had said about ambition: that she was going to be a movie actress, a dancer and a singer.

It is quite possible she thought that it would be a way of getting out of the clutches of her mother. In the late 1970s, I interviewed Donald O'Connor for *The Times* newspaper. He told me: 'She hated doing so many of those shows and not having time to play with her friends. But her mother told her: "If you don't stop crying, we're not coming back for you in this hotel." She never forgot it.'

'I kept crying,' she told O'Connor, who was frequently on the road at the same time, 'because I was so lonely and the hotels were so Mickey Mouse.' But they had to go and do their show, with her mother saying, 'Stop crying!'

She didn't think she had done all that well in *The Big Revue*. It has to be admitted that if there had been any reviews of the *Revue*, so to speak, few critics would have thought so either. Had it not been the film debut of Judy Garland, no one would today know of its existence. However, it went down well enough in Lancaster and Great Rapids. When the girls sang 'That's the Good Old Sunny South', their parents, the former Jack and Virginia Lee, Sweet Southern Singers, must have thought this was history reprised.

There was nothing star-like about the sisters. How could there be? For the moment, they were still living in Lancaster. Not just living there, still working in their old home town – and making great progress in their locality, which now did have radio. As Glen Settle told me: 'The greatest thing was to listen to them on our local radio station.'

At first, being heard on the radio by the Lancaster residents was enough. To them, *The Big Revue* was really The Big Time. When they saw the picture at the Valley Theater they couldn't suppress their excitement. They nudged each other in the stalls and in the balcony and screamed in support – even though, in truth, the girls were mostly drowned by the other children in the cast, most of whom came from the same dance school.

But that wouldn't remain the case for long. Having made the movie, the girls were able to qualify for the title of Hollywood people. So much so, the Gumm Sisters were now being billed for a stage show as part of *Flynn O'Malley's Hollywood Starlets*. Ethel wasn't altogether pleased about them joining another organisation. After all, where did she herself fit in with the new regime? The answer was that she, too, got a job with Mr O'Malley – accompanying the girls on the piano and working as a vocal coach. 'They can't do without me,' she said, wreathed in smiles, when the contract had been signed. No longer was she living quite so vicariously. Only if she had become one of the Gumm Sisters herself could she have been happier. As for Frank, so what? He was misbehaving, as she always knew he would, and she had taken a lover who was keeping her content enough.

Paul Rabwin says that his father, the doctor who had been responsible for Ethel not having an abortion, knew all about it. And so did his mother. 'My mother used to talk about the relationship Frank and Ethel Gumm had,' he told me. 'And Frank apparently was fairly outspoken about his homosexuality. Ethel would confide to my mother that the marriage wasn't a particularly good one, but she wasn't going to leave Frank. She figured she was going to stay because of the careers of their kids, to keep the family together as much as she could.'

But then, meanwhile, there were other priorities. The stage mother was preparing for battle. She had no doubt she would win it with her 'Baby'. Whether the studio would be such an easy walkover was a different matter. Time would tell. Which turned out to be something of an understatement.

Actually, time dictated another movie contract. Her association with MGM proved to be short-lived – at least, for the time being. Instead, she was moving to Burbank, headquarters of Warner Bros. and its sister organisation, First National. She was to make a movie with the help of the Vitaphone system, the first serious method of recording sound movies on discs which – hopefully, but not always – would be synchronised with the pictures. Warners proudly boasted about that – and, as the motto on their water tower proclaimed, that they were the studio that combined 'good citizenship with good picture making'. Both organisations were run by Harry Warner, who liked to consider himself the big boss, Albert, who would have preferred to have been running a clothing company but was the titular head of sales and the firm's theatres, and Jack, 'head of production' and generally considered to be a comedian – which is what he would have liked to have been. He told terrible jokes and made even worse speeches, but he was the public face of the studio. Sam, the brother who was the technical genius and the one who brought Vitaphone to Warner Bros., thus making it possible for the Gumm girls to go before their cameras in the first place and be heard as well as seen for three 'shorts', had died the day before the premiere of the first 'talkie', Al Jolson's *The Jazz Singer*.

Warner Bros. took the film to be made with the Gumm Sisters as simply something to be done. It wasn't even part of the parcel, more a stocking filler, a tangerine that would only have been noticed had it not been there. Jack Warner handed over full responsibility to an underling who would see his bosses if something went wrong, but not otherwise. He didn't receive any complaints about the Gumm shorts and so wasn't called into Warner's office.

Of course, Judy would have liked it if these films had been completely forgotten, but they were carefully stored away and produced to her total embarrassment when Warners were ready to release their only other Garland film, *A Star Is Born*. But without them, it is possible to surmise that *this* star would never have been born.

There was a whole string of these shorts starring the girls, with titles like *The Old Lady and the Shoe* (guess what that was about), *A Holiday in Storyland* (ideal kiddie material), *The Wedding of Jack and Jill, La Fiesta de Santa Barbara* (a Spanish language title) and, finally for this contract, *Bubbles*. They fitted in beautifully in holiday-time children's programmes, the sort that were dubbed 'suitable'. *The Wedding of Jack and Jill* was particularly suitable. It was predictably stacked with nursery rhyme characters and there was no billing for either Judy Garland or the Sisters. Judy didn't even play Jill. She simply stood in the chorus behind the leads, Johnnie Pirrone Jr playing Jack and Peggy Ryan as Jill. But Judy did get to sing a song that might have seemed to augur something. It was called 'Hold on to a Rainbow'.

No one in the movie business really had sought her out as star material, but they needed children and the girls were on hand. 'It was inauspicious,' Judy later remarked in what could have been described as an understatement. A few hundred thousand other women would have given their all for such an inauspicious moment. There were three other 'shorts' in the contract. As for Ethel, she was enthralled. She had invested so much in her 'Baby' and the sisters and now was ready to take the dividend. Her self-taught role was as astounding as Judy's impact. There were no schools for stage moms, but then Ethel Gumm's instincts were not something that could be taught. In any case, like all members of that species, she considered she knew best and would not have dreamed of taking any advice that might, just might, not fit in with her own decisions and opinions. Frank Gumm had long ago known that and so had the citizens of Grand Rapids and Lancaster. As Glen Settle told me: 'When Ethel went to Hollywood with Judy, we were glad to get her out of our hair.'

As for the Hollywood producers, it is probably true that she got in their hair, too, that she demanded things for her daughter no self-respecting company would willingly offer, but she forced her way through locked doors like some female Houdini. What she learned, above all, was that you don't take no for an answer. The fact is that once a producer said 'Yes' he wasn't likely to regret it – apart from letting Ethel Gumm into his life. The Gumm Sisters were not yet a name, but the youngest of them certainly had enough about her to make audiences talk. There are no secrets in showbiz and what those people talked about leaked before long to the production companies.

Not that it was always a smooth-running race. At the 1934 Chicago World's Fair, the sisters had what has to go down in history as their first blooding. One gig at the fair was a show at the Old Mexico nightclub in Los Angeles, starring a certain Skippy Real ('the sensational fan dancer'). Looking at the poster, six acts from the bottom, in very small type are the words, 'The Gumm Sisters'. Whether the older Judy Garland would ever admit that she helped pack a bill for a fan dancer isn't on the record. They were good enough, but their employers for what should have been a major booking were not. Frank Sinatra said on many occasions that a lot of the stories about his associations with the Mafia arose simply because the places where he sang were 'not exactly run by Christian Brothers', which is more than a little simplistic. The people who employed the girls were the kind who legend decreed had twisted noses and wore long overcoats – with pockets bulging not just with all the cash they were making but with a collection of machine guns, too, probably with the safety catches switched off. There were no guns pointing at Mrs Gumm and her offspring, but she came across her most serious opposition to date – and lost.

As her youngest daughter would later write: 'Mother tried to collect what they owed us. They told her to "shut up and stay healthy."' That was one of the kind of things she was to write about her mother – in later years, she was to dub her the 'original wicked witch of the west'.

The Chicago fair may not have been a great success, but there's reason to believe that it was the most important engagement that Frances Ethel Gumm would ever have. Norma Gurber might have said 'Who knows?' about how that name – along with 'Baby' and 'Gummy' disappeared. But by all accounts it was in Chicago that the name would change for ever when Jessel persuaded Ethel to change her daughters' title – all of them. From that moment, the girls were officially the Garland Sisters.

But it didn't happen in time for the posters for the city's Oriental Theatre. Jessel was the headliner. 'Gumm Sisters' – not *the* Gumm Sisters – were down the bill. The interesting thing is that they replaced another girl trio, called The Andrews Sisters.

If Jessel's word meant anything, Judy and her sisters were on their way to stardom. It didn't happen like that. As the mature Garland sang in *A Star Is Born*, she wasn't exactly an overnight sensation. Unless, that is, one accepts that overnight took a year or two – which, in the scheme of things, was the equivalent of a lunch break.

Later in 1934, the 12-year-old Judy and her siblings toured America's Midwest. They appeared at a place that has also earned a place in entertainment lore, the Cal-Neva Lodge, a hostelry where a line in one hall divides the room between California and Nevada. There's gambling in the Nevada side of the building, none at all a couple of feet away in California. In later years it was there that its owner, Mr Sinatra, held court, gave concerts and collected a small fortune from his gangster pals and it was there that Marilyn Monroe, supposedly after affairs with Robert Kennedy and the Mafia boss, Sam Giancana, was spirited out, only to die very soon afterwards. When the Sisters appeared there, there were, seemingly, nothing but flowers in their way – big, big garlands of them.

From there, they went further south, back to California – and back to Down Below, Los Angeles. There were rumours that the act was about to break up. Mary Jane, now known as Sue or Suzie, had met a man while at the Lake Tahoe resort and was already saying she was going to give up singing. But that was not for then. Ethel would never have allowed it. There was no doubt that Judy was the central attraction, but what she was selling was a threesome and she wasn't about to spoil such a potentially good thing.

At one stage, it seemed that they were going to go back into the movies. There was a contract from Universal Pictures to take part in the biopic of the most influential theatrical producer of the early 20th century, *The Great Ziegfeld*. The trouble was that before the film could get on to a Universal lot, MGM decided that the great Florenz Ziegfeld – he of the *Ziegfeld Follies* and, in historical terms, probably the most important name on Broadway – would be even greater under their control and signed another contract, giving them the right to say if they wanted to use the previously arranged Universal cast, including the Garlands. They didn't.

So the chance of Judy Garland joining the studio with the legend above its portals that it housed 'more stars than there are in the heavens' was not to be. At least, that was how it seemed as the little girl shed enough tears to soak a dozen or so handkerchiefs. But that wouldn't satisfy the queen of stage moms. Ethel, with the help of a newly appointed agent named Al Rosen, one of those tough businessmen who looked as though he lived on a diet of hard-boiled eggs took what was perhaps the most important step in Judy's professional life. Rosen heard that MGM were holding auditions for child actors. He also knew Ida Koverman, who was officially Louis B. Mayer's secretary, but was far more than that. She didn't take shorthand, and she didn't bring in the tea in the translucent sets that were de rigueur when he was talking to his stars (although the really big players *were* always assured of Ms Koverman's personal attention). Moreover, she was an electric fence against unwanted intruders into the mogul's life. Most significantly, she was his principal talent scout. Mrs. Gumm was happy enough to put her daughter's career prospects in the hands of a professional like Rosen. What she didn't realise was that, with Ms. Koverman aboard, it was the beginning of the end of her own role in Judy's life.

One night she was persuaded, along with other MGM executives, to go to a show at the Wilshire Ebell Theatre near Beverly Hills. The idea was that she would take a particular look at the sisters named Garland. She conferred with the others, most notably Roger Edens, the musical arranger who would become one of Judy's greatest defenders at the studio in future years. He later said of Judy: 'She had that rare vocal quality of *breaking* hearts.' Ms Koverman came, she saw, but wasn't exactly conquered, although the smallest of the girls did seem to her to have something.

Going on to any trail involves what the business knows as 'reckies' – reconnaissance trips. My first footsteps on the Judy Garland Trail, a few years before, led to New York's Dakota Building, the apartment block near Central Park where John Lennon was shot. It was there that the songwriter Burton Lane recalled for me his first experience of seeing Judy Garland at work. 'I was there at the Ebell when the Garland Sisters were playing. They were a so-so act, until you realised that the little girl at the centre – she must have been no more than eleven years old [she was actually twelve] – was so good. But that voice! It rang out that evening.' In later years, Judy would say that she owed everything to Lane – her father apart, of course. It was a nice thing to say. She owed a great deal to a lot of other people, but it was gratifying to the composer of numbers like 'How About You', which would be featured in her film *Babes on Broadway*.

He was there with Ida Koverman and the MGM executives. 'I remember leaning over to Ida and saying that here was one youngster she ought to take under her wing. She said she knew something about her. For the studio people, the act was an audition – and one that wasn't what they were looking for. I said, why not forget about the other two? The little one shouldn't be held back because of her so-so sisters. I think she took it to heart.'

Ida did take it to heart. Yes, she thought, she would tell Louis Mayer about the girls, but agreed with Lane's verdict that didn't hold out much hope for a three-person act, at least not this one. To prove that her hunch about Judy was correct, she called the child to a meeting on her own – with Ethel in attendance, of course. This was a woman who was never intimidated – and for once Ethel was forced to take a back seat. In effect, Ida Koverman was now giving Judy a personal audition. The song they agreed should be featured in this one-girl show was 'Dinah'.

As she heard Judy stretch out the syllables of the rhetorical question, 'Is there anyone finah?' she realised this was something special, a girl with the voice of a young woman, singing with the verve of a top Broadway star, but who still looked just what she was – a little girl with a bow in her hair and a dress that came down just above her slightly knobbly knees. This, she would report to her boss, was a charming child who had no pretensions about her age. She also told him the girl had a mother. That would not be a recommendation, but Louis B. Mayer had had experience of those and would take no nonsense. If there was going to be a battle of wits (some might have called it more a battle of cats), Ida Koverman felt secure enough that she was going to win. If Ethel thought she would be able to interfere, the formidable Ms Koverman had other ideas.

The MGM executive was not the only one to spot the young talent. Louis B. Mayer himself, head of the studio but not its owner (a fact which would later get him dismissed) even though he was said to be the highest paid man in America, was ready to be wooed by little Judy. Other executives also advised him that he ought to take Ida Koverman's advice to heart.

So much to heart that the MGM dragon, as some people knew Koverman, turned into the Metro fairy godmother. She interviewed the child once more and then asked for Mayer to meet her – but only after giving her some commercial intelligence. The studio head could be relied on to be bowled over by the old Hebrew–Yiddish tune, 'Eli Eli' ('My God! My God!'). That was not the sort of number she would have known in Grand Rapids or

Lancaster. Certainly, Frank Gumm would never have dreamed of singing it in the Episcopalian church.

Judy was already sufficiently imbued with showbiz to know that when it came to getting a job, a mere suggestion from someone in authority had to be taken up – and taken seriously. She went away and learned the song, in tongues she doubtless hadn't even known existed. Latin, she had probably heard of. But Hebrew? Yiddish? This was a world away from the life she had known. And so was MGM.

But with Ethel's coaching – it was a *very* new experience for her, too – putting all the heart into it she could muster, she was going to succeed and face the dictator of Culver City. Mayer was not a religious man, although he insisted that his mother's chicken soup recipe was on the MGM dining room menu each day. His real religion was his studio and all – the money, the fame, the influence that made him head of the Republican Party in California – that it brought him. He regarded himself as the father – if not the emperor – of all he surveyed; his employees were his children.

When he heard Judy sing the plaintive song, tears rolled down his cheeks. This in itself was not unusual; when he interviewed long-serving stars to tell them they had served *too* long and were about to be fired, he could be relied on doing so while constantly dabbing his eyes. Judy was at the start of that journey. Yes, he agreed, the child had something. 'Give her a contract.'

Her money, initially, was $100 a week, an amount that was actually negotiated not by the agent and not by Ethel, but by her father. Frank had taken her to this audition and proudly mouthed the words he wanted her to say – and sing. He was delighted, he wrote back to Lancaster, that she would get a rise every six months: 'A very attractive deal'.

She would always say that this most influential contribution to her career stayed with her for the rest of her life. She had him to thank for everything, she said – which would not have pleased Ethel at all. Certainly, this new link with Frank Gumm couldn't have come at a more poignant time. Within weeks, meningitis had struck and before 1935 ended, he was dead.

Not many years later, when Judy was already a big star, the teenager would sing about being 'just an in-between', a girl too old for Mickey Mouse but not old enough to go out on dates. This, she remembered, was her fate at MGM, a studio she believed was only interested in females who were either too young to go to school or too old to go to college. As she once recalled: 'They wanted you either five years old or eighteen, with nothing in between.'

US law decreed, however, that she had to go to school, and a whole repertory company of 'in-betweens' sat at desks at the studio's own schoolroom. The teacher Mary MacDonald had probably one of the most envied jobs in her profession, but she tried not to let it go to her head. She dressed severely, wore no make-up, and tried to give the impression that she was treating her pupils no differently from how she would have taught youngsters in the school down the street. She gave them the usual tests, supervised by the State of California, but none of the kids was likely to win a university place as a result of her teaching. However, there are no records of complaint, and they willingly submitted to publicity shots of them being hard at work over their books.

The children were also subject to parental supervision. Ethel Gumm wouldn't have allowed anything now that would spoil Judy's career, any more than she would have done when she was on the way up to MGM stardom. But she wasn't the only stage mother getting in on the act. Jackie Cooper's mother had seen the way Judy had performed on a radio show in which her son also appeared and arranged with Ethel for the kids to get together. She was already marking out a prospective wife for her son. Ethel was happy to go along with the idea. Young master Cooper would be a good catch. He was a star himself, and they would play together in *Ziegfeld Girl*. And besides, think of the trouble that might avoid in the future. When Jackie's mother had a date all arranged at the Gumm residence in Los Angeles, she hired a car and a driver to take the boy there. The mothers weren't the only ones pleased with the possible match. The studio had its photographers as busy as they had been in the schoolroom, delighted in the news prospects of a romance.

Judy made friends there who would stay with her for the rest of her life. Ethel, now the sole parent, represented a strange kind of dichotomy in her life. On the one hand, she was still a severe taskmistress, determined to make sure that her daughter became a big star. On the other, she wanted her to live some kind of semblance of a normal life. Perhaps it was for that reason that they continued to live in Lancaster.

Those days still form part of conversations in the Lemon Tree restaurant in Lancaster when the old folks get together. It is plain that they regarded Judy's success as reflecting on the town itself, which by all accounts needed it. Certainly, she gave the local paper plenty of copy. There was glamour about her now, and not just focused on the Gumm girl, as they still called her. She brought her MGM friends to come and stay at her house, which Ethel could only believe was good for her future. Ethel knew who was likely to make it and issued a whole series of invitations.

As Daphne Myron recalled: 'Once in a while, she would bring some of her acting friends here as she got older. Mickey Rooney came up here and they'd go to the matinee on a Saturday afternoon. They would get up on the stage and sang and did a dance and things. I remember Donald O'Connor coming up once. They would sing and dance. Everyone went to those – what we called – horse operas. That was an experience for them. They would stay one night and sometimes, girl dancers would come, too.' Much of the time, however, Judy and her mother were living in rented accommodation in Los Angeles.

All the time that Ethel was working on her youngest daughter's career, she was also on the MGM payroll, 'guiding her career along' as she saw it. But, as far as the studio was concerned, it was a way of keeping Mrs Gumm quiet – better to get her inside the tent than throwing rocks from the outside. There were times when the studio bosses would have reason to regret that decision, but on the whole, the ruse worked.

Donald O'Connor and I talked about Judy and MGM. 'It was a wonderful nursery,' he said. 'Just try to imagine what it was like going to school with Judy Garland and Mickey.'

The young performers would go to Lancaster when they didn't actually have pictures on which to work. Trouble was, from the start, Judy herself didn't have any pictures to make at all. That worried Ethel, particularly when she saw the enthusiasm that MGM producers seemed to be directing at another pretty young girl on the lot. Her name was Deanna – at least it would be; at the time she was called Edna Mae Durbin, another singer who, when she opened her mouth, threatened any crystal glass that was lying around. Her bell-like soprano voice was different from Judy's, more pure in its way, almost operatic. But there were those at the studio who believed they could be complementary to each other. They made a test reel and MGM put them together in a film called *Every Sunday*.

The 1936 movie was the real beginning of Judy Garland's career.

CHAPTER FOUR

MGM

MGM stood, as everyone knows, for Metro-Goldwyn-Mayer. I still think that it would be equally appropriate to think of it representing those words 'Makers of Great Musicals'. Not that this was the only explanation on offer. There were others who considered the most easily recognised form of letters in Hollywood to be a tribute to nepotism. This was, after all, the studio where it was said 'the son-in-law also rises'. So MGM stood, they declared, for 'Mayer's Ganzer Mishpochah'. The words were Yiddish and translated as 'Mayer's entire family'.

Judy would never have known that or thought that the studio where the boss's son-in-law David O. Selznick (there was no apostrophe in his name; he was Jewish, not Irish) had held court was practising anything strange. She did know, however, that in 1936, when the 14-year-old Judy was given her seven-year contract, musicals were already the backbone of the studio where she was to earn a starting salary of $100 a week – a veritable fortune.

Meanwhile, Louis B. Mayer himself decided that Judy could be a part of that spine. Putting her in a 'short' was, he reasoned quite logically, a marvellous way to start. She may not have realised it, but this was a standard training exercise. People like James Stewart and Robert Taylor had begun their careers by appearing in those tiny films. If she passed this test, the sky over the Culver City lot was the limit. The message given to Deanna Durbin was much the same.

The 20-minute short was set around a bandstand, said to be

much like the one Mayer himself had enjoyed visiting when he lived at St John, New Brunswick, in Canada, and gave both girls the chance they needed to show their vocal talents. They sang together and separately. Both Judy and Ms Durbin were charming and came over well, with Deanna looking rather more mature and, it ought to be admitted, more beautiful.

In one of those moments in a man's life when he signs a piece of paper and then regrets what he has done, Louis B. Mayer declared that he didn't want both girls to be MGM stars. He thought having two young females playing roughly the same kind of roles, particularly at a time when 'in-betweens' were not exactly in great demand, would be just too confusing. Why have the problem of trying to decide which of the two should make the same kind of film? The answer was to offer a contract to just one of them. So who would get the deal? Mayer decided it should be the girl who made him cry.

Judy Garland was given a contract to sign for a new short. The document came without a screen test. For years afterwards, Mayer was sorry for his decision – not that he had Judy Garland on his books, but that he didn't keep Deanna Durbin too.

He might have been spared a great deal of aggravation had he chosen Durbin instead of Garland. Had he kept her alongside Judy, one might have been played off against the other. What he didn't consider was that Deanna would decide to retire while Judy was still riding high.

He ordered that Judy's contract be extended to the customary seven years. That was not enough in itself to guarantee Hollywood success. It was an agreement where the most successful thought they were the most hard done by. Stars went to court to protest that they were being subject to slavery – but by the same token, for every star there was an actor who either was confined to tiny bit parts or was never to be seen on a screen. Yet for seven years, he or she was paid a generous salary.

Certainly, Mayer was aware that Judy Garland was a marketable commodity, even though he didn't give her a great deal of work to start with. In a way, it was like the 'Phoney War' that preceded the German occupation of France in 1940. But there was that matter of big business. 'He didn't know what to do with us,' Judy commented about her boss. However, Mayer's thoughts were on his investment. He didn't want to waste her. She may not be getting any work for the moment, but the studio boss had already worked out a schedule for his new commercial commodity.

Phoney stardom at first, maybe, but Mayer decided he was going to get full use from his new discovery. Deanna Durbin was, therefore, free to accept an offer from Universal. That annoyed LB (as those who were privileged not to have to address him as 'Mr Mayer' called the studio boss) more than anything. If she couldn't get her contract at MGM renewed, what right had she to go anywhere?

Deanna later went into retirement as a mother and housewife. She once wrote to Judy, asking: 'Why didn't you get out of that business, you dumbbell?'

The truth was getting out of the business was the last thing Judy Garland wanted. The real problems were in the future and she was as keen on performing in the late 1930s – and, in truth, for the rest of her career – as when she couldn't be dragged off the stage in Grand Rapids.

The story of the other Gumms was much more one of being shunted out of the limelight – but that, if they were to be believed, was the way they wanted it. Judy's two sisters were finally out of the picture, able, before long, to marry and live the lives of contented *Saturday Evening Post*-type housewives – before getting divorced. The youngest of the three was about to embark on a career that brought fame, fortune and disaster. £4 husbands

The 'short' declared a success, the 'exam' considered passed, her 'phoney' contract days were over. Now she was going to be put to work. Louis Mayer's investment was going to be made to pay off.

She could not possibly know either how hard the work was or how devastating it would turn out to be on her life. She could have got some idea from the schedule that was initially arranged for her – into the studio early in the morning, school, then working all afternoon. Not bad for the occasional movie, but the success of a film for which she was lent to Twentieth Century Fox was fairly unexpected. *Pigskin Parade*, in which she supported Stuart Erwin in the story of a farmboy who becomes a football hero, proved that hers was a career that was going to be excessively busy.

It was quite an introduction to feature film making. Nobody had told her that she could be let out to another organisation for a sum of money far in excess of her contract, an amount that she not only was never able to see, but from which she would never get a cent. Most important, however, for the first time she was getting close to 'real' grown-up stars – like Betty Grable and Tony Martin.

Not that MGM had any plans to let her go permanently. She was told that her 'own' studio had big plans for her. For once, the studio with the 'super, colossal' boast were not lying. The most glamorous outfit in Hollywood were pulling out all the stops to fulfil their promise and to emphasise their optimistic plans for her.

It was a fact enhanced when she was recruited to participate in a party MGM were throwing for the birthday of their number-one male personality, Clark Gable. It was a typical studio affair. Every one of the stars were there on the biggest MGM sound stage to pay tribute to the actor whose work in movies like *It Happened One Night* and *Mutiny on the Bounty* made him a big box office hit. *It Happened One Night* was actually made by Columbia, to which Gable was loaned after a scandal – he killed a woman while driving home drunk; proving his immense power, Mayer had hushed up the whole affair and arranged for another studio employee to go to jail instead of the star (the story – queried by some, although it was much discussed by those supposedly in the know at the time – nevertheless would be a fair representation of Mayer's power).

There were always Hollywood parties, which people did not throw or attend simply to eat, drink or even have a good time. You didn't go to them to enjoy yourself. You went because to be invited was a demonstration of status. The main object of any guest once the women had handed in their newest white mink coats (even in summer) and the men had deposited their London–made hats was usually to see who was in and who was out. They were usually held in the drawing rooms of stars or senior executives, places big enough for a sufficient number of guests to be around to assess the success or otherwise of people in the industry, a sort of opinion poll from within.

The studio had Judy, and at first Deanna Durbin, on its regular guest list. As at every big Hollywood 'do', guests were expected to sing for their supper before the compulsory showing of a film in the private screening room. Judy was the singer who probably deserved that meal in return for services rendered more than most of the others, although she rarely got it. She was dolled up in a beautiful dress, supplied by the wardrobe department at Culver City. But she wasn't treated like any of the other guests. No champagne and caviar for her. Just lemonade and a pastry or a dish of ice cream, which was frequently melted by the time it reached her. In the days when Deanna was working at MGM, she and Judy were always invited together. There was no pretence that they were there other than to work. Judy would write: 'We would be taken over and we would wait with the servants until they called us into the drawing room where we would perform.'

The Gable 'bash' was bigger than all the rest. At this one, which she and those who had replied to the gilt-edged invitations would remember for the rest of their lives, Judy performed a routine that lived long in memory. Little Mickey Rooney introduced the girl as 'the finest voice you'll ever hear' and with the famous Ben Bernie orchestra backing her, she sang a specially written version of 'You Made Me Love You' – in the midst of which, she dictated a letter to 'Dear Mr Gable'.

If it were possible for a singer to bring a house down, MGM would have had to call in the builders and carpenters to reassemble the wreckage. It was an amazing triumph – so much so that she reprised that performance in her first big solo MGM role, *Broadway Melody of 1938* (which was originally supposed to be *Broadway Melody of 1937*, but wasn't finished in time). She was such a hit in the film that other roles in what could be called 'Hollywood Melodies' followed.

After the great success of her 'Dear Mr Gable' routine on the studio lot, Mayer now brought Judy to parties at his own house on her own accord – for other guests to meet her and to fawn over her. They were always held as much as business occasions as social events. In addition to the best Krug champagne offered by flunkies in full dress and a dinner that would earn a restaurant a Michelin star or two, there was always *that* film to be shown – one that had not yet gone into any cinema – and, of course, the 'live' entertainment, too. Fred Astaire would dance with Ginger Rogers in Mayer's private ballroom, George Gershwin would play 'I've Got Rhythm' for the first time on his grand piano and Judy would sing from the balcony, which was a kind of minstrel gallery. The fact that she was now not merely invited to perform but to enjoy proceedings that were intended for people far beyond her age group proved that she was already regarded as a star.

Back home in Lancaster, to say nothing about Grand Rapids, people flocked to their local picture houses to see just how good the local girl had made. Jean Denzil told me: 'I don't suppose there was anyone in Grand Rapids who didn't see those movies. We waited for each to come out and then stood in line to see them.'

In Lancaster, it provided the local paper with real 'copy' at last. Recording the success of their own 'Baby' was more interesting, its editor had to admit to me, than telling about the ice cream soda she bought at the drug store or the time she narrowly escaped being knocked down by a truck.

Norma Gurber said: 'Lancaster was such a small town, but when a Judy Garland film was shown, I'm told by the old people here, it seemed to grow bigger. The place almost literally swelled with pride. When she came home, they virtually waited in line to talk to her.' Daphne Myron told me that day when the trail took me to Cedar Avenue: 'We were just very excited. We loved to talk about her and to tell people how we played with her.'

They were not concerned about such things at Culver City, the home of MGM. They liked the local-paper publicity, but needed it to be copied in thousands of other papers in towns, small and large, all over America. And not just America. Good Hollywood films went all over the world. And all over the world, there were gatherings of people who paid tribute to little Judy Garland by seeing her films and buying her records. For that was another part of her success. Decca, along with RCA and Columbia one of the big three in the recording industry, had had her in mind for a contract earlier in the decade – thus being able to list the name Judy Garland along with stars like Bing Crosby and Al Jolson – but then thought better of it. Yet then, after the success of *Broadway Melody,* the label decided they had been right all along and signed her to a contract. It was a wise move. People spent good portions of their wages or their pocket money on 78 rpm discs and now, as a result of the contract that Ethel signed on her behalf, they were buying Judy Garland records. There was also her face on sheet music. But it was the records that were big business and from smart department stores to the local Woolworths, there were boys and girls and their parents waiting for a new Judy release, even before they heard it played on the radio. That was a special kind of fame. Now, the folks up Lancaster way didn't have to wait to hear her at a local concert. She was there all the time.

Louis B. Mayer was not everyone's favourite Hollywood personality. He might have wanted to be considered father to his contracted children, but actually he was much more like the owner of a stable of racehorses he thought stood a good chance of finishing first in a race, or a farmer with prize cattle to fatten up. With that thought in mind, he was ready to turn his attention, if only momentarily, from Clark Gable and Greta Garbo and from Myrna Loy and Robert Taylor to the kid from Grand Rapids and Lancaster.

He had to worry about her welfare. The law said that. He made the odd trip to the MGM schoolhouse and, if there were a photo opportunity in it, he could be seen smiling benignly at Judy and her young friends at their desks. But without the public eye on him, the private one was looking at the books. After *Broadway Melody of 1938,* they were distinctly in the black. Judy not only sang about Mr Gable, but proved she could act. In fact, she out-acted Sophie Tucker, which was not altogether difficult.

Ms Tucker, who was a top vaudevillian and a former Ziegfeld star, was exceedingly popular during her stage days and was still a pull as a nightclub entertainer. But a good dramatic actress she was not. However, every big star had to do films. Some made it, some did not. After that *Broadway Melody* movie, it was quite clear that Judy Garland was one of those who would succeed.

People believed that Sophie Tucker could only look jealously at the young girl who was playing her daughter – and do so coupling that envy with feelings of bewilderment. But to her everlasting credit, she didn't allow any jealousy to show and did what she could in newspaper interviews *and* in private conversations to say how much she admired the younger star. Years later, towards the end of both their lives, Sophie said she hoped that Judy would play her in a biopic movie.

When I interviewed her in London shortly before her death, she told me: 'I'd like to think that Judy had something of what I had, the thrill of entertaining. She may even have been better than I was.' That was really saying a lot. If there was real admiration, it was infectious.

Judy was having a strange effect on the studio head. Mayer never lost his interest in her as a business asset, but he found her endearing at the same time. There were those in the studio and to whom I spoke on *The Judy Garland Trail* who noticed the change in his attitude to her. He knew that her father had died, he appreciated that Ida Koverman was keeping Ethel out of his hair, and yet when he talked about her being one of his children, there was indeed something fatherly about him.

She needed that fatherly touch more than she would let on. The veteran singing star Margaret Whiting told me that her friend Judy was devastated by Frank's death. They had had a very strong relationship, which had partly succeeded in keeping her out of her mother's clutches. Now, Ethel was exercising every ounce of control at her disposal. Mayer tried to put a stop to too much interference, as he saw it. He did not, however, see the backbiting at home, Ethel's determination to give her daughter 'lessons' that she patently did not need. Vicariously, she may have been enjoying her youngest daughter's stardom, but she wasn't sure that Mayer was doing enough to foster her. He, of course, said that wasn't true. All he wanted was what was right for her.

He was even ready to lend her to David O. Selznick for a part in *Gone with the Wind* – no, not as Scarlett O'Hara, that would have been too much for the citizens of Grand Rapids to take, but as her sister. The role eventually went to Ann Rutherford. LB was more concerned with keeping Judy Garland under his personal supervision. Besides, he had big plans for her.

For that reason, he was not about to leave her to some underling to watch over her career. Now, he had the right vehicle for her – a series of movies that would forever after be summed up in the name 'Andy Hardy'. Andy was supposed to be a cheeky chappie who frequently got into scrapes. He was the centre of the kind of all-American family that was dreamed of by the all-American Louis B. Mayer (who actually was born in what is now Belarus), chairman of the Republican Party of California, donor to a dozen good all-American causes.

It was a part made to measure for Mickey Rooney, whom Judy had met at school, but who first worked with her in the 1937 movie *Thoroughbreds Don't Cry,* made soon after the *Broadway Melody* picture. In that, Mickey had played a jockey. Sophie Tucker, teamed with Judy again, played the landlady of a boarding house for riders.

LB told her he had an Andy Hardy movie on the lot waiting for her. But while they were getting prepared, he had other projects in mind – notably *Everybody Sing*. If *Broadway Melody* made a huge impact, *Everybody Sing* did almost as much for her. She was against such seasoned veterans as Fanny Brice (the critics put them together as stealing the show) playing her iconic 'Baby Snooks' routine, Allan Jones and Billie Burke (who was the last Mrs Florenz Ziegfeld), but the audience reactions as they signed the comment cards after the various previews and premieres declared they couldn't get enough of the new girl. When she made a live appearance at the Miami showing, singing tunes from the movie, the audience erupted. As the broadcaster Joe Franklin told me: 'She was competing with as well as dancing with Fanny Brice. She was singing grown-up songs really for the first time and she was sensational. She had that throb. That pulsating sound, a great, great, grown-up sound when she was so young.'

If anyone doubted that MGM were working this frail young girl hard, the catalogue of work she was doing proved it. All three of those movies were made in the same year. What was more, her work was not restricted to appearing before the cameras or recording new ten-inch shellac discs. There were, of course, the statutory personal appearances and now she was being boosted as a radio star. In the days before television, this was the primary home-entertainment medium. With regular appearances on the film comedy star Jack Oakie's *Oakie's College* show about a mythical university, with Oakie featured as the dean, she could have written the words 'radio personality' in her CV as justifiably as she could claim to be a film star. Then, following the success of the Oakie programme, there were regular appearances on the studio's own weekly radio show *Good News* – needless to say, the title of an MGM movie.

It was *Love Finds Andy Hardy* that proved how useful Judy was as a stock character. It was the fourth film in the series and – because of Judy's arrival – the most popular. She was assigned the part of his next-door neighbour. Actually, her principal role was to keep the series going. It was incredibly cheap to make and equally incredibly popular with audiences in Middle America. The citizens of Grand Rapids and Lancaster not only went to see the movies, but saw their own small towns come to a new kind of life on the screen.

The films all told the story of the good, decent, clean-living Hardy family – old Judge Hardy, Andy's father, much older than one would think this young boy would have as a dad, played by Lewis Stone, his mother by Fay Holden and his girlfriend, Ann Rutherford, back from Atlanta and *Gone with the Wind*. When Judy Garland came along, the stories had to be given a new look. The youngsters from the MGM schoolroom were working together on the same set. 'Working' was the operative word for what Judy did on the studio lot – going to school as well as making movies. Her day at lessons wasn't the easy run-through that a lot of people thought, but the camaraderie with other children in the same business could be exciting.

By the time Judy Garland made her first – and only – trip back to Grand Rapids in 1938, she came as a star, albeit a star who was not appreciated quite as much as she thought she would have been. In a broadcast interview she had said how much she loved the town/village of her birth. The love she probably quite genuinely felt was distinctly not returned by the people who were friends of her parents but who thought the young girl was perhaps a little too big for her tiny shoes.

There are two factors that usually play a part in a local hero or heroine's arrival. One is that people like to claim friendships that never really existed. The other is a sense of jealousy. In both Lancaster and Grand Rapids, the citizenry deny that either of those things occurred. At least, most of them do. As John Kelsch told me: 'Most people were delighted to see her when she came and the town made a great fuss of her. But there were one or two who did not. I suspect there was a certain jealousy.'

The visit to her birthplace followed a highly successful US tour. She had been to New York, Chicago and a trip round Ohio, concentrating on Cleveland, home of Bob Hope, who sent her greetings. The tour had been extraordinarily successful – not least making her solo debut at Loew's State on Broadway. It was nothing less than a sensation and Roger Edens, who was now accompanying her on the tour, wrote back to MGM, saying it had been a tremendous boost for the studio. After all this big-time stuff, going to small-town Grand Rapids seemed to be easy meat. It wasn't.

Lilah Crowe puts most of the problems of that visit down to the very unusual experience of very ordinary people meeting someone who was now an international celebrity. It was rather like poor old Joe Gargery in Charles Dickens's *Great Expectations* going to meet his wife's nephew Pip once he had become a 'gentleman'. Gargery did not know what to do with his hat or which cutlery to use. That wasn't Judy Garland's problem in Grand Rapids, but the citizenry had other things to concern them. As Lilah Crowe told me: 'She was a budding star and she did wear a lot of make-up. In 1938, in a little town like Grand Rapids if you wore make-up, you were not considered part of the community. You were after something.' So Judy was regarded as a kind of 20th-century Jezebel? 'Right! You got it.'

There were dances for young people in Grand Rapids and you might today just find a man in his nineties who can recall doing a foxtrot with her in the school hall. Until recent years, a group of them would get together and remember when they danced with Judy Garland. Lilah Crowe put it like this: 'The guys liked her, but it was really hard on the older local people, because they weren't used to that.'

The ramifications spread. 'Some people did look at her as a star. Others looked at her, saying, "This is out of our realm". They pretty much stayed back.'

As she said: "You have to put yourself in the concept of 1938, of what was going on in our world, our community here. There wasn't this "Oh! A star!" It was "Oh, this is the one who left and made herself up". Ordinary people just go on with living their lives. They kinda struggled to make a living in a northern community town and she never did come back.'

Jealousy, without doubt, had a lot to do with it. 'Oh, I'm sure,' Lilah added. 'Theirs was a struggle merely to survive. For them to travel to Hollywood was unheard of. For them to travel out of town to go to Minneapolis was like a miracle.'

So, on the whole, the older people made her feel very unwelcome. And there was another dimension: Judy found out why her father had to leave town.

If that was a difficult time for her, already the pressures of work were getting too much. It was clear to the MGM people that she had problems. She was always tired – not difficult to work out why. She lacked confidence – so unlike Mickey Rooney's astonishingly large capsule of energy, which was equally obvious off the set as it was on.

It seemed clear, bearing in mind the list of projects to come, that

MGM were thinking of a permanent partnership between Rooney and Garland. But, like all sensible business operations, the studio were covering their options. In *Listen Darling*, a lightish story about children looking for a wife for their widowed father, she was partnered with Freddie Bartholomew, who had made a reputation playing very nice little boys with cut-glass English accents, like in the 1936 *Little Lord Fauntleroy*, a movie with which he would always be linked – his name was rarely printed without the film role in the same sentence. In *David Copperfield,* the year before, he had first shown what he could do with what would become typecasting. But he was getting older, too old to wear an Eton collar, and MGM wanted to test how he would shape up as an all-American teenager. They also wanted to see how he would get on with Judy. As it turned out, Mickey Rooney had nothing to worry about.

But Judy was unhappy and showing signs of that overwork to which she was subjected.

What to do about it? What Louis B. Mayer authorised was a step that would ultimately be his new star's ruin. He introduced her to a doctor. The doctor prescribed drugs.

When I spoke to Judy's daughter Lorna Luft, many years before the trail started winding, she had no doubt that the behaviour of the studio was responsible for so much. 'They gave her downers to make her sleep and uppers to get her to work.' It was a roller-coaster regimen that contributed to her roller-coaster life and the inevitable question in this 'trial' of a trail: how could a performer be so wonderful so often and so disappointing at other times? No psychiatrist was necessary to put those troubles down to her childhood and early youth.

On the other hand, there were a great many people I met on the Judy Trail who cast doubt on that received 'wisdom'.

One, Meredith Ponedel, niece of Judy's favourite make-up artist Dorothy Ponedel (who had moved from Chicago to Hollywood to get big parts in silent movies with Mabel Normand), told me about the 'big girl' to whom she would look up whenever she came to visit her aunt. Meredith has assessed all the sides to Judy's

MGM relationship story. 'In my opinion, [Louis B. Mayer] was definitely not looking after Judy's welfare. He just wanted to turn out a commodity. You can't do that with people who were talented on a level that Judy was talented.'

On the other hand, she dismisses the notion that LB was all evil. Judy, she maintains, did not think that. 'I've heard both sides. I know that Dot (Dorothy) never had a problem with him. Judy also very much liked his brother Jerry Mayer. If Judy needed something, she'd go to Jerry who would then tell Louis: "We need this, we need to do that." Dot was always fighting for Judy to have more time off, to have a break. I know there were rumours when Judy was much younger at MGM about her not being fed properly, not being allowed to eat in the commissary. Dot said that was nonsense. She would bring Judy food herself and she knew she could eat.'

Indeed she could. But Meredith did not doubt those stories about the uppers and downers. 'They were not a fabrication. To a degree, they were necessary, and Judy was not the only one to use them.'

Between checking designs and looking through swatches of materials, Judy's TV designer Ray Aghayan used to discuss with her the drugs she took at the behest of MGM. He, too, agrees that the legend was not confirmed by what the star, with the benefit of hindsight, recalled. 'Her problems were not all MGM's fault. Not according to her. I heard all sorts of naughty things about almost all the people at MGM, Louis B and all of them. It was never as people have written – at least, according to Judy. She wouldn't think so.'

So nothing from Judy Garland about Louis.B. Mayer being the real villain of the piece? 'She didn't feel that way. She made fun of it. She thought it was funny. She never talked about the pills and all of that. She didn't seem to resent it.'

Nevertheless, the use of drugs by Judy has come to serve as a warning to young people – not least of all, in her old home in Grand Rapids. John Kelsch said he believes they were originally prescribed to her as cures for her asthma. 'Hollywood just embraced those drugs,' he told me. 'We had a seminar about the dangers of prescription drugs.'

But then everything in Hollywood was fantasy. Meredith Ponedel, who at aged three and a half, would experience the fantasy of Judy Garland close at hand. 'I remember meeting her for the first time. We had two record albums. All I knew was that there was a very pretty lady on the covers. And then Dot introduced me to this rather dishevelled-looking lady who one day came down the hallway and Dot said, "This is Judy Garland". And she said this was the same lady I listened to on the records. I looked at the records, this beautiful woman, and [then] I looked at this woman with the hair sticking out and no make-up on, she had just come from goodness knows where and I said, "No, that's not her." They both started to crack up. They couldn't believe that here I was, this little monster, looking up and saying no, that's not who you are.'

That was MGM's job. To convince people that she was not who they thought she was, that an adolescent was really a child. Making a well-developed, 17-year-old woman play a girl of 12 was taking things a little far. Except there was a wizard on hand to make it all seem reasonable.

CHAPTER FIVE

The Wizard of Oz

The story of Judy Garland and *The Wizard of Oz* is one of a triumph that probably came too early. In a way it was similar to that of Orson Welles with *Citizen Kane* two years later. Both featured young stars at the beginning of their careers. Both of those actors would always be remembered for what they did at that stage, but they were people who, despite all their obvious talents – more talented than a host of other famous actors put together – would in some people's view never live up to that promise.

Of course, Judy Garland was luckier than Welles, who was a genius who perhaps tried too hard. Everything he did would be compared with his *Kane* role – and rarely favourably. He had arguments with producers who changed his movies out of all recognition and was fired from film after film.

Judy had a string of successes after making *The Wizard,* mostly all forgettable but all making her more and more loveable. Yet her problems were similar to those of Orson Welles in so many ways. She would be sacked from films, behave in ways that were determined to be unprofessional, fail to turn up for jobs and find that even close friends, who totally understood why she had her problems, despaired of her.

Whereas Welles was cocky and overconfident, spending most of his time nurturing a superiority complex, Judy was always unsure of herself, labouring under feelings of inadequacy. Unlike Welles, she was no genius. She had a wonderful, thrilling voice and could act beautifully, but whatever she did after walking along that yellow brick road would pale into insignificance in the public memory – excluding, of course, the memory and adoration of her fans. When she gave a concert, the audience cried for 'Over the Rainbow'. As I discovered working on a 'vox pop' in a New York subway asking people what the name Judy Garland meant to them, the answer was always summed up in four words, '*The Wizard of Oz*'. That is, if they knew the name at all. Such is fame. She had plenty of good, perhaps brilliant, achievements as she grew older. Without them she would never have become the cult figure that she was. True, much of that would come from her live performances, but her fans, thousands of them, saw everything she did on the screen. Some of that body of work, such as her performances in *Meet Me In St Louis* and *A Star Is Born* and, towards the end of her life, in *Judgment at Nuremberg,* was quite brilliant. Yet she will never be remembered specifically for those roles in quite the same way that she still is for *The Wizard*.

Was she lucky to get the part of little Dorothy Gale in *The Wizard of Oz*? Of course she was, but nevertheless, she was on the way to creating a monster for herself.

When MGM awarded her the big prize of Dorothy, they began, in the process, not a yellow brick road to happiness, but a sad trail to mental strife, overwork and final disaster. Would things have been easier had she not played the part of little Dorothy in the film? It is possible to pose the thought that had she not bound her mature body in sheets of linen to make a 17-year-old girl look like a child of 12 – which presented its own problems – she might not have become the superstar into which she did metamorphose. She could well have gone from Andy Hardy's next-door neighbour into a competent, charming actress in the kind of middle-of-the-road musicals that the MGM factory produced with great finesse but not much thought for posterity. But that was not what the studio had in mind.

The search for a Dorothy was treated much like the one that David O. Selznick instituted for a Scarlett O'Hara in *Gone With The Wind*. There was a great deal of pre-publicity for the movie version of Frank L. Baum's story about the girl from Kansas who ends up in a land of fantasy – almost as fantastic, it has to be said, as the life of Judy Garland.

People remember the film not so much because of its entire story, but because of its characters. The cowardly lion (played by Bert Lahr, an old vaudevillian) the tin man (Jack Haley) and the scarecrow (Ray Bolger) have become so iconic that they now symbolise a movie and an era of cinema that people who never actually saw the whole picture firmly believe they remember. Of course, along with her three friends, there was the omnipresent 'Toto', her faithful and ever-loving dog. Millions who have never seen the movie – even on its numerous excursions on television – can point to the scene where Judy, in pigtails and a gingham dress over a blouse with puffed sleeves, danced down the yellow brick road with Toto and her three fabulous friends. That is a ciné moment that few other films can replicate. Perhaps only the moment when Dooley Wilson sang 'As Time Goes By' in *Casablanca* could compete with it.

What was it that made *The Wizard* so important? It would be nice to just say it was Judy singing 'Over the Rainbow'. Surely, that was a song moment that made her career, that solidified it, that made it her signature – like Al Jolson singing 'Mammy', Bing Crosby warbling 'White Christmas' and, yes, Liza Minnelli's performance as Sally Bowles rejoicing about life being a cabaret. And, like them, people associate the song with her, not with the film. It is because of that number that the picture has gone down in history. Its effect was to make this and the scene with her three friends a double whammy. To win on both counts was an achievement.

Did Louis B. Mayer, sitting in his all-white office suite at Culver City, predict that? He did not. Did he think that with Judy Garland he had a sure-fire hit? There was nothing to indicate that he did. It could all have been a hunch, which in the movie business was perhaps the most valuable asset a mogul could possibly have.

On the surface, the cards were stacked against this picture as a successful project right from the start. For one thing, it was going to feature a Technicolor sequence at a time when a film in colour was almost a risky operation. There were very few colour movies and until 1939 when both *The Wizard* and *Gone with the Wind* went before the cameras, the results were usually awfully unpredictable – or predictably awful. So, like a man who wears both a St Christopher's medal and a Star of David, Mayer was covering all his bases. There would be just one reel in colour and the earliest moments would be in sepia. If this and the colour didn't work, he could let people praise the more conventional photography in between. If it did work, then he'd reap the benefit of the adventurous idea he was promulgating.

But the colour option wasn't the only reason for LB and his executives to scratch their greying heads. For one thing, the story had been filmed before. There had been a 1925 (silent and black-and-white, of course) version which hadn't exactly made many film lovers rejoice, and is as far away in the world of film master-pieces as could possibly be imagined. So there was risk number two – could a comparative flop be turned into a huge success? No one knew.

Mayer felt he needed an insurance policy. There was no more popular child star in America than Shirley Temple and it was she whom he wanted. Certainly, the role of Dorothy would be as perfect a fit for her as the little dresses she would be expected to wear. Shirley herself might have thought so, but Twentieth Century Fox wouldn't release her from her contract obligations so that she could work for the enemy – no one at Fox thought in terms of MGM's having already lent Judy for *Pigskin Parade* and that perhaps it would be nice to return the compliment. But, then, Hollywood is like that. Shirley's studio may have seen something in the film that Metro didn't and hated the idea of its own star possibly being responsible for Mayer's outfit having a big success. That was a lucky thing to happen. Can we today imagine the little girl who sang about 'The Good Ship Lollipop' providing anything like the plaintive rendering of 'Over the Rainbow' that Judy was able to offer? Hardly.

Deciding Judy should have the role was an inspired – and, again, risky – idea. She had never done anything as big as this before.

There were the very well-developed bust and hips that Judy now had to disguise. She had to be bound and strapped into her little blue check dress with the white puff sleeves. She had to have her by now very attractive hairstyle altered to a 1930s set of pigtails. At first, she was made to wear a blonde wig, but she hated that and was, before any damage could be done, allowed to alter and dye her own hair.

Temple wasn't the only first choice who had to end up not getting the part she wanted. Buddy Ebsen – who famously danced with Shirley and in later life became well-known on American television as the head of the *Beverly Hillbillies* Clampett family – was to have been the scarecrow. But he switched to playing the tin man, and then had to give way to Jack Haley because he was allergic to the aluminium dust. Ray Bolger turned into the scarecrow and became the one who sang, 'I could while away the hours – conversin' with the flowers'.

Then there were other problems – not least, that of the director. For the first 12 days of shooting, Richard Thorpe was Mayer's choice and began giving the instructions from the other side of the camera. But nobody seemed happy with him and after those 12 days he was replaced by one of the outstanding directors of the time, Victor Fleming. But actually, he wasn't the director *all* the time. Those sepia moments earlier on and at the end of the picture were directed by the equally valued King Vidor. Oh yes, and some of the costume and make-up tests were given to George Cukor, Hollywood women's favourite director, to supervise.

Even the role of the Wicked Witch, another iconic part, wasn't settled in one go. Edna May Oliver, an established actress used in film after film as the kind of woman who looked as though she had always flown into a scene on a broomstick – and had scored great personal acclaim as Betsey Trotwood in *David Copperfield* – didn't last the course either. She was replaced ultimately by Margaret Hamilton.

MGM were not exactly the kindest outfit to the people who were as essential to the picture as any of the others but who they reasoned didn't need to be spoiled. The Munchkins were the 'little people' (today, it wouldn't be considered politically correct to call them, as they were at the time, 'dwarfs' – the first full-length Disney cartoon movie, remade today, would presumably have to be called *Snow White and the Seven Small Ones*).

All over America, notices were printed in local newspapers calling for volunteers to go for auditions to be considered for the parts of 'little people' welcoming Dorothy to Munchkin Land. One of them was Jerry Maren, who was approaching his 90th birthday when he told me proudly: 'I was the one who greeted Judy when she arrived in Munchkinland on the Yellow Brick Road.'

He remembers his time on *The Wizard* as being the most important in his life – it led to hundreds of other roles. But he doesn't recall it as particularly happy for him and the other citizens of Munchkinland – although he says that Judy was lovely to them. 'She'd come on stage and say, "Hi, gang. How are you all today?" 'We would love to have seen more of her, but somehow that didn't work out, except for one occasion. I suppose you could say that she was typical of any school kid her age.'

He has less than kind thoughts about the studio that employed both him and Judy. 'MGM was not the benevolent institution that Louis B. Mayer would like to think it was,' he told me. But he soon got back into the spirit of remembering his own involvement. 'Me and my partners were in the crowd when she got on the yellow brick road. I said: "We represent the Lollipop Guild. We wish to welcome you to Lollipop Land."' With that, he took a giant lollipop from behind his back and waved it, as he had done in the movie 70 years earlier. He was once again living his role. It was easier to do that than to remember the preamble to his getting his role.

Maren told me how he got involved in the project. 'We're from Boston. My sister, Rae, read an article that they were looking for little people for *The Wizard*. She wrote them a letter and told them about me.'

Jerry Maren, 3 feet 6 inches tall at the time, was the only one of his family to be 'little'. There were 400 to 500 people like him needed to audition. In the end, just 124 of them turned up. 'We had to be under four-feet-five. They wanted more people, but they couldn't get any more.'

They were all herded on to buses at Times Square in New York and then began the long gruelling trip to Los Angeles. 'We were told to have the correct clothing and they introduced me to seven or eight little people. It was fun meeting them. I'd never seen other little people in my life. I could look them in the eye while standing up, instead of looking up all the time.'

He didn't look up to the MGM executives. 'We had a long talk on the bus, all the way to Culver City. There were people from overseas and people from Texas, who I expected to be huge. They were smaller than I was. But the journey they inflicted on us was terrible. We slept on the bus for five nights and thirty-five of us stayed in a Culver City hotel. I slept in a room with three other guys. Three of us in a pretty big bed. In the morning, I heard a band. I looked outside and there was a big parade. The other guys said, "Listen, they're welcoming us to Culver City, wake up." They didn't realise it was Armistice Day.'

But there was little sign of an armistice from Louis B. Mayer's henchmen, who ordered them about as though they were subhuman – even if they did pay them all of $50 a week each.

Maren had always wanted to be an actor. But the life wasn't what he had expected it would be when he went to dancing lessons with his sister. That was when he first dreamed of a show-business career. 'We worked on the film for about six weeks. A week of preparation, make-up, wardrobe. It was horrible. We each had to wear a skullcap. Then they put wigs on us and I ended up with spirit gum all over me.' That was not the only humiliating factor. Before they did their singing and dancing, numbers like 'Ding Dong, The Witch Is Dead', they had to record their speeches and their songs – with their voices distorted to make them sound as the director believed the Munchkinland citizens ought to sound.

The mitigating factor was meeting Judy. 'She was working all the time. They demanded so much of her, she could hardly keep up. She was a lovely young lady. She was charming. She was an angel. We all loved her.' Not that they were allowed to socialise with the young star. In fact, Maren only remembers one occasion when he and his pals were invited into her dressing room. 'She gave us a big box of chocolates.' Not a big box each, but *one* chocolate each, a box between 124 of them. 'The chocolates were in her dressing room and she had told us: "I want you all to come over. I want to give you a chocolate. She gave us a chocolate and an autographed picture of herself." '

The film was not the big hit of 1939 that Mayer had been hoping for. It was greeted sympathetically by large audiences, but seemed to come and go. What few people realise is that it took a while for its cult status to be achieved. Gradually, people began to talk about it. The result was a whole series of reruns for generations who were not around at the time it was made. Television, of course, has given it a whole new lease of life. But Judy had achieved universal fame – and a special Oscar for 'the best juvenile performance of the year'. 'Over the Rainbow' won an Academy Award for best song and Herbert Stothart, the musical director, was given one too.

The film itself was nominated for best picture, but was beaten to the Oscar by *Gone with the Wind*. (It was in good company; other losers included such immortal titles as *Goodbye, Mr. Chips*, *Ninotchka*, *Wuthering Heights* and *Mr. Smith Goes to Washington*).

There was no doubt that Judy was now made both as a star and as a national symbol of perfect girlhood. Joe Franklin, one of New York's best-known television personalities, told me: 'I interviewed Judy Garland many times and she always spoke about *The Wizard of Oz* and was very proud to have done it.'

MGM felt much the same thing.

CHAPTER SIX

The Hollywood Years

Louis B. Mayer was basking in the response to a film from people whom he respected – although he would have respected the *paying* public more if they had set a few box-office records, which they didn't. But there were plenty around who considered him to be the real wizard of the piece. After all, he was the one who made the *Oz* story a practical proposition.

As for Judy, there would be another 20 pictures to come in the following decade. She was plainly now being sought as never before. And she was being given the best people with whom to work. It was while appearing on a radio show that she met Kay Thompson, who was to become a tremendous influence on her. Kay was currently appearing in the Broadway show *Tune-Up Time* and Judy was promoting *The Wizard*.

Before long, the sometime actress, comedienne, singer and pianist was adding the job description of 'Judy Garland friend' to her resumé. MGM decided to appoint her as more or less resident consultant and arranger for Judy's future pictures, of which they assured her there would be many. The appointment was made from almost the moment the first coins for *Wizard* seats tinkled on to the box-office counters.

'They immediately became friends,' Sam Irvine, who is working on a Thompson biography, told me. 'More important, she became a huge influence on her.' As he said: 'Judy never had much of a childhood at all. She relied on Kay in so many ways as a mother figure and as a friend, someone she trusted implicitly. She knew that Kay would never betray her as other people in the studio were to betray her. Judy needed a support system and was given it by people like Kay Thompson.'

Indeed, it was an important relationship. It is possible to see Kay's influence in Judy's TV performances, something that people who saw her on stage should have been able to appreciate. Judy would stand on stage with the poise that Kay taught her. Style in show business is all-important. The upraised arm that Liza Minnelli and dozens of other women stars have adopted since Judy appeared to make it her own trademark was also a Kay Thompson style. As Sam Irvine put it to me: 'There was a style of singing that Kay Thompson minted at a high-octane level, which was very ener-gising and uplifting for the audience. Kay was known for wide gesticulations, very frenetic movements.'

If Thompson was a great friend, she was not the only one. It seems that the girl who was so under the influence of the men at MGM, from Louis B. Mayer down, made no secret that she sought friendship from other women – and was plainly able to confide in them in a way she had never been able to do in the studio, or even with her mother and sisters. Her family, to no one's regret, were now drifting into the background, although from time to time they all shared the same Beverly Hills house. Judy needed a particular kind of girl-to-girl friendship away from her family and she found it with another singer called Margaret Whiting.

Ms Whiting was not a star in the way that Judy Garland was, but she was an important singer on records, radio and television and was one of Bob Hope's cast of friends who were also performers when he made his World War Two trips to entertain the troops. She also recorded with him.

In a smart New York apartment, Margaret Whiting told me how seeing Judy in *Pigskin Parade* ('I had never seen anything like it in my life and never will') made her an instant fan. But they got to know each other through one of those Hollywood parties, not an MGM affair, but one thrown by her father, the songwriter Richard – 'The Good Ship Lollipop' and 'Hooray for Hollywood' – Whiting. They talked and talked then – and made up their minds to be friends. Richard Whiting died in 1938, but his wife,

Margaret's mother, continued to host the parties every Saturday night. Judy attended them with a great deal more alacrity than she did those sponsored by the studio.

The friendship the two girls had became one of those associations that go beyond mere idle gossip. 'My mother gave us a party every week and it was a hang-out for New York and for movie people who were doing pictures. The folks came every Saturday because it was a ball and we had every pianist in town and every great singer. I was not aware that Judy was having problems at this time – because we were having fun.'

Because the parties were so obviously a chance to guess who was 'in' and who was 'out', frequently the arrival of guests was announced out loud by those who had arrived early. 'We would shout, "Hey, Mel (Tormé) has just walked in. Here's Judy!" She would come in and she would sing, just like at one of those Hollywood parties you hear about. And my mother said, "I have to cook for you and your friends. Stop inviting people."' Mrs Whiting was not serious, because the invitations to people like Judy Garland and Mel Tormé continued and the hostess was enjoying them as much as anyone. 'But it was at one party in particular that I realised Judy was very unhappy and very complicated – and I realised she had never really had a happy life and probably never would.'

It was a time when, as far as the opposite sex was concerned, Judy had stopped being an in-between – and it was painful. Margaret Whiting was suffering along with her. That became clear when they were guests at other people's parties. 'I [eventually] got to know she was an unhappy woman the night she and I were at Ira Gershwin's house for a party.

'I went upstairs to the bathroom and as I walked into the room I could see Judy was sitting on the floor next to a fire that was burning in the adjoining bedroom. She said, "Sit down with me, Margaret." So we sat down and talked, girl to girl, about life and about who wrote the best songs.'

Neither of them could avoid talking shop.

But there was, Margaret told me, 'a wistfulness in her voice as the conversation got round to men – and what she wanted and what I wanted. And we spent a good hour sitting on the floor in front of the fire at that party. Then somebody came upstairs and said, "Will you broads get out of here and come back to the party." '

There were other conversations in the years that followed, often showing that same wistfulness. 'A woman can tell when another woman talks about her life. She liked having fun with Mickey Rooney and she *had* fun, but there was no man in her life at this time, no one who knocked her out. I could tell that she was missing something. Women know that when they are with other women. We talked about what we would do when our prince came along. Every woman, when we are young, thinks that some man who will be gorgeous and tall, your own prince, will enter her life. You've sung those songs, you've played those parts. We were daydreaming in front of the fire and dreaming at night, thinking of the men we idolised. Maybe they were actors we had seen on the screen. She wasn't happy and neither was I.'

Judy's problems were becoming obvious to other friends. Paul Rabwin, a man closely connected with Hollywood people and their difficulties, told me: 'There was a camaraderie when she was with Mickey Rooney. [MGM] tried to make a good environment for them. But going from one project to another had a toll on her even when she was very young. You don't suddenly get worn out by business. It's an ongoing pervasive malady, but when you start as early as Judy did, you show it.

'She may not have been taking drugs or drinking in her teens, but I feel pretty certain that [work] was taking its toll and she started having problems in her personal life. She didn't have a release point. She just found herself ultimately trapped. It was a very toxic environment, particularly when she was regarded as a commodity. The studio were totally controlling her whole life. It was very dangerous [for anyone in movies] but much more so for children if you don't have a secure family life to go back to and it was difficult for Judy. She didn't have a strong family life and for her it was very difficult.'

Meanwhile, intentionally, the impression given by the studio was that this was a very happy young woman thoroughly enjoying all the success that had come to her. What was more, this happy youngster wanted nothing more than to show how much fun she was having as a teenager. Therefore, *Babes in Arms*, her first picture after *The Wizard*, was made to show all the glories of being very young. It also cemented Judy's position as the perfect teenager – and, in particular, as the perfect partner for Mickey Rooney. It was the beginning of a sequence of movies that, in retrospect, just seem to be parts of the same film, not even prequels or sequels. 'Come on, let's put on a show,' became a line copied, mangled and used in film after film.

Judy appeared at live performances on Broadway and home in Los Angeles. Bob Hope, who no longer had to explain to the citizens of Cleveland who she was, had her as a guest star week after week on his Pepsodent radio show. No more perfect proof of arrival could there possibly have been. Louis B. Mayer might have wanted her to act the perennial teenager, but on those radio programmes she was as grown-up as she looked. The people of Grand Rapids might have muttered 'Jezebel' again, but it didn't matter. When they saw pictures of her at movie premieres, arm in arm with Mickey Rooney, they doubtless swooned and squealed and clapped as they went about their business. They felt as proud as did Ethel Gumm, who was finding it difficult to reconcile her daughter's achievements with her own position and was shoved more and more into the background. But Judy's mother had a compensation. She married the man with whom she had been sleeping for years (even while she was still married to Frank), Will Gilmore. Judy was not pleased. She and Gilmore did not get on at all. He was not the sort of man she wanted for her mother and certainly not the kind of stepfather she would have appreciated for herself. He himself revelled in being able to say that his step-daughter was Judy Garland.

Studying the extramural or off-set activities of the stars, it is revealing to contemplate the problems experienced by youngsters like Garland and Rooney. The MGM publicity department pulled no punches in emphasising how joined at the hip (but only at the hip) the pair were. Had Judy had her own way, they would have had a love affair. She adored Mickey and would have loved to have set up home together. She was very sexually aware and talked about going to bed with him before he ever understood that beds were not just for sleeping in. But he showed no interest in that sort of a relationship. Had they been older, LB himself would have tried to invent a romance and get them married at one of the famous Hollywood churches, with a dress for Judy made by one of the couturiers who were on his books. But there was the big dichotomy – he would have liked to say there was a puppy-love romance going on, on the other hand, he was in the business of celebrating their youth, young people who never got into any kind of trouble – if they had difficulties, as Mickey did when he bought himself a Cadillac and Mayer ordered him to get rid of it, they would be suitably chastised. These had to be seen as clean-cut kids who, like Andy Hardy, celebrated good American family life, who rode bicycles not sedans, who quaffed ice-cream sodas not champagne and who, if they got into trouble, were never more than merely naughty.

In late 1939, the studio publicity department organised a lunch for the two at the Waldorf Astoria Hotel, New York's most fashionable watering hole and, as they did with all good publicity stunts, plugged it in the press. They invited people to join the young stars at the celebration of their achievements. Just 120 people came along – there was no room for more – out of the phenomenal number of 200,000 who hopefully sent in requests for invitations.

Plainly, Judy's stock in trade was being a teenager. Yet there was something of an undercover battle she was waging – to show that, while making money as a growing-up child, she wanted to be seen much more as a *grown-up*. As she later wrote: 'I wanted to look glamorous.' The occasion for the comment was when she reached the pinnacle of show-business success, the triumph of having got to the top – by reaching, as it were, to the bottom. She was selected to get her hands and feet sticky and dirty, doing just what she had done at Lancaster – but a lot more publicly and legally. Judy became what was virtually an entertainment immortal by placing her prints in the cement in the courtyard of Grauman's Chinese Theatre on Hollywood Boulevard. Her gold star on the pavement would follow years later.

On the day of the Grauman's ceremony, she did her best to look as glamorous as she dreamed of being. She wanted to have long fingernails, like Joan Crawford's. So she had artificial ones fitted for her by a manicurist. But the cement got stuck under the nails, fixing them apparently permanently like some kind of superglue to her real ones. She vowed never to do that again.

For Mayer, being glamorous was the last thing he wanted of her. It wouldn't have gone down at all well alongside his efforts publicising *Babes in Arms* and its successors, *Strike up the Band* and *Babes on Broadway*.

Certainly, the Hardy films that followed, *Andy Hardy Meets Debutante* and *Life Begins for Andy Hardy*, wouldn't have benefited from that glamorous look one little bit.

Already, the pressures were being felt. Mayer was persuaded to look into her case and agreed that the commodity that was Judy Garland needed more than just cosseting. He agreed that she should get looked over, kindly and not too intensively, by a nursing home in Boston. He paid for the treatment, which was not at all the sort of thing to be fostered by the studio's PR department. The people in the untidy, paper-strewn press room were exercising their responsibility by keeping names and stories out of the news at the same time as publicising their films and stars.

She went and she came back. Back to work and back to the pressure. Margaret Whiting would have appreciated it had she known about the hospitalisation. She was young and, like Judy, hoped that her friend's condition was nothing more than anxiety over men, just as in any of their 'girlie' conversations. When they were a little older and Judy suggested lunch between them, it seemed a good idea.

'One day she called me and said, "I'll pick you up." I lived in Beverly Hills in an apartment. She came down the alley at the back of the apartment, which we had said would be an appropriate place to meet. She opened the door [of her car] and we decided to go to the Brown Derby [restaurant] in Beverly Hills. She started to drive and then said, "While I'm going back through the alley would you look through the glove compartment. You can help me get rid of a few things." There were handkerchiefs and make-up. There was also a box. She said, "Open it up and see what it is. It if doesn't look very promising, throw it out." As I stopped, she said, "Oh my God. It's my false teeth that I wear in pictures. My career just went out of the window!"' Margaret promised not to tell – until now.

That was quite a revelation. Look at stills from her young-girl movies and her teeth were as perfect as her make-up. See a news picture of the time and her uneven teeth – and the odd space where a tooth had once been – were quite obvious. It wouldn't happen today. Stars may not be quite as starlike as they were in the 1930s; male actors, in particular, seem to care less about their clothes than ever before – but they all make sure that their dental work is exceptional.

As far as MGM, the studio which liked to think of itself as the most perfect in Hollywood, was concerned, everything had to be exceptional, especially its stars.

The 1940s seemed to be the era when Judy Garland showed herself as potentially the most exceptional of them all. Very sensibly, the studio were going to aid her career with every dollar they paid to their publicity department. Equally sensibly, they came to the conclusion that, while Garland and Rooney looked great together and liked each other enormously, this was a brand that could tire. Just as Paramount loved having Bing Crosby and Bob Hope teamed together in the *Road* films – which were made at the same time as Judy was moving from *The Wizard* – but not all the time, the policy regarding Judy and Mickey was that they were a great team, but they were good enough to be treated as stars in their own right. No one wanted to see them as a new Astaire–Rogers 'partnership'. Fred himself told me that he hated that word: 'It sounds like a team of horses.' Mayer agreed they should be in different stalls in his stable.

Audiences did want to see them grow up – although not too quickly. Mickey Rooney was still Andy Hardy in films that did not feature Judy, and he had also been doing pretty well in other roles. He was still the impish character that audiences had got to love, but he was already making films like *Young Tom Edison* and was graduating to *Men of Boys Town*, a sequel to one of his own big successes, the title itself confirmation that he was growing up.

As for Judy, she was being allowed to get older, if older meant prettier and more sophisticated. In the 1940 film *Little Nellie Kelly* she actually played her own mother – a young mother who died in childbirth – as well as the title role of her younger 16-year-old self. The most notable feature of the film was not so much the double part, but the chance to give out, as they liked to say in the trade, with the song 'Singin' in the Rain'.

The real break from the past came in 1942 with *For Me and My Gal*. It was the beginning of US involvement in World War Two and MGM did what all the studios did to be topical and boost morale – it went back to World War One, which at the time was still a conflict to which people could relate. It included Judy in a figure-hugging Army-type uniform, complete with forage cap, entertaining a lot of very smart soldiers dressed as their fathers or elder brothers would have been before being sent off to France in 1917 (only their uniforms were better made and better pressed).

Gene Kelly always maintained that he, a newcomer to Hollywood – he arrived on the day that Japan struck at Pearl Harbor, 7 December 1941 – after a Broadway triumph in *Pal Joey*, got the role of Harry Palmer specifically because Judy had asked for him. It began a long friendship between the two and also Gene's wife, Betsy Blair. It did not, however, as we shall see, mean that he would avoid criticising her. George Murphy, who shared billing with Kelly – Judy Garland's name blazing at the top of all the posters and newspaper advertisements above the title – was originally supposed to have had Gene's role, but Judy was the one who suggested that it was Gene who should be the romantic interest alongside her.

This was a grown-up musical with a very grown-up Gene Kelly

as her co-star and lots of grown-up songs to sing. No more was she an in-between. Their version of the title song is still played on musical archive radio programmes on both sides of the Atlantic and features every time someone feels like taking a duster to the MGM archives and playing a clip.

I interviewed Gene Kelly long after he had officially put away his dancing shoes, but not his memories. 'It was easy to love Judy Garland,' he told me. 'But it was also easy to hate her. She was supposed to be this lovely young lady who behaved herself perfectly, but she didn't. For a time, she wanted to argue, to show that she was the star of the film. I was really terribly disappointed – and yet as a performer she was superb.'

Kelly might have been critical of her behaviour at times, but never of her dancing. He always said he thought it remarkable how she, with no real professional dancing experience, picked up the required steps so easily.

The arguments with Gene didn't last and they returned to their friendship. Those with the director were more permanent. Busby Berkeley was in charge and Judy and he sailed into very troubled waters. Judy vowed never to work with him again. He said much the same thing about filming with her.

Plainly, she had become what she and her mother Ethel had always wanted her to be – a star. Her boss, Louis B. Mayer, had, of course, received daily bulletins about her work and occasionally visited the set, but while she was working, she was making money for him.

Yes, Judy Garland really had now grown up. And to prove it, she got married, which astounded her public and seems to have caught the studio unawares. If she had joined in holy matrimony with another MGM star, Mayer might have been a little anxious about a young girl getting wed (it could mean her becoming pregnant and so lost to the studio, and some of her audience might question her marrying so young). But at the age of 19, she became Mrs David Rose after numerous romances – or affairs, depending on the way you looked at it – with people like the multi-married bandleader Artie Shaw, who asked her to marry him but changed his mind without telling her. (Instead, Shaw decided to wed Lana Turner – in time, the list would include Ava Gardner, Evelyn Keyes and five others. He was the man who once said he got married so many times because in those days it was the only way to have legal sex, which seems to indicate that he and Judy did not go to bed together). Then there was the actor Tyrone Power, who was alleged to have had an affair with Errol Flynn.

Judy's activities all seemed to confirm her yearning for a man in her life that she and Margaret Whiting had discussed so openly. When she and David Rose, one of the most talented Hollywood musicians of the age, announced they would marry, the shock of 19-year-old Judy declaring she would be taking the seemingly irrevocable step caused the studio to rock and roll and Louis B. Mayer almost to explode. JUDY MARRIED IN 1941.

There are those who say that Judy married the British-born Rose simply to show that she really was her own woman (even to be able to show that she was a woman and not a young girl, a thought that had a certain piquancy about it). She made it clear she was fed up with being told what to do. When Mayer heard the sequence of events, the squeaks from his chair as it started revolving could be heard in the next room. The normally polite mogul used words that had never been heard from his mouth before.

When Mayer met Judy again after the marriage he noticeably did not call her 'darling'. There were compensations. The studio had no difficulty in persuading film magazines like the highly influential *Photoplay* to feature Judy on their cover. That was proof that she was now regarded as one of the top women stars. MGM's publicity boys watched what she wore and encouraged the press to use her as a model for new fashions, even if she herself didn't realise that this had been the purpose of so many of the photographs for which she was posing.

All the stories about Judy's troubles give the impression that the pressures of her life made her hate her life. But that cannot be true. When she was well, she enjoyed being a star, with all its fringe benefits, the chances to meet interesting people, to say nothing of the adulation of fans. That would always be the case, even if the facts of this truth tend to interfere with a good story. On the other hand – and there was always another hand with Judy Garland stories – it is true that there were moments when she could play the girl next door and wonder about the experience.

Her experiences with her return home to Grand Rapids might give the impression that she was above all that. It would be an unfair judgement. The stories of her relationship with Dot Ponedel and her niece Meredith give a perfect example of the way she could let her hair down – and happily, not in quite the morose way as Margaret Whiting tells it. Her old Lancaster friend Irma Storey told me about a meeting they had in Hollywood. 'It was at the time she was married to David Rose. I ran into her in the street and we just went into a drug store on a street corner and had a soda and talked a bit. One of her sisters lived near the girls I was visiting. Later that day, her sister brought me a record of "Somewhere over the Rainbow". I don't know what I did with that. I had really treasured it, although I didn't play it very much.'

In later years, it would seem that Judy's experience with marriage to David Rose would look like the replaying of another very old record.

Rose was a very successful composer with a definite style, using strings where other music men would never have dreamed of placing them. Future pieces like 'Holiday for Strings' and 'The Stripper' would become instantly recognisable. And so, in Hollywood terms, would his – and her – style of marriage. In practice, it lasted for just a matter of months. As Rose told me just before his death: 'Judy wasn't interested in marriage as such. I think she just liked the idea of becoming a wife, but more she thought it would bring her a degree of independence, which she had never had.' That was undoubtedly a big part of the story. In 1943, they separated and were divorced the following year.

The effect on Judy was catastrophic – at least, more catastrophic than her previous problems. At the studio's behest, she again saw a psychiatrist, who put her on a regimen of pills, to be taken in conjunction with all those other drugs without which she felt she could not survive. The idea of starting a day without a pill to pop and going to bed without another tablet was unthinkable. Combine that with working all day and going out all night – either because the studio required it or because she was getting into the habit of living at night, something that would become another problem – and she needed every session on the couch she could get. If she could have had those sessions without the accompaniment of more pills, she might have found a happier outcome at the end of that particular rainbow. As it was, she was developing yet another difficulty. She was putting on vast amounts of weight – to the extent that dresses she'd had made for the beginning of a film turned out to be too small by the time the last scene was shot. MGM's solution was to put her on a fat-blasting diet, which led to horrific depressions.

But she was now, despite that, very much her own woman – and now she was *giving* the parties she had previously attended at other people's invitation. They were the best Judy Garland performances ever. If she could afford to coast on public occasions – and she had not yet 'learned' how to do this – she could decidedly not do so when she was among her peers. Just as the guests still came to see who was who and who was not who, they were the severest judges of how fellow professionals performed. If they had been no good, word would have found its way to the 'trades', *Daily Variety* or *The Hollywood Reporter* (even if the editors of those august journals had not been invited themselves, a risk no responsible host would dare to take).

The stars came and so did the starlets. A few years later, a popular guest at Judy's parties would be a young blonde woman who would before long suffer similar problems to Garland and would deal with them (or not) in similar ways – Marilyn Monroe. When Marilyn did start going to them, her exquisite beauty and her insouciance was the talk of the town, literally. But for the most part, it was the entertainment before the film show that the guests enjoyed – once, that is, the gossip had ceased and the food had gone. Anyone who was anyone came along. Gene Kelly, who held his own weekly open-house parties every Saturday night, would often be on hand. Occasionally, Fred Astaire would go to those but hated the affairs – because, as he told me when I was working on his biography, 'There's always some matron there who wants to be able to say that she danced with Fred Astaire.' Danny Kaye, then at the top of his tongue-twisting form, was always a popular guest.

Judy professed to be the perfect hostess who loved having the parties, but on more than one occasion she could be found hiding away in the kitchen, tears streaming down her face.

Audiences, on the whole, were unaware of her difficulties. Only the most astute would have noticed how different she looked at times. If MGM had ordered her to take a year's break, go off and have a vacation somewhere, things might have been different. But 'different' to the studio might have meant the people who paid their cents and shillings at the box office beginning to forget her – and that was a problem with which they didn't want to be faced. Besides, why lose her services if they didn't absolutely need to do so? It could not be considered. Judy Garland, commodity, could not be spared.

Actually she was now doing an even more prodigious amount of work than she had before. There were still the first nights and other 'show-off' occasions, still the radio broadcasts. As for the films, there weren't necessarily more of those, but the ones she was making required more and more effort. She could no longer be excused as one of those child stars whose performances would cause people to wonder, even if they weren't especially brilliant – much like a dog taught to walk on its hind legs yet not doing it terribly well (Judy, of course, did everything terribly well on screen) the remarkable thing being that it could be done at all. She was now a fish in a big pool, competing with other actors and actresses who were willing to give her no advantages. Playing adult roles meant doing the things people like Katharine Hepburn and Olivia de Havilland were doing so well. And Judy had to sing, too. She did that in *Ziegfeld Girl*, as much a demonstration of escapism – as America wondered if it was going to get into World War Two – as a trip back to the great days of Mr Ziegfeld and his *Follies*. That this film about the lives of girls in the chorus wasn't a folly in itself had a lot to do with Judy. She was excellent in combining a fair dose of nostalgia with some pretty effective acting. Charles Winninger, a genuine veteran of old Broadway, was delightful teaching Judy to sing 'properly' and even James Stewart and Lana Turner were around. A young Dan Dailey, later an essential for the big movie musical, had a featured part. The interesting thing about the film was that, despite their previous mutual reservation, the dance director was Busby Berkeley, famous both for his geometric panoramic routines and for his hatred of Judy Garland. Judy said that he shouted at her. He said she messed up his carefully planned routines. It wasn't a case of no chemistry between them. More, it was very bad chemistry, the kind that caused explosions.

She did well enough in *Presenting Lily Mars,* in a part originally earmarked for Lana Turner. This was about a small-town girl who stars on Broadway. It might seem like the biographical tale of the girl from Grand Rapids who went to Hollywood, but it had little of the sad realism of the real story.

More truthful were the 'shorts' *We Must Have Music, Cavalcade of the Academy Awards* and *Meet the Stars,* all made between 1941 and 1942 and all demonstrating that without Judy Garland on view MGM would be seriously losing out. That could have been their thinking when Judy made her own contributions to the war effort. But when she went on war-bonds drives and served coffee and doughnuts and danced with soldiers about to be shipped out to the war zones, she was proud to be doing her bit and made numerous broadcasts to emphasise the fact. The coffee, doughnuts and dancing were at the Hollywood Canteen, which had been established at a former Hollywood livery stable. The idea was that film stars would entertain young men in uniform who perhaps the following day would be on a ship to the South Pacific or flown to Europe. The girls – Marlene Dietrich, Rita Hayworth, Deanna Durbin and Judy among them – danced with the troops but were not allowed to date any of them. Every able-bodied star working at the studios was expected to take part. The evidence from her conversations at that time was that Judy would have been there even if the MGM bosses had not ordered her to go along to the canteen.

What was really expected of stars was that they went out to the actual battlefields themselves. Judy stayed in America. MGM were not keen on allowing her overseas because of the risks – not just from the Germans or Japanese, who were rather unpleasant critics of the shows, but also from other entertainers, some of whom (Bob Hope in particular, who had girls lined up waiting for him when he arrived at military bases) saw trips away from home as opportunities to misbehave. But she did an exhausting tour around America, singing to troops in camps and, notably, in military hospitals. She also did programmes for the American Forces Network and made records specifically for Army, Navy or Air Corps troops on the specially produced 'V' discs.

At the same time, there were the films that topped the bills at cinemas all over the parts of the world not occupied by the Germans or Japanese. They were mostly morale-boosting pictures intended to make people forget the war, easier for civilian audiences than for the service personnel who were sent the movies to be shown in military camp halls or outdoors in the shadow of firing lines. Judy made three of these in 1943: in addition to *Presenting Lily Mars*, there was *Girl Crazy* and *Thousands Cheer*. *Girl Crazy* had the songs of George and Ira Gershwin. *Thousands Cheer* may have been a good title – Irving Berlin had a show called *As Thousands Cheer* – but many more thousands jeered, even though both pictures featured Judy alongside Mickey Rooney. *Thousands Cheer* also starred Gene Kelly, Kathryn Grayson, June Allyson, Eleanor Powell and Lena Horne, among many others. It was typical of what Hollywood studios believed was demonstrating its patriotism, featuring a series of performances in an Army base. What more could anyone want in 1943? That was not a question the publicity scribes wanted asked and less did they want to answer it.

But the reaction of people who saw the movie proved that perhaps MGM did have to think again about making these portmanteau pictures, films that were made, as far as the studio economists were concerned, because they were stacked with contract players working in very basic settings. People who saw it were not nearly as enthusiastic as Louis B. Mayer seemed to be.

The critic James Agee didn't like it at all. He called it 'a thoroughly routine musical distinguished only by Gene Kelly with nothing to use his talents on, a terrible piece of trash by Shostakovich and the unpleasant sight of José Iturbi proving he is a real guy by playing the sort of boogie-woogie anyone ought to be able to learn through a correspondence course.'

That was, as they say, telling them, although whether Judy told anyone is not on record.

What were well recorded were Judy's numerous live appearances, particularly those in 1943 with the Andre Kostelanetz orchestra. She seemed remarkably ordinary and unsophisticated on the concert platform. No exotic gowns, no particular regard for her hairstyle. It was as if she was respecting the need for wartime austerity. Or perhaps, since most people were so far away from the stage, she felt more relaxed without worrying what audiences thought, except what they thought of her singing. That was as good as ever. She sang popular songs and always a patriotic number, like Irving Berlin's 'God Bless America', which every now and again seems to push the 'Star Spangled Banner' into second place as the country's national anthem.

The following year came a movie that possibly would have gone down as Judy's most popular ever musical – if it weren't for that film about a wizard. Except that, at the time, it was much, much more popular.

Meet Me In St Louis was one of a whole genre of movies set at the turn of the 20th century, so popular among film-makers at the time. Whether it was a yearning for the simpler things of life or simply that the 1900s were colourful (for those not on the breadlines, that is), when young men wore striped blazers and straw hats and girls wore flouncy white dresses, there is no doubt that they were loved. Like the later films *Cheaper by the Dozen* and *On Moonlight Bay*, this was one of those movies that was a paean to parenthood, a time when children were naughty, but really knew their place. They called their fathers 'Sir' and doffed their caps when their mothers and other ladies were met in the street. There was usually a maid, a dog and – always – the boy next door.

Fathers read the papers and drove big open cars they had to start with a handle, mothers told cooks who always worked in a cloud of steam what to put in their pots and never seemed to get their own hands dirty, and the older girls of the family – who always looked a little too old to be siblings of new babies born into their clans – sang songs that sounded a little more 1940s than 1900s.

That was what Judy Garland did in *Meet Me In St Louis,* a multi-coloured project that, given half the chance, would have had half the young eligible males in America rushing to accept the invitation. But it might never have happened. She at first turned down the offer of the film (as much as she was allowed to turn down anything – refusal would not have made LB happy and the time that the picture took to make would have been added to her contract). But after sufficient cajoling from Arthur Freed, who ran MGM's musicals unit, with promises of adjustments to the scenes she said she didn't like (which have never been specified), she agreed. It might have been merely a fit of pique on her part, a decision to put her foot down over *something,* merely to show that the big star of a big film called *The Wizard of Oz* was entitled to a say – and perhaps needed a little more respect. So she finally said yes. It was not a decision to regret. But even after she had agreed and had started work, she was not an entirely happy lady.

Meredith Ponedel told me about what she'd heard from her aunt, the make-up expert Dorothy Ponedel. 'Dot told me a lot of stories about Judy. There was one she loved to tell about the time she had come over and Judy was already in the house, door wide open all the time. Dot knew something was up by the look on Judy's face and she said, "What's going on?" Judy held up a bottle of Clearol and said she didn't like the way she looked in the rushes. She was working on *Meet Me In St Louis*. "I would like you to give me a different hair colour," she said.'

That was easier said than done. For one thing, changing hair colour or style in the midst of a picture being made could cause major continuity problems. For another, there were rules for those who did make-up and hairstyling. Meredith told me about Dot's reply: 'You know I can't do that. It's against union rules, just not right.'

But there was nothing quite as persuasive as a shmoozy, anxious Judy Garland. 'You didn't say no to Judy if you were wise. The next day she looks beautiful. She does the shoot and someone calls Dot into the office and asked how come Judy's hair looks different? She stuck up for her. "Maybe, the lighting was off."'

Dot was, remarkably, regarded as pretty convincing. The story did not end there, according to Meredith. 'Years later, I came across some letters from MGM, a memo from the hair department to the camera department saying, "Miss Garland's hair looks different today. Will you please check into it?" I laughed my head off. It was a matter of protocol and ethics that hair people didn't do make-up and vice versa.'

Judy didn't have that sort of relationship with a lot of other people. But Meredith explained: 'Judy was twenty-five years younger than Dot. She was in a state of flux and needed a mother figure. Dot, having no children – her husband was shot down in the war – they sort of gravitated to each other.'

It did take quite a lot for a big star, in the midst of the most glamorous business in the world, to deny her beauty. Of all the charges of unprofessionalism and other difficulties assigned to her, allegations of narcissism were not among them. Meredith added: 'Dot was very proud of the make-up she did because Judy was so hard to please. Judy never felt she looked beautiful. When Dot did her, she thought she *was* beautiful.'

In the movie, she was one of two older sisters (the other was Lucille Bremer) of little Margaret O'Brien, who had equal billing with Judy above the title and who looked dangerously like the girl who would succeed her in the poll for everyone's favourite female child star. Judy sang to her (notably a rather nice novelty number called 'Under the Bamboo Tree'), brushed her hair and looked every bit the way teenagers (which at 22 she no longer was) were 1944 supposed to look in those turn-of-the-century days – helping Mama (Mary Astor, demurely throwing off the scandals of her racy diaries that caused a sensation just a few years before) do the things Mama was supposed to do herself. All the time, she was cast as the girl dreaming of the boy next door, played by Tom Drake – about whom a wistful Judy would sing 'The Boy Next Door'. The setting was the St Louis World's Fair, where everyone rejoiced that her father (Leon Ames, looking very Papa-like) had changed his mind about moving to New York. An extra bonus was Harry Davenport completing the family (along with Marjorie Main as the crusty but adoring maid) by showing they had a grandpa too.

The scene everyone would remember was the one when she sang 'The Trolley Song', full of colour and other pretty young actresses who all seemed to have wonderful voices. Judy, in her 'high-starched collar', and the hat which was about to be blown on to the line below, was truly convincing as the girl being swept off her feet – as the lyric declared – by the crowds on the trolley car, if not by the young man who doffed his hat to her. 'Clang, clang, clang, went the trolley' was the famous line – originally a caption to a photo of a trolley car discovered by the film's lyricist Ralph Blane, who found it in an old newspaper cutting.

There was another song in the picture that was notable, one which became hugely popular, and was the only hit that would, in years to come, be sung by virtually every popular entertainer of the age, Frank Sinatra and Bing Crosby included. This was 'Have Yourself a Merry Little Christmas', which Judy sang to Margaret O'Brien. If ever Irving Berlin's 'White Christmas' had a rival, it was this. And if ever Judy Garland was going to have to look to her laurels it was with the presence of this cute little girl on her lap, the one with an attractive lisp. Indeed, Ms O'Brien was very popular and made a number of films, but, unlike Judy's, when she began to grow up, her career began to fall down. Ask people today who they remember more and there is no contest. Most would say Judy. As for her 'rival', unless we're talking about real movie experts, it's more a case of 'Margaret Who?'

No one, however, imagined that when the film was announced or when it was released.

The most notable feature of the making of the movie was the continuous stream of arguments between Judy and the director. Not, as had happened before, over her tardiness, coming in late, failing to turn up at rehearsals, all the usual things. This time she was appearing to be unprofessional in a totally different way. At one stage, the director complained that she was trying to direct the picture herself. She demanded retakes if she said she felt she was standing in non-existent shadows or if her make-up was not suitable – or if another member of the cast was getting better positions in a scene.

If the director felt she was trying to tease him into taking her more seriously than had others in his position, he was right. And he was angry. Their relationship would change, however, after the film was wrapped up. The director's name was Vincente Minnelli. They worked on a few other projects together after *St Louis,* the biggest creation of which was that of a little girl called Liza in 1946. Kay Thompson became Liza's godmother and gave the baby a gold bracelet to mark the christening. Judy would later be buried wearing it.

Kay was, as Sam Irvine put it, 'part of Judy's extended family'. He admitted: 'I think there was a little jealousy about being the wings behind the wind of people like Judy. But Kay was able to give her the comfort that she needed. She would be there for Judy – for her albums as well as for her films.'

The film – and, alas for Judy, the marriage to Minnelli – set a standard for virtually everything that followed in the next four years. They were nice, easy to watch and simple to listen to musicals that MGM, made under the guidance or dictatorship – depending on which side you took – of the famous Arthur Freed unit, which was virtually a studio within a studio. The marriage of Judy and Vincente had a less successful outcome. Nobody depends on a film lasting for ever, but weddings are supposed in all the best fairy stories to go on till death tears them apart. The Minnelli–Garland marriage was to be a death in itself, with Judy's fans gathering around its bedside, mourning what they hoped would not also be the death of her career. But at first it looked as though she might have found an investment in both her happiness and her work.

As far as the films were concerned, the only exception to the 'Makers of Great Musicals' recipe of Mr Freed was the 1945 black-and-white movie *The Clock,* which gave Judy her first opportunity to play a dramatic role without a single song to sing. It, too, was directed by Minnelli. It also showed the film business what Vincente most wanted to prove – that he could direct a film that did not depend on lush landscapes, beautiful homes, swish cars and actors who would find an excuse for a song every time they walked down the street or were conveniently standing by a piano. When he took over as director from Fred Zinnemann – later to be the much-acclaimed director of *From Here to Eternity* – this story of the lovelorn girl who falls for a soldier on his 24-hour leave, and marries him soon after meeting under the clock at Penn Central Station in New York, was not brilliant but it did demonstrate the times shown on that clock.

Minnelli made a lot of changes to the film as originally planned. Judy's hairstyle, for one, was changed. Then he abandoned the idea of filming at the real station – which he now recreated in the studio – the actual place would look too real, too busy and too untidy for an MGM movie. And so was the love between Judy's character and the soldier played by Robert Walker, looking very handsome in a tailor-made corporal's uniform, the like of which was never seen on a parade ground. Nobody suggested that they were lovers off the set, too, but then in 1945 you didn't read such things in all the papers that featured stories about a nice married lady like Judy.

She and Minnelli had, it seemed at the time *The Clock* was being made, a secret: he could direct her virtually without speaking. All he had to do was give her 'the look' and she knew what it meant. An eye in one direction guaranteed that she would raise her voice; another to the other side indicated that he wanted her to move back a bit. It was a process that mystified the other players but the couple knew what was meant and that was all that counted.

But in real life, Judy was about to hit crisis time once more. The pills were doing their evil worst and again she was introduced to the psychiatrists and nurses at a sanatorium. She would become very familiar with the places that she got to call 'my nut houses'. She wasn't being disparaging of other people who had to suffer those institutions – it was a combination of the mores of the time and her own sense of humour.

MGM wouldn't let her off the hook, however. Incredible as it might now seem, despite her hospitalisation and the slow, agonising progress of another marriage heading towards the rocks, the studio had three films for her in 1946. *The Harvey Girls* was the best of the three, featuring a number that always looked as if it had been left over from *Meet Me In St Louis*, 'The Atchison, Topeka and the Santa Fe', a train song that was on the right lines and gave plenty of opportunity for whistle-stop noises. It also won the writers Johnny Mercer and Harry Warren an Oscar for the best film song at the 1947 Academy Awards evening.

But Johnny Mercer didn't get one other prize he yearned for at this time: Judy herself.

Ginger Mercer discovered that her husband, the songwriter, was having an affair with Judy. It was more than an affair. Mercer later admitted that he carried the metaphorical torch for her that was still burning at the end of Judy's life. The affair ended when Ginger stormed into Judy's dressing room, telling her to lay off. Mercer was still crazily in love with Judy and once told me he had dedicated in spirit one of his most famous songs to her, 'I Thought about You'. Ginger certainly told Judy what *she* thought of her. But Johnny thought about Ginger, too, and decided there was nothing for him to do but continue his marriage. It did not mean he could fall out of love with Judy.

It is possible that Kay Thompson also told Judy to remember her responsibilities as a married woman. In the studio, she coached Judy through the difficult bits. There were other things about *The Harvey Girls* that should have been better received than they in fact were at the time: like the partnership between Judy and Ray Bolger, renewing their professional relationship that had been established in *The Wizard*. He was better dressed than he had been as the scarecrow in the earlier movie. A few years later, visiting her fan club in London, she spoke about Bolger: 'No Astaire he!' But they got on well enough.

The love interest was mainly between Judy and John Hodiak, but it was being with Bolger again that really was more exciting to audiences – if not totally so to Ms Garland. One of the reasons the film succeeded was that Judy looked stunningly beautiful in the movie – again thanks to Dot Ponedel. 'She changed the look of Judy altogether,' Dot's neice, Meredith Ponedel told me. 'That was according to several people, not only what was obvious on screen.' As a result of the Ponedel treatment, one would no longer compare pictures of Judy off duty with the ones issued by the MGM publicity department.

'Before Dot started doing what she did, Judy's eye make-up was very dark. Dot didn't like to use anything that made her eyes darker. She used lighter make-up to bring the eyes up. She would work with the hairline. She didn't think the hairline was correct. She would tweeze it out. She was very good at contour and shading. She would change the shape of Judy's lower lip in order to make it blend with the lighting. If Judy was having a bad week, not feeling well, if she lost a pound or two, Dot was able to change that by shading and highlight.'

That would sometimes change with the films on which she was working. 'There are certain colours that were better for her than others. Before [this time], she was basically a blonde, so you had to change everything else. Now, her hair was its normal, reddish colour.'

More important, there would be no more funny incidents like the time Margaret Whiting discovered Judy's false teeth. 'She freed Judy up from a lot of the prosthetic devices that had been made by other make-up artists, teeth caps [note, not sets of dentures], things to make her nose wider. Dot took one look and said, "What the hell are these?" Judy said, "Well, that's what so-and-so says." She said, "Throw 'em out. You don't need them."'

There was a scene in *A Star Is Born* in which make-up teams, like a battery of surgeons working on a complicated operation, changed her make-up – using all the prosthetic devices they could muster – only to have her co-star James Mason do exactly what Dot Ponedel had done.

Ziegfeld Follies, directed once more by Minnelli, had the kind of story that made some critics go running for the nearest sick bag – and which any self-respecting director of Vincente's standards should have seen for what it was the moment he was handed a script. Was anyone expected to take seriously the idea of Florenz Ziegfeld sitting on a cloud and planning one more big show? It was just one more excuse to use the studio's repertory company – Judy along with Lucille Ball, William Powell (as Ziegfeld), Jimmy Durante, Lena Horne, Red Skelton, Gene Kelly and, best of all, Fred Astaire – with he and Kelly reprising the Gershwin duet that Fred had performed in *Funny Face* on stage with his sister Adele. This was the famous 'The Babbitt and the Bromide', their only teaming until they got together in the same routine in the marvellous *That's Entertainment* compendium. Judy had one number in the picture, doing a superb take-off of Greer Garson holding a press conference. Four years later, she would reprise it in her smash performances at New York's Palace Theatre.

Judy was not a political person. Indeed, in an age when some stars were becoming highly politicised, there were those who considered her more than a little naive when it came to the post-war situation, the start of the Cold War and the coming re-election campaign of President Harry S. Truman. But she did take part in one particular activity in which she seemed to be nothing less than passionate. In 1947, a score of movie stars clubbed together to take part in a radio programme called 'Hollywood Fights Back'. It was, they hoped, their answer to the anti-Communist vendetta (which would come to be known as 'McCarthyism'), which was threatening, in their eyes, to ruin the film capital and its principal business. The House Un-American Activities Committee (HUAC) had held a series of investigations into what they claimed was Communist infiltration in the motion picture industry. Nine writers and a director (Edward Dmytryk) were being harangued in Washington and were about to be jailed for contempt of Congress. Their crime was to refuse to answer the question: 'Are you now, or have you ever been a Communist?' They became known as the Hollywood Ten.

A group of Hollywood personalities, including Humphrey Bogart and Lauren Bacall, John Huston and Danny Kaye, chartered a plane and flew to Washington, calling themselves The

Committee for the First Amendment (the First Amendment to the US constitution is the one that guarantees the right to free speech) and taking a petition calling on HUAC to respect the men's rights and not pester them any more. For their part, the studios decided that the Committee for the First Amendment were showing contempt for Hollywood and the stars were ordered to go back to their commitments or lose their jobs and have their names put on the infamous blacklist. All but a handful reneged – including the Bogarts – and went back to work, writing articles at the same time saying how loyal they were and how they were 'duped'. Judy was not one who made the flight. But she did take part in the radio show.

She told a national audience that she and her colleagues could accept criticism of their work but could not tolerate anyone calling them 'un-American'.

Whether Judy was really politically committed to the cause or merely did not want to feel left out is open to speculation. But she did not take it any further. Had she done so, she would have been laying herself open to possible blacklisting. Mayer was in the forefront of the moguls' campaign to emphasise their Americanism. At any time, he was ready to run up the Stars and Stripes outside the Culver City studio and even, if one were available, no doubt to wrap himself in it for good measure. On the other hand, Judy was still a commodity and one he did not want to lose. That did not mean that everything was coming up roses in the way she and her employers regarded each other. She still thought she was being overworked and they still felt the solution would be more drugs – which she now began taking without any medical supervision.

If she was worried about her relationship with MGM, life on the recording front was a lot easier. Most of the tunes she had sung in the movies were given airings by Decca, which not only brought her publicity for the pictures but spun a great deal more than was on the turntables that young people were winding up at home or while sitting on boats or on the beach. As now, the best way to plug a record was on the radio. So Judy's records were being exposed to potentially new audiences and so was her talent, making her more in demand than ever before. Over 100 sides bore the label, 'Judy Garland, vocal'.

There were other radio performances without discs. One of the most popular shows on the air was the *Lux Radio Theater* – a programme, usually introduced by Cecil B. DeMille, sponsored by Lux toilet soap, broadcast live, which was a scripted version of movie successes. In 1942, she had starred with Walter Pidgeon in a radio play in the series based on the 1937 Janet Gaynor/Fredric March film *A Star Is Born*. Afterwards, she suggested that it would make a very good new movie. Mayer was not impressed. He said it would never work – words that 13 years later he would wish he had never uttered.

But the films were her core work. Judy and Fred Astaire got to perform together in another of those movies that crop up on television year after year. *Easter Parade* wasn't a particularly great demonstration of the Garland acting ability but featured one number that she was to reprise till the end of her life with a variety of other partners in live concerts and on TV, show after show – Irving Berlin's, 'We're a Couple of Swells'. It hasn't quite reached the heights of an 'Over the Rainbow' but people did scream for it. *Easter Parade* was much more Astaire's picture than Judy's and probably would have been Gene Kelly's, too, had he not had to bow out because of a broken leg. Both Astaire and Judy carved themselves a new niche with the number in which they were seen with ragged evening tail suits, bashed-in top hats, dirty faces and, in her case, blacked-out teeth. They may have had to walk down the avenue because they couldn't afford the fare, but for this song alone they were entitled to a lifetime limousine service on MGM's bill.

When I was working on my biography of Irving Berlin, he told me he prepared the score for *Easter Parade* because he dearly wanted to work with Judy Garland, who, to the surprise of most people in the business, was billed above Fred. 'I've always said that I'd rather have Fred Astaire sing my songs than anyone else,' he told me, 'but every time I heard Judy sing I always had a special tingle. Until then, she hadn't sung much of my work, but the tingle came back tenfold when she did.' The title song, along with such oldies like 'When the Midnight Choo-Choo Leaves for Alabam', 'Snooky Ookums' and, best of all, 'I Love a Piano' were enough to gladden the songwriter's heart – and his bank account. They were virtually a catalogue of much of Berlin's repertoire over more than 50 years, sandwiched as they were between this story of a leading nightclub dancer (Fred) training a new girl (Judy) to take the place of his usual partner (Ann Miller). Judy might even have allowed the thought that if Frank Gumm had joined the heavenly creatures from the earlier *Ziegfeld* film, he would be pleased, too. The *Easter Parade* collection was made up of numbers that some time or other had featured in the Gumms' repertoire.

Charles (Chuck) Walters, who once told me it was the best thing he ever did, directed the picture and was indulgent to the extreme when Judy occasionally allowed her insecurities to show – coming late on to the set and complaining when *everything* didn't go so well. Sometimes, she seemed to complain because things *were* going well. Sometimes, the problem was that she was left far too often to fight her own battles.

Certainly, it is true that Judy needed people to lean on. Kay Thompson was one. Dorothy Ponedel was another. She lived in Judy's house for a time – ostensibly to make sure that the star left to get to work on time. But there was a time when they fell out. Maybe they had been too close for too long, or perhaps the fact that 'Dot' was living with her at the same time as Vincente Minnelli had something to do with it. But, as Meredith points out, the time had come when Dot 'wanted a break and Judy didn't want her to have one and Dot said, "I'm out of here."' Judy looked for a peace offering and found one in a framed photograph of herself. She inscribed it: 'Stay with me, Baby'.

Dorothy reacted immediately: 'What did you think?' she asked. 'I was going to leave you?' The matter never came up again, for which Meredith was always grateful. 'When I came up the driveway from school and I knew that Judy was in the house, I would go flying up the driveway because it was such a joy to know she was there. Because I was going to play with her.

'She could be coiffed to her nines and I would go and sit on her lap and mess up her hair. She actually sat on the floor with me. She would sit on the floor, cross-legged, and Dot would say, "Get up from the floor." Then Judy would say, "The kid's on the floor. I can stay on the floor." She was fantastic.' But the relationship the two women had, the younger and the older one, had an important aim as far as Dorothy was concerned. As Meredith puts it, 'Dot was the protector of Judy's reputation.'

But not Meredith's. As a very small child, the young Miss Ponedel decided to take a leaf out of her aunt's book and offer to make up Judy the way she thought she had seen Dot do it. As for Judy herself, she took it all in the spirit in which it was completely inappropriately intended.

'I wanted to see if I could do it as well as Dot. Judy was game with me and Dot had kept a lot of her old powder puffs. She got some out – together with whatever face make-up my dad [who was also a leading make-up artist] had. Then came the final touch. That was powdering Judy – not compact powder, but loose powder. Well, I must have got too much on because I started to giggle. Then she started powdering me. I powdered her some more and she powdered me some more – and before you knew it, we were throwing powder at each other like you wouldn't believe. The bathroom was covered in powder. We were roaring with laughter.'

Dorothy Ponedel had by then been struck with multiple sclerosis and was confined most of the time to a wheelchair. 'Dot, who had been in the kitchen, comes wheeling her walker into the room. "What the hell are you two doing?" she asked. Judy's having a blast. I was having a blast. There was powder up Judy's nose, powder up my nose. Dot put an end to it. Judy was having a wonderful time and then went into the kitchen. I said to her, "Wait minute. I have to clear all this up." She said, "Yes, you do!" She never helped me. I had to clean up. I cried.'

Louis B. Mayer, on the other hand, was not going through one of his *crying* periods. After all, he had Irving Berlin, the man who wrote 3,000 songs, on hand.

There were those in Hollywood who hoped that *Easter Parade* would turn out to be an Irving Berlin biopic but they had to be satisfied with a long list of songs run off like a stream of continuous stationery.

There were hopes to see a Berlin biography on celluloid for the next 40 years, but the man himself would never approve the idea, perhaps in belief that having a filmed life story would mean the end, not immortality, a superstition that, once the story had been filmed, there would be no more life to live. Had he agreed, he would have been in good company. It was the era of songwriters' biographies – all of them totally fictitious and mostly pretty bad. George Gershwin was 'honoured' by *Rhapsody in Blue* (one of the better ones) in 1945, Cole Porter's life followed the following year with a travesty called *Night and Day*, and in the same year came the even worse *Till the Clouds Roll by,* which was supposed to have been the story of Jerome Kern who had recently died. Kern would never have recognised it as having anything at all to do with his own life. But it was saved by Frank Sinatra singing a rather original version of 'Ol' Man River'. (Kern, who used to play the piece on his piano before making a trip, just for luck, forgot to do so the day in 1945 when he flew from Los Angeles to New York – and collapsed and died, unrecognised, on a Manhattan street.) Judy did her own impression of Marilyn Miller, an old Broadway star, by almost getting lost in a big production number of 'Who?' and was then seen standing over a wash stand as she sang 'Look for the Silver Lining'.

She could only hope there would be such a silver lining with her next film.

Arthur Freed paired off Judy with Gene Kelly in *The Pirate,* the sort of picture that usually went under the heading of 'a Technicolor extravaganza'. Again Minnelli directed, but little of it seemed to come off. There was just too much fantasy, too many stagy effects in this story of a travelling player in the West Indies whom Judy tells herself is really a pirate.

Looking back now all these years later, it seems as if Gene's reservations about Judy were strictly about her behaviour, not about herself, and certainly not about her talent. In one of those wonderful self-contradictory statements that makes talking to people about their pasts so enticing, he told me: 'I cajoled MGM to let her do *The Pirate*, despite all the problems I knew we would get on the set and her weight difficulties – she seemed to go up and down from one day to the next. One moment she was very happy, the next she was weeping.'

Nevertheless, he gave the impression that if she had not been his co-star, he would have done his share of weeping, too.

The best part of the film was Cole Porter's score – which poses a very strange question and problem: the best of these best was the song 'Be a Clown'. No one has ever worked out why Porter, a man who searched for perfection and usually found it, who even told Frank Sinatra not to mess around with his lyrics (for 'The Lady Is a Tramp' in particular), could allow Arthur Freed to quite literally steal the number for his masterpiece *Singin' in the Rain*. It was the same tune, with an easily recognisable new title – 'Make 'Em Laugh' – with precisely the same message; but never was a bad word said publicly about it. The composer issued no writs and Freed took full credit in the second film, along with his partner Nacio Herb Brown. (A possible explanation was that Freed and Brown wrote the original number and allowed Cole Porter, whose writing of the score for the entire picture was given full credit, not to make this an exception.) Porter was, after all, a prestigious name to have attached to any movie.

If nothing else, it would help him forget *Night and Day*. But that had been a Warner Bros. movie and now he was at MGM, which helped him a great deal while building up a relationship with Arthur Freed and his unit.

In case anyone thought that the phoney songwriter biography was a busted flush, MGM set out to put them right. In 1948 came *Words and Music*. This was (supposedly again) the story of Richard Rodgers and Lorenz Hart, starring Tom Drake (who had grown a little more mature since *Meet Me In St Louis*) as Rodgers, and Mickey Rooney as Hart. It wasn't as bad as the other pictures and there was a chance to hear some wonderful numbers – not least of them the iconic 'Manhattan'. It was, above all, another opportunity for Mickey to work with Judy. She was only in the film for

11 minutes – enough to give a beautiful rendition of 'I Wish I Were in Love Again'. Audiences were in love with her again, too. Her studio, however, was not so sure. Was it a good idea having Garland and Rooney together again?

Mickey and Judy represented the old days when people went to see them because they were the most attractive kids on the block. Now, quite reasonably, MGM wanted to plug them as adult stars – from whom they wanted something totally different. Gene Kelly and Judy Garland had been, in Freed's eyes, a great team with major potential for the future, and he had plans for them, which was as good a reason as any why he had wanted them to star together in *Easter Parade*. Kelly's broken leg had, for the moment put an end to that – and all the enthusiasm Freed had had for that pairing he was now transferring to the idea of another outing for Garland and Astaire.

Gene had taken himself out of the equation and Fred was willing and very able to repeat the success of the earlier film. In the firm belief that there was nothing like copying yourself to ensure a success, the studio had a project made to measure for them – the story of another top stage couple who have a professional reunion. It was to be called *The Barkleys of Broadway*. Yes, it was to be virtually an action replay of *Easter Parade*, with Charles Walters again in the driver's seat and Arthur Freed in his customary position in the producer's office.

Judy, unfortunately, was in *her* customary position – which was showing she couldn't cope with all the demands made of her, while still putting on a great performance. The trouble was that her behaviour was so irritating any residual sympathy from her previous 'performances' had by now been used up.

She claimed that MGM had promised her a holiday after *Easter Parade,* a pledge manifestly broken when they announced they were immediately setting her to work on the *Barkleys* film. This was followed by another statement – Judy was unwell. That was true. But being unwell meant more overdoses of drugs and more hospitalisations. She would later write: 'By now I was just a mechanical hoop they were rolling around. I was sure I wasn't going to make it, but it didn't matter. The rehearsals began and my migraine headaches got worse. I went for days without sleep but I kept on. Then I started to be late for rehearsals and began missing days.'

The studio decided that this was the breaking point. Judy Garland, the pride of MGM, Louis B. Mayer's favourite 'child' of all in his so-called family, was fired from the film. Judy was incensed. 'They didn't even give me the courtesy of a call or a meeting or a discussion,' she wrote. 'They sent me a telegram.'

The piano player-cum-sarcastic comedy actor Oscar Levant, who was one of the last links with George Gershwin, would maintain that Freed and Mayer called round to Judy's home in Stone Canyon Road on the famed Bel Air estate to discuss the problem, but she wouldn't open the door. Neither would her mother, who was also living there at the time.

Meredith Ponedel puts a lot of the blame on Dore Schary, who had taken over from Louis B. Mayer as head of production and was at the start of his ongoing war with the man who was nominally still the boss – although within a couple of years LB would be ousted with his nemesis appointed in his stead.

Meredith told me that her Aunt Dorothy knew the star was not getting enough rest. Schary, she said, 'was not looking after Judy's welfare. He just wanted to turn out a commodity.' The old charge again – with a new face on the target board.

The film went ahead without Judy and with Fred apparently as happy as a sandboy – at least, one who was able to dance his way around any sand that was there and, particularly, on a shiny, newly polished dance floor. His 'new' partner was Ginger Rogers. The old 'team', the term Fred still didn't like using, was back in business. (One of the discoveries I made when researching the Astaire book was that it was clear Fred and Ginger didn't like each other very much; when I asked her to explain the magic of the Astaire–Rogers movies, she said, 'Don't you mean the Rogers–Astaire movies – it's customary to have the lady's name first, isn't it?')

So the partnership between Astaire and Garland was over. In truth, the ace perfectionist would never have stood for what he would have regarded as Judy's arrant unprofessionalism. As for the partnership between Garland and MGM, it had turned sour – and would never be really sweet again.

CHAPTER SEVEN

Troubles and Triumphs Ahead

At first, things didn't look so very bad. The astonishing fact was that the studio which fired her still wanted to use Judy for new projects. Other people in other jobs, once fired because they were troublemakers or just no good, stayed fired. Not in Hollywood.

A casual observer might have wondered whether MGM were gluttons for punishment or were simply using their investment for as long as they could. The latter was the more likely scenario.

The year 1948 may have seen the fiasco of *The Barkleys of Broadway*, but just a few weeks later there was *In the Good Old Summertime*, which Judy *did* make. It was not a good picture by any account, being yet another retread of a story that has had almost as many incarnations as MGM sent telegrams to erring stars. It was basically the old *Shop Around the Corner* tale, which began life as the tale of a pair of shop assistants in Budapest who don't get on, but then discover they have been writing love letters to each other under assumed identities. The original film starred James Stewart and Margaret Sullavan. Now, the drapers shop was changed to a music store in 1906 Chicago (yet another turn-of-the-century yarn) and co-starred Judy with Van Johnson, which seemed to most people to be a reasonable combination.

The production number 'I Don't Care' was one of the best features of a film that, probably deservedly, is now all but forgotten. But it had its historic interest. The final scene in which Judy holds the hand of her baby daughter, was Liza Minnelli's movie debut. Admittedly, she didn't show any signs then of becoming

Sally Bowles in *Cabaret,* but Liza got just under $50 for her day's work, which Judy decided wasn't bad money for a three-year-old. As she once said: I never forgave myself for letting her hang around the house for the first two years of her life, doing nothing.'

Summer Stock in 1950 featured the classic Garland routine of Judy in a very feminised version of a man's dinner jacket, accompanied by tights that emphasised her legs from ankles to thighs in a way never seen before. On top of the ensemble, there was a rather strange fedora hat, which has become another of her signature 'looks'. It's what people remember about that film – along with the number she sang while wearing the ensemble – 'Get Happy'.

It was a strange time. America had few of the inhibitions shown in Britain during a period when the BBC censored records, deciding what could be heard and what could not. It was a virus that was caught by the distributors of *Summer Stock,* which in Britain was called *If You Feel Like Singing* – the term *Summer Stock* (roughly comparable to British repertory theatre, but generally limited to the summer months), quite fairly, didn't mean anything to audiences in the UK. But censoring the 'Get Happy' song was something else. The British branch of MGM had been warned that Brits wouldn't take kindly to the words 'Judgement Day' at the end of the number, not that (as far as anyone can now tell) any of them were asked. So for British consumption, the words 'Judgement Day' as performed in *If You Feel Like Singing* were changed to 'jolly day'. Judy wasn't available to make the new dubbing, so some unknown, and forever anonymous, woman was employed to 'sing' those two words. Ken Sefton, who edited Judy's London fan club magazine, recalled for me discussing the dubbing with Judy herself. 'She was so intrigued,' he recalled. 'She said, "I never knew that."' Ever since, fans have been trying to find out who the lady was, as though they were archaeologists seeking to discover the origin of some ancient artefact. The anonymous woman no doubt did have a jolly day – getting happy.

If only that had been a call to Judy herself. She was decidedly *not* having a jolly day and was certainly anything but happy and it showed in a film in which her performance was on-off/off-on.

Once more, her weight was unpredictable and, to the annoyance of her co-star Gene Kelly, she again failed to turn up for rehearsals. 'It was very hard work trying to get her to be professional,' he told me. 'Whether this was because of her health I never really knew.'

They were words that, as we shall see, came from him with something of an inner shudder. Actually, he did know it was very much a question of health — and like Judy herself his statement coincided with a mood swing. At other times he was full of sympathy for her.

The miracle was that Judy was in the film at all. It should have been a June Allyson role, but she became pregnant and the studio were frightened it would show. As it was, Judy could have been with child herself and then the victim of a miscarriage, looking fat one moment, incredibly slim the next.

For all that, Kelly and Garland certainly looked great together. What Mayer really wanted was to pair Judy again with Fred Astaire. He felt Fred could be persuaded to give it another try and he had just the project for them — *Royal Wedding,* a second movie originally scheduled for June Allyson that was interrupted by her pregnancy. The film was about a trip to London in time for an event supposedly based on the wedding of the then Princess Elizabeth (now the Queen) and Prince Philip of Greece, who had become Lt Philip Mountbatten (now the Duke of Edinburgh). Britain was going to be sensitive about that picture's title, too, the people at Culver City were advised. So there it was to be called simply *Wedding Bells.* Actually, it rang all too few bells on either side of the Atlantic.

When work began on the film, nobody seemed to doubt that it would work. Judy herself was delighted with the plan — until she was primed for a not terribly important scene, dolled up in finery and make-up and was walking through one of the studio's corridors. It was then that she bumped into Arthur Freed, who asked her simply: 'What are you doing here? You're not in this picture.'

Judy retired to her dressing room in tears, looked around her dressing table and cut her throat with a piece of broken glass she had either just discovered or had stashed away for a moment like this. It wasn't a spur of the moment decision. Indeed, it wasn't much of a cut and if she had really planned to take her life, it wasn't done very expertly, as those who have attempted a serious suicide themselves pointed out. What it was was a cry for help, which didn't come very readily.

Dot Ponedel, for one, never thought Judy was trying to take her life. As Meredith told me: 'It was a little scratch across the throat. Dot was there at the time. It was in the bathroom soon after she had been dumped. Dot said it was absolutely nothing. The media were blowing it out of all proportion. As far as the drugs were concerned, Dot did see her hooked up to IDs at times, but I think she called it glucose and Judy would take her uppers, nothing major.'

That in itself was a revelation. Drugs – if that was what the intravenous devices *were* being used for – had previously come in tablets from a bottle.

The movie was running behind schedule. It was not released until 1951 and finally starred Jane Powell opposite Astaire, who achieved even more acclaim than he had before in his praise-loaded life by devising a scene in which he appeared to be dancing upside down on the ceiling. Judy would have loved to have been part of that scene, if only to gaze at the way Fred actually was dancing on a platform in a large drum complete with firmly-affixed scenery that revolved around as he moved.

For Judy, *Royal Wedding* represented a disaster, although she tried to laugh it off once the minor throat cut had healed. When she talked about the film that for her never was, she had her own perfect explanation: 'Leo the Lion bit me,' she declared. Actually, the name of the lion in question was Louis.

That big cat and its unpredictable cub, Dore Schary, kept on biting. But if Leo was responsible, he was aided by someone else, someone very close to Judy, who – had it been revealed at the time – would have had quite a bit of explaining to do for actions that were motivated entirely for her own good.

Paul Rabwin, revealing the story for the first time, told me that his father, Dr Marc Rabwin, actually went to see LB pleading with him to let her go. 'My father had determined that she couldn't deal with the politics of the studio, the pressures. She was showing up late. He said, "Mr Mayer, you have to let her out of her contract. You're going to kill her or she is going to kill herself." He literally went to L.B. Mayer and asked him to give up millions of dollars by giving up her contract. And Louis Mayer did. A lot of people have feelings about studio heads, but this man was willingly giving up his contract to save her life. She was claiming that they were overworking her. She was taking alcohol, drugs.'

The good doctor knew that the broken-glass incident was just a symptom of something more dangerous and feared she would do it again and that next time she might succeed. There are those who think that this first incident (and there would be many others) was no more than a cry for help and, like Meredith Ponedel, believed that she never had any intention of taking her life.

MGM actually kept her under contract, although letting her off *Royal Wedding* allowed her a few moments of respite. Before *Royal Wedding*, though, there was an even bigger disappointment for Judy, over MGM's movie version of the big Broadway hit, *Annie Get Your Gun*. It was going to be such a big film that the very idea of her being contracted to make the picture seemed to confirm that all was forgiven and that she was as big a star and as important a name as ever. The trouble was that, once more, what Judy got was not a gun but the bullet.

This was a real tragedy for Judy. She had a great part in what looked like being a great movie. After all, how could it fail? For more than three years people had been singing numbers from what was, for a million or more of them, their favourite Broadway musical. The tunes were played daily on the radio. Records by Ethel Merman as Annie were still selling by their thousands and the new long-playing disc was still in the windows of music stores on both sides of the Atlantic.

Merman would probably have wanted to play the part in the film herself, but she wasn't photogenic enough to play a young girl on the screen. There was no doubt in the MGM offices that they had found the right star to take what Merman had always considered to be *her* role – and hers alone.

Certainly, the movie version of the hit Irving Berlin show had seemed to be made to measure for Judy when the cameras first started turning in 1949. The story of Annie Oakley, the girl who really did use firearms to try to get her man (and a place with Buffalo Bill Cody's famous circus), had a perfect plot, which had wowed stage audiences since it first opened. The score was one of Berlin's best – with hits like 'Anything You Can Do', 'The Sun in the Morning', 'You Can't Get a Man with a Gun' and, above all, the number often described as the national anthem of the theatre, 'There's No Business Like Show Business'. It is doubtful if, before or since, any other Broadway show had as many bestselling songs – practically every number was a smash – as this.

Plainly, however, things didn't look good from the moment Judy heard that the director was going to be her old *bête noire*, Busby Berkeley. Here was a definite target for the gun she was learning to handle so expertly. She filmed a number of scenes, most notably the one where she was dressed in Indian costume to sing 'I'm an Indian, Too'. She recorded enough tunes from the soundtrack to make a fairly decent album. And when Berkeley was fired, to be replaced by George Sidney, Judy was delighted. But her pleasure was short-lived.

There were, it seemed, too many results of Berkeley's work hanging around for her liking. As Meredith Ponedel told me: 'They knew Judy could not work with Berkeley. When you take a star of Judy's magnitude and her amazing immense ability to portray what she could on the screen and then place her with someone who couldn't work with her...' She left her sentence hanging there, seemingly lost for words, but the implication was that it had been a disaster. It was something Judy and Dorothy Ponedel talked about a lot. 'I remember,' said Meredith, 'her saying that if things had gone right, it would have been fine. But they were not looking after Judy properly.'

Judy, with her get-up-and-go and a voice that had never

sounded better, had an enthusiasm that seemed to promise a really good movie. Except that she was a girl behaving badly and throwing her ever-changing weight around, all demonstrations of a temperament that was more than the studio could take. Judy was fired.

Her part went to Betty Hutton, who was not nearly as good as Judy would have been, but she was reliable (although Fred Astaire, who worked with her on another picture, thought otherwise). The role had almost gone to Betty Garrett, who probably *would* have been as good, but she was blacklisted after the House Un-American Activities Committee decided she was still a dangerous Communist (she had been a member of the party, along with her husband Larry Parks, who had recently starred in *The Jolson Story* and *Jolson Sings Again* and was also on the blacklist). For her part, being blacklisted was precisely how Judy Garland felt at the time – blacklisted by the people for whom she had done so much, and who had done so much for her.

Again, Judy would use her amazing sense of humour to tell the story. It was a sad moment in the tale of what had once seemed the perfect relationship between a studio and a star who had achieved that status purely as a result of their own fostering. Yet, in the retelling by people who were in receipt of the tale, it all reads like the script of a very funny story indeed. George Schlatter, who was to produce Judy's television show, told me about it.

'They really ripped her off when she did *Annie Get Your Gun,*' he said. 'She worked hard and did her best, but they thought she was difficult. Yet nobody would tell her. They decided to fire her on a Friday afternoon before a long weekend and when everybody had gone home. They sent a little guy down to the set to tell her, "Miss Garland, you've been fired."'

That was an old Hollywood trick. Part of Tinseltown lore has it that Jack L. Warner, head of production at the studio he controlled with his brothers, would disappear when an employee was about to get sacked. It got so that every time Warner took off unexpectedly for some unknown destination, people would ask, 'Who's got fired now?' The answer would come when the assistant usually assigned to the firing task would reveal the name of the latest victim.

Few of those ex-employees would react as Judy did, with that very unusual sense of humour that, strangely, came to its fore in the midst of some disaster or other – although it did take time for this firing to get the Garland touch. As George Schlatter explained to me: 'She was dressed as an Indian in war paint. She went through the halls of the Thalberg building at MGM looking for someone to attack. She had a tomahawk and was wearing moccasins and buckskins, running through the halls saying, "I'm going to find them and scalp them".'

It would have been even funnier to have been a fly on the side of her tepee at that firing moment. She told the gofer that she was being left high and dry. She didn't know what tribe she belonged to, so where was the reservation to which she had to go? The man, who didn't see things the way she did, just shrugged his shoulders and walked off, unaware of the humour. There are some people who just can't take a joke.

Plainly, Judy was furious. George Schlatter understands how she felt. As we shall see, he would not be immune to the peccadilloes of showbiz bosses himself. 'In Judy's case, they were cowards. They were all terrified of her.'

Vincente Minnelli did not need any pleading to let Judy go. In 1951 the couple were divorced. Margaret Whiting told me she wasn't surprised – but, like most of Judy's friends, she was upset. 'I always felt that she felt very close to Vincente,' she told me. Indeed, that was the general opinion – a couple who felt close to each other, but not close enough to share a home – which would have been too close. No one was surprised at the news of the break-up. In truth, they had not been getting on for a long time and the fact that Minnelli was gay brought a strange dichotomy. As would be proved later, Judy had no more devoted fans than homosexuals. On the other hand, she had an enormous sexual appetite, perhaps sometimes even reaching nymphomaniacal levels, and it was obvious her husband could not satisfy her in bed. There were those near her who were frightened for her future, afraid that she would marry just any man whom she thought would fulfil her needs in that direction, rather in the way she believed that her drugs were making her a happy woman – which they patently were not.

The trouble for Judy was that her problems were all in the public eye. She couldn't just sneak away for a couple of days if she felt under the weather. She was always working – even when she had been fired from a particular film, she was still a machine in the MGM factory and Dore Schary was the foreman. Later, she said that Schary was responsible for the ending of her contract. She never knew what Marc Rabwin had done. But if in her mind it was Schary, she had an explanation for it. As she said: 'Schary came into Metro and wanted to prove that stars weren't necessary.' After 16 years under contract, Dr Rabwin's advice was acted upon and she was finally let go, as the contemporary term for being given the sack has it. MGM would be doing without her.

But was it worse for her when she was an MGM employee? She had to reason just how bad it was. It was not enough to remember that if she were sacked from a project, the whole world knew about it. If she was carted off to a sanatorium, the news was public property. Even worse, there were no secrets from her friends. If she was feeling down, she couldn't – and didn't – keep the fact to herself. The broadcaster, Joe Franklin recalled for me: 'I went to see her once when she was living at a friend's house, a psychiatrist's home. She was upset about something and started throwing things about the house. She broke a mirror. So she was very nervous.' There was something ironic about that. It just had to be at a psychiatrist's house. There was treatment at hand, but the pathos of it all was obvious. Her host must have had thoughts about this, and would have had to have been particularly obtuse not to see her behaviour as a cry for help.

Yet there was always the need for a satisfaction that no psychiatrist could ever give her – unless he was ready to be struck off the medical register. As Margaret Whiting told me: 'She had nowhere to go. There was no man in her life and it hurt.'

If Judy wanted a way out, a chance to do something entirely different came with an invitation to play the most important vaudeville theatre on Broadway. And also to go to London.

Both places had theatres that were called in the trade 'temples'. An appropriate word, because what she received in them was something close to worship.

In both cities she discovered something she could only have guessed at before: the love she was both giving to and receiving from ordinary people, folk who asked no more of her than a few songs – and a lifetime of memories.

CHAPTER EIGHT

A Star is Reborn

J udy had always liked performing live. Incredibly for someone
who could be wracked by stage fright, she believed there were
fewer pressures than she experienced on a movie set. But,
hitherto, making stage appearances to plug her movies had never
been more than an ancillary job – not something she took all that
seriously. But now it was going to be different. Judy Garland, film
star, was about to become Judy Garland, concert artist.

Of course, there would be pressures. But those pressures, the
insecurities and the depressions, would have new focuses. And she
would also find new audiences as well as a new love affair. Had
there been a serious man in her life, he would have discovered that
his principal competition would have been in the stalls and the
balconies of live theatres, people who had seen Judy on the screen,
but who were now for the first time getting an opportunity to see
her for herself, to hear songs they had never heard her sing before,
to experience her reaching out to a brand new public.

She was also finding out how much she needed all the adoration
she was receiving. Most encouraging of all, that reaction was not
all at home. Thousands of miles away, people speaking with new
accents and having different manners were clapping and cheering
as though they were being introduced to a totally new talent; a
talent who was overwhelming them.

On 9 April 1951, Judy Garland joined a select band of American
entertainers who were confirming their reputation as supremely at
the top of their profession They did it simply by accepting an
invitation to what the Brits called the temple of variety, the London

Palladium. Ever since its opening in 1910, the leading British show personalities of their day knew they had finally made it when they topped the bill at the Palladium. There were music halls all over the country when the theatre opened – 60 of them in London alone – the principal entertainment centres for the working man and his wife, smoke-filled venues smelling of the beer they sold while comedians tried to get over the punch lines of jokes the audiences had heard a dozen times before. There were singers in top hats and full evening dress suits that looked as if they had been borrowed from some waiter making a few coppers on the side. The women frequently looked not unlike the girls standing on street corners as they sang about an old man who told them to follow the van.

The Palladium was different. It made variety, as it was now being called, respectable. It was a theatre with Doric columns outside, the seats were red plush, there was a gilt veneer on the walls and the stage was huge. Perhaps it had to be to provide, as it did in 1930, the setting for the biggest stars of the land, the entertainers who played before the King and Queen at the annual Royal Command Performance, just as their descendants do to Queen Elizabeth II or other royals to this day. Most significantly, it was immediately recognised as the theatre that was comfortable for the people who normally chose to see productions traditionally considered more dignified, the shows that were called 'musical comedies', as well as straight plays. It was the only variety theatre where people were happy to visit in full evening dress and to be spotted as they left their chauffeur-driven cars. The real success was that 'ordinary' working people were equally comfortable there.

In the first post-war years, it all got more exciting than ever. The Palladium was more important than it had ever been before – because it was packaging the most important stars in the world, not just those from Britain. Mostly, they were Americans. Americans had always come to the Palladium, but only in dribs and drabs. Irving Berlin had brought his show *This Is the Army* to the theatre and Joe E. Brown, Sophie Tucker and Jimmy Durante had played there. Now, however, they had virtually taken over the theatre and the public could not have been more pleased.

It was a daunting task that was now facing Judy. She was asked to follow in the footsteps of people like Jack Benny, Laurel and Hardy, Burns and Allen and the Andrews Sisters – and, above all, Danny Kaye, who had come to the Palladium in 1948 and received the kind of adoration probably no British act had ever experienced. This was austerity Britain, when people mostly came to theatres by bus and train. Kaye and the others brought sunshine to a city that was still drab and grey – with holes where buildings had once stood, thanks to the German Luftwaffe. For Danny Kaye there had been lines three or four deep around the theatre block day and night, made up of people who in those days were used to queuing for everything they bought – nylon stockings, cigarettes, bread. Queuing for tickets represented luxury. When the King and Queen came to see Kaye – their younger daughter Princess Margaret was in the same seat in the third row of the stalls every night – it was a stamp of approval not only for this very unusual star, but for the Palladium itself and the kind of acts it was booking. But Kaye's was quite an act to have to follow.

After his performance – or rather performances; he came back twice more – the American stars lined up to follow him. Only one megastar said no. Al Jolson said, 'Everyone's a sensation there. I like to set records.'

Judy was ready to set records in London herself. But there was probably, to quote a song lyric, a warning voice at the back of her mind – telling her that there had been disappointments there, too. Not least of these was the man Danny Kaye followed at a moment's notice, her old friend Mickey Rooney, who didn't complete his engagement.

There was no risk of that happening to Judy. At least, not after the first ten minutes or so of her Palladium debut. Those first minutes could have been horrendous. After standing in the wings, twisting her damp hand, running her fingers through her hair, she came on stage – and fell flat on her bottom. Her legs had got tangled in the hem of her long, trailing skirt. The gasp coming from the wings, where Kay Thompson was on hand to give her the necessary dose of confidence, was audible. But amazingly it did not presage trouble.

If the audience had not been sympathetic, they might have laughed. Instead, they clapped and cheered as much as a polite British audience could be expected to do.

When her pianist Buddy Pepper helped her up, she was at first flustered, but then began singing. From that moment on, the Palladium audience claimed her as its own.

'There was an electricity in the audience that night. The audience loved her for her vulnerability,' Chris Woodward, the official Palladium historian and author of a book about the theatre, told me.

For the second house, Woolf Phillips, the theatre's resident band leader, conductor of the Skyrockets Orchestra, went up to her and told her to sit on the apron of the stage – Danny Kaye's favourite routine – and just talk to the audience. She was so happy with the reaction of the people out front that she kept that in her act for the rest of the tour. For the next four weeks, the name Judy Garland on the posters for the London Palladium proclaimed that she had arrived. The career that had begun singing on a stage at the age of two in Grand Rapids was continuing after a 16-year hiatus. And she was better than ever before.

Chris Woodward was taken to the theatre for the Judy Garland show by his parents. He told me: 'She was only twenty-nine at the time and she did a wonderful job. I think this was the pinnacle of her career at the time. Val Parnell, who ran the theatre, wanted to get the top stars and he was never less than delighted that Judy was one of them.'

Today, British fans remember that Palladium show as though it were a milestone in their own lives, which it plainly was.

Dennis Sykes, a retired legal executive, put it like this: 'After her time at the Palladium, she realised this was a big comeback opportunity, which she grabbed with both hands. After that, she always had a yen for London audiences because they were so sympathetic to her. They loved her.'

And it really was a lifelong love affair for many of them. There was no more devoted 'lover' than Brian Glanvill, who helped run a children's theatre in London and was a Butlin's holiday camp 'redcoat'. He confessed to me that he had first fallen for her when he saw *The Wizard of Oz*, 'like most people'. But the adoration for his idol went further than a mere confession of love. As a child, he said, 'I decided, when Judy and I were married, how many children we would have.' Such was the devotion of a Judy Garland fan. After that first Palladium performance, he stood outside her dressing room and was 'patted on the head' by the then leading British comic Max Bygraves, second on the Garland bill. He didn't talk to Judy that night, but later on during other British visits, they got to know each other in a way few stars and their fans have been able to experience.

Beverley Baxter, one of the most respected critics and columnists of the time, reported: 'This sturdy young woman bowed and smiled as the cheering went on, but there were no tears, no trembling of the lips or wobbling of the chin. She was a trouper who had come to give a performance. That was what mattered to her.'

What mattered to her audiences was simply that she was there. People who paid from three shillings and sixpence (17½p in today's money) for a balcony seat to £2.18s (£2.90) for the best box wondered if they would be able to see her at all – the theatre was so big and she was so small. But that never happened. They came with opera glasses and those who didn't have them were still able to appreciate the magic of it all, as though that personality of hers provided a magnification of its own.

There were other performances in London before she moved on to some of the biggest theatres in the British provinces. She opened the second half – with Buddy Pepper at the piano again – of a memorial benefit for the comedian Sid Field, a big British star who in his prime had briefly taken over from Mickey Rooney when the Palladium run was cut short before Danny Kaye could arrive. Field had hit hard times before dying in 1950. The midnight show staged a year later was put on by Laurence Olivier and ran until 3am. As Chris Woodward recalls: 'Almost every big name you could think of took part.' Big names that included Danny Kaye again, Count Basie, Margaret Lockwood and Frankie Vaughan as well as Olivier himself. Which was further proof how great Judy

131

had been during the four-week Palladium run. It was the first of nine appearances at the theatre.

The audiences in the provinces reacted precisely as had the people in London. It wasn't all easy going. She may have been told that provincials would like her because they liked anyone who came to visit them – much like those in Grand Rapids and Lancaster who had nowhere else to go. But she was sensible and didn't try to coast.

Maybe she had been advised that the people who paid for tickets in Glasgow, in particular, were the toughest in the world. True, many a career had been ruined by crowds at the Glasgow Empire, who treated acts they didn't like the way they would players from the wrong football team. But they loved Judy, as did the audiences in Edinburgh. The old cliché about there not being a dry eye in the house when she sang 'Loch Lomond' would be overplaying it somewhat – but people did take both the high road and the low road to the theatres where she played and were delighted they had done so. The trademark break in her own voice went with the tears she was displaying herself on those nights in Glasgow and Edinburgh. They were real enough. And so were the cheers and claps from people in Manchester, Blackpool, Liverpool and Birmingham. When she crossed the Irish Sea to play in Dublin, she couldn't have been better treated if she had gone on to kiss the Blarney stone with a pint of Guinness in her hand. When she sang a medley from her *Little Nellie Kelly* movie there, they went wild. As she sang, it was a great day for the Irish.

She was happier than she had been for years, perhaps happier at any time since Mr Mayer had politely clapped when she sang 'Eli Eli'. But there was a reason for that. The man in her life that Margaret Whiting had said was so obviously missing had now arrived. He was her new manager, the man who had organised the British tour for her in the first place. On this trip, he was managing her whole life and she couldn't have been on a higher cloud. His name was appropriately Sid Luft.

Luft was the handsome son of Jewish immigrants, born in New York in 1915. He was a former Royal Canadian Air Force pilot, a test pilot, showbiz entrepreneur, manager for the Hollywood dancer Eleanor Powell and the one who convinced Judy Garland that she should say 'F... 'em' to MGM.

They had both just gone through divorces and their meeting appeared to do both of them a lot of good. As Paul Rabwin put it to me: 'Sid had found his pot of gold.'

Judy had been instantly attracted to him and allowed Luft for the next few years to be her guardian, saviour, Svengali and in-house devil. The year after the British tour, they married and had two children, Lorna and Joey. Meanwhile, Sid treated Liza, too, with a great deal of obvious love. She called him 'Pop'.

Much has been written about the demands made by Luft and his apparent cruelty to Judy, but he had a lot to put up with and the facts lean heavily towards his obvious care for her. It could be said that he was, like the men from MGM, merely protecting his investment, but there is also a great deal to say that there was much kindness from him.

His surviving elder sister, Peri Fleischman, an artist of remarkably unusual talent, living in a small apartment in Los Angeles surrounded by her paintings and sculptures, told me that she wasn't at all surprised at anything her brother could do – including marrying a star like Judy Garland, whom she says she always thought was 'wonderful'.

'I wouldn't be amazed at anything he would do, because Sid was very adventurous,' she told me. 'He explored many avenues. I was always pleased they married – despite their different religions. She brought more colour into the family. She was brilliant and talented, very nice and pleasant, very unusual and very good with me. We liked each other.'

So why the unpleasant things said about Sid? 'Unpleasant? Oh, I hope so! Everyone would be jealous of him, wouldn't they? Jealous of anyone who had such charm, so many opportunities, so many interesting confrontations and problems.' I thought at first I detected an element of sarcasm there. But no, she meant every word.

So was he a good husband? 'He took good care of her, so to speak. If he were a good lover, he was a good husband. The truth is he was a very self-centred, needy man. He was a good husband because he took care of her. He did right by her and gave her what she needed when she was with him. He was a selfish, spoiled guy because he was good-looking and people were always interested in him and he was charming. He was a charmer. Even when he was a kid in school, the teachers knew he did what he wanted to do and could get away with murder.

'He was a good actor, too – and he liked being important in certain ways, so he got a lot of attention. He was a very good man at home. How could he be bad? People who say he wasn't a good man must have been jealous. They have to give a reason for saying that.'

But as a businessman, there was plenty wrong with him. 'Absolutely he was interested in money and he took advantage of Judy. He took advantage of anyone he could because he was interested in money. He spent it when he had it. And he dressed well and took good care of himself. He ate well. He did everything like a real sport. He was a great sport. But whatever he was, people liked him and wanted to be near him, wanted his company. He was seductive.'

And had always been seductive, she maintains. 'My mother was full of life and energy – and she taught him to dance. She was crazy about him. She didn't like me that much. Perhaps she was jealous of me – because I was pretty smart.'

Pretty smart – that was Sid, too. And because he was pretty smart, he decided that the time had come for Judy to repeat her London success in New York – at the Big Apple's equivalent of the Palladium, the Palace. As Judy would later sing, 'Vaudeville's back at the Palace and I am on the bill'. More significant was that other line from the song with which she opened her act: 'If you haven't played the Palace, you haven't played the top'. Well, Judy played the Palace later in 1951 and showed that she could be as close to the very tip of the top as she had been in London.

The opening of the Palace show was treated like a film premiere, with all the panoply of press receptions and interviews broadcast from coast to coast. She didn't actually say another line from her opening number, 'until you've played the Palace, you might as well be dead', but she could be forgiven for thinking, if only briefly, that she had never lived this well before.

Louella Parsons, one of the resident Hollywood bitches of movie columnists, went to New York for the opening and interviewed her with the requisite amount of shmooze and praise. 'Welcome home,' she declared, and made sure she added a feminine touch: 'You look wonderful. Your skin is wonderful after your British triumph.' Judy was truly appreciative. 'I've just lost fifteen pounds.' For a young woman constantly told she was putting on too much weight, that was exceedingly important.

The opening was sensationally successful, singing about how glad she was to be back in America and performing, for the first time, the old Jolson standard 'Rockabye Your Baby with a Dixie Melody'.

One of the most exciting scenes in the show was a replay of the 'Get Happy' number from *Summer Stock*. She looked as good on stage in her tuxedo and tights as she had on screen. There was also a montage sequence, featuring periods in Judy's career with a particular reference to New York and her associations with the *Ziegfeld* films.

If Britain had been a big success, the Palace run was that in capital letters and every superlative that could be conjured up by critics who loved it. The *New York Post* critic described it as 'the greatest act ever to have played the Palace'. The four-week Palace run was extended to an unheard of 19 weeks.

It was an event that became engraved on her soul, one she would remember in her dark days, which may not have been such a good thing. It wasn't healthy in later years, when she was riddled with drugs, to have to say, 'I was so great at the Palace.' It just emphasised how low she could sometimes fall, even if, after a time, she was normally able to pick herself up again.

Of that Palace show, she later admitted, nothing had frightened her more. She was scared beyond measure. Not just because it was the most important theatre still playing vaudeville in America – she hadn't sung live to a significant audience in her home country for years. The Palladium had been wonderful, but that was far away and had she flopped there, she could have written it down to experience. But you couldn't keep secrets in New York in those days. It was an era before mass media, half a century before the Internet. But a bad review in the *New York Times* alone could have ruined her career forever. But it wouldn't be like that.

'Pandemonium broke out when she appeared at the Palace,' Martin McQuade, a Broadway historian told me, as we stood outside the very theatre, now barely a shadow of its previous self. 'The crowds were enormous. Thousands and thousands of people, royalty and the common man, were lining the streets to see her. When she appeared here, her career [in America] was sagging. Her movie career had pretty well gone by the wayside, but her appearance here at the Palace in 1951 completely and utterly revived her. She felt as if she were alive again.'

In fact, she told an interviewer: 'I really think I am Judy Garland once more.'

That prompted another question to a man who has seen all the big Broadway moments for decades. What was the secret behind it all? He told me: 'I think, basically, it was the emotion that she was able to convey to people. I think it was the sense that she was able to associate herself and connect with people who were misplaced in their own lives.'

As the comedian Alan King, who shared countless bills with Judy, put it: 'She was the heroine of the misplaced.' Martin McQuade confirmed that statement from a New Yorker's point of view. 'She had a certain zeal to be loved, a zeal to be revered. The audiences immediately hit on this. You could almost hear her say, "Please love me". It was the emotion she was able to convey.'

Actually, it *was* simply love. Other big entertainers played, wonderfully successfully, to their audiences. She, however was one of those few who made love to them – a love that was instantly returned, and at the same time Judy was rewarded. Not since Jolson had wowed them at the nearby Winter Garden Theatre when he actually told audiences to 'Watch me, I'm a wow', had there been such a transfer of love from one side of the footlights to the other –

and passed straight back again. It was like a successful series of volleys at a tennis championship. Spencer Tracy was in an orchestra seat and said afterwards: 'A Garland audience doesn't just listen, they feel they have to put their arms around her when she works.'

Not just their arms. They were smothering her in – quite literally – *garlands* of adoration.

The show brought Judy her first 'Tony' award. She shared the stage the night of that presentation with Richard Rodgers and Oscar Hammerstein, Gertrude Lawrence and Yul Brynner, all for *The King and I.* It was an important night for the American theatre. Certainly it was for Judy.

The tributes from her peers was the nicest thing of all. In June 1952, the Friars Club, the best-known show-business club in America, gave her a testimonial dinner – complete with Frank Sinatra singing 'You Made Me Love You' to her.

It was all part of the triumph of her Palace show. Before long, an album called *Miss Show Business*, which included a medley of Judy's songs at the Palace, would be one of her most successful records ever. The theatre showed its appreciation of that, and all the other publicity she brought, by putting up a brass plate outside what had become her inner sanctum, declaring it to be 'Judy Garland's dressing room'.

It was astonishing that at what had seemed to be the nadir of her career, Judy had made a comeback, the like of which had rarely been known before. It was not enough for her to say – as those making that sort of new return often do – 'I've not been anywhere'. In her career, she had been, seemingly, *everywhere.* But now she was somewhere else and did not want to leave. She had realised that this was now what she wanted to do. This was, she would say, the new Judy Garland. At 29, Judy Garland, concert artist, had been born. But she was thinking about a new movie, nevertheless. One away from MGM. One produced by her husband. One called, highly appropriately, *A Star Is Born.*

CHAPTER NINE

The Roller-Coaster Years

P lainly, Judy was the darling of her own masses. She was one of those very few artists who could quite genuinely have had people crawling at her feet as she read the telephone book. If she recited 'Little Bo Peep', they would have gone crazy. There was a very select band of performers who were like magnets to piles of iron filings. Judy was one of them. To her fans at the live shows that followed the Palladium and Palace triumphs, she was the only one who could ever attract them into her own magnetic field. It was as if for those supporters who treated her like a close relative, not merely a friend, loving any other artist would have been a gesture of disloyalty to *their* Judy.

They had plenty of opportunities to show they were anything but disloyal in those early years of the 1950s. In San Francisco and Los Angeles, Judy repeated her Palace triumph. And that seemed to be the way of her private life, too. Giving birth to her second child, Lorna, in November 1952, she repeated the success she had had as a mother with Liza's arrival. It was also good for the marriage she had with Sid. She was an adoring parent who was determined not to repeat the experiences she had had with her own mother. She was not going to be a showbiz mom. Or so she thought. As for Sid, he was quickly showing himself to be a devoted father. His sister Peri Fleischman told me: 'He was wonderful to the children. He loved them. Always loved children. He was crazy about them.'

But being married to Judy wasn't easy. 'I think being married to a star is very hard. Two people who are both stars at the same time are *tres difficile*. My brother was a star, too. Charming, aggressive and ambitious.'

During these early stage shows, Peri worked with Judy herself. 'I sat and waited at the shows. I worked backstage, taking care of her while she prepared herself for the performances, so I thought a lot of her. I always admired people who were intelligent and gifted and she was both. We were friendly and we respected each other. I used to help her dress, be next to her. Actually, I didn't have to do much because she cared about herself, put on her own make-up and all that – she wore very good eyeliner, nice black up and down and around. And she was very funny. She'd pinch my behind going upstairs.' But only after a show. Before going on stage she was her usual bunch of nerves.

She was feeling her way into what was virtually a new profession, even if it were something she had been doing practically all her life. What she was realising was that she had created a new Judy Garland with a new style. She could do things on stage that she had never been able to put into practice on screen, when she had to perform within the parameters of a story line. Now, she was liberated from screenplays. She was her own woman and that was how people wanted her to be. This was obvious in how she performed her numbers.

No one expected that she would just stand on stage and sing with a microphone in front of her. That could never work for a performer like her. Some great singers were doing it. Frank Sinatra and Bing Crosby had turned a microphone into a musical instrument. When they started doing so, it was the modern way. It was not Judy Garland's way. In that respect, there was something distinctly old-fashioned about her. She 'gave out' like the old-time vaudevillians did, but in her own unique way. A perfect example was the rather beautiful song 'Just in Time' which, it could be argued, was easy enough to croon. Not for Judy. For the first few minutes, she was holding out her arms, beckoning people to be with her. She was calling to her audience, almost pleading with them to come and cuddle up a little closer, as she had sung years before. Then, once she knew they were there and she was hugging them to herself, she did a little dance with them – and with those inviting arms. Finally, she was ready to give the number all the diva-like strength and force at her command. Few, if any, other entertainers had ever given three performances in one as she was doing with that number. It was that which her public loved so much and which assured her of her amazing success.

If everything looked wonderful, the shadow of her mother still loomed. At a time when Judy was thinking she could put all those examples of her interference behind her, Ethel attempted suicide and it was only Dr Marc Rabwin's attention, which saved her life. He might well have secretly wondered about the curse of the Gumms.

Publicly, Judy was undoubtedly the darling of Broadway. It was a fact proved by radio presenters and the television producers who had finally come to grips with their new medium. They wanted her to have shows of her own, but she – and principally Sid Luft – had turned them all down. Sid had other things in mind for her. But she was wonderful when she guested on other people's programmes.

Joe Franklin, New York's 'Mr Radio', loved having her on his programme. He told me so in an office surrounded by piles of papers, record sleeves and almost everything else one could imagine – everything, it seemed, but Franklin himself, who was hidden somewhere behind the six-feet-high mountain of material that began at his front door and ended only where it began on the return journey out of the large room. ('When people want video tapes or photographs from me, I know they're buried here some place. Many times I know the order of my disorder.')

Judy was plainly one who escaped his disorder and was one of his number-one people. 'I guess when people ask me my favourite female stars, these days I have to say Judy and Barbra Streisand – in that order. I used to tell her, "Judy, you were born in a trunk, born to entertain." It was so sad that she never had a child's life.'

But not sad that she had found this new life for herself on the stage. It had repercussions throughout the world of show business. She might have been fired by MGM, but her films were doing well on reruns and Cecil B. DeMille made sure that she and Fred Astaire were available to do a radio version of *Easter Parade* – not an easy thing to do. Fred was the only man who danced on radio – literally, his footsteps had to be real and in the precise tempo. The *Lux Theater* programmes were all live and this hour-long show had to have about ten musical numbers. Irving Berlin, sitting in his New York apartment, was delighted when he tuned in his set and heard how his songs from the movie were coming across. So was Groucho Marx, who appeared with her on the *Big Show* radio series. 'Judy Garland?' he said at the time, 'I think I'll make her an honorary Marx Brother.' He, too, had found the magic in her sense of humour.

But she knew when she could entertain and was never better than being interviewed in those days after her Palace triumph.

'She was always a keen wit,' recalled Joe Franklin, reprising what so many others had said. Never more so than when she and the very large Sophie Tucker renewed their old acquaintance on his show. 'Sophie said, "You know, Judy and Joe, I've just come back from London, where I was very big." Judy replied: "Sophie, you're still big." '

The strange thing was that the waiflike Judy Garland was often compared with Ms Tucker, who weighed in like a prizefighter but resembled a Mrs Blobby. 'Judy asked her, "What's on the agenda, Sophie?" and Sophie replied: "I've got people to sponsor my own radio shows. Two companies want to make me record for them. They want me to write a book for them." Judy replied, "Don't worry, Sophie, you'll get something soon" .'

For a time there was talk of her making a film of Sophie's life, but it never happened. Sid Luft didn't want her to do it. It's possible he thought people would start thinking of her as Sophie Tucker and forget that she was Judy Garland. Her own radio and TV shows would have assured that never happened.

On 30 October 1952, Bing Crosby realised that his wife Dixie Lee was dying. For one of the few times in his life, he was unable to do his radio show. He asked Judy to host the programme in his place. She took to the task as if she had just been offered a new mink coat and a Cadillac to carry it in. The money wasn't bad, but nothing like enough for all that, and she would have done it – had Sid agreed, which is highly unlikely – for nothing.

She and Bing were close friends and Judy had appeared on his show 15 times, as well as recording with him on Decca. As Martin McQuade, who is regarded as the world's number one expert on Crosby, told me: 'They went so well together. So much so that he wanted to be in a movie with her.'

In fact, Bing had the project all lined up – a film called *Just for You*. 'It was one of the great might-have-beens. But Sid said she shouldn't accept it because it would interfere with her concert duties.'

Besides which, he had *A Star Is Born* ready to roll – although that would take a little longer to get on to a film set. But it was going to be as important to her husband as it was to Judy herself. The understanding was that he would be the producer. A producer who knew who he wanted on his team – the best. George Cukor, who still had the reputation of being the best 'woman's director' in the business, was signed up. The writer was going to be Moss Hart, better than whom few people could imagine – although, in truth, he merely adapted the screenplay written by Dorothy Parker for the first version of this archetypal Hollywood tale. That was in 1937 with Janet Gaynor in the title role, when Judy herself was just settling in at MGM.

It would turn out to be the best thing she ever did on screen, although so much was removed from the version shown to the public in 1954 that people would be forgiven for not thinking so. She performed beautifully and superbly sang the songs written for the movie, one of which, again, has outlived the film itself. 'The Man That Got Away', written, as was most of the score, by Harold Arlen, reprising his 'Rainbow' triumph, and Ira Gershwin. (The scene in which she sang this, standing next to a band after a night-club show, was shot three times – with Judy dressed differently and with alternative hairstyles each time. George Cukor was demonstrating his demands for perfection; the woman's director had a woman whom he felt he could repackage.)

The difference between the two songs, 'Over the Rainbow' and 'The Man That Got Away' was that few people think of the newer number in connection with the film, whereas, as we've seen before, 'Rainbow' and *Wizard* remain irretrievably married to each other in the public's mind.

The song got an Oscar nomination and has been recorded by dozens of other artists, none of whom has ever been able to put into it the verve and pathos that Judy achieved. It will always be Judy's song.

Some say the pity was that Sid Luft, the man in her life, didn't get away like the anonymous fellow in the song. But he gave her a vehicle that made her a new kind of film star all over again.

He came along at what was probably the best time for her. But it was a complicated, difficult moment too. On 5 January 1953 her mother died. She had been ill for some time, although no one thought seriously. Ethel, the epitome of the stage mother who had guided Judy's career, who, in fact, had invented Judy Garland, and who had been responsible, some might say, for all her problems, was no more. Judy was saddened. Actually, she was very much more than just that. At the funeral, she couldn't hold back the tears and threw her arms around whoever was there, wailing bitterly. But she now had this new influence in her life. She did not think in terms of Sid doing everything Ethel had done all those years before. But he was – and perhaps doing it tenfold.

Again, Judy had weight problems. For most of *A Star Is Born,* she is the lithe and sometimes seductive – particularly in tights – star of stars, born to be great. In one scene, however, she appears to be so fat she is almost unrecognisable. That was when she was merely the as-yet-unborn star, whose real name was Esther Blodgett. In that sequence, as she wrestles with all the problems of being made up by the studio 'surgeons', she begins to learn what Hollywood can do to a girl.

The film was made by Warner Bros. She had been rescued from MGM and was not about to return there, although when that studio heard about it, they did their best to try to entice her back. It was the last thing she wanted to do. The brothers Warner, however, were not spared the rows and the difficulties of employing Judy Garland. Jack Warner, the head of production, was as forceful a character as Louis Mayer (or Dore Schary) but was able to joke about most things, usually in highly questionable taste. Certainly, he had no taste for Sid Luft, but in him he had met his equal in the demands business and, incredible as it was to the mogul's hangers-on, Luft usually won.

Some of the problems were the fault of neither man. Judy again was having trouble dealing with the schedule. She found it over-taxing and there were the usual days of coming in late or failing to show up. But producer Sid Luft was not about to sack his wife.

Then there were technical problems. It was going to be shot in the normal screen ratio. But then the people at Burbank, Warner Bros. headquarters, began to think about it. Wide screen was all the rage and Cinemascope was the medium audiences were now coming to expect. It was not a comfortable size screen for either director or cameraman – too shallow and too wide for close-ups. But that *was* what people expected. So, two weeks after filming began, everything so far in the can was discarded and work began again from scratch.

There had been casting problems, too, mainly about the man who was to play her co-star. Certainly, James Mason, who was British, was neither the best-looking nor the most popular star in Hollywood. Sid wanted either Humphrey Bogart or Cary Grant for the role of Judy's husband, but terms could not be agreed with either. So Mason got the job. Nobody could argue with the fact that he was a superb actor (if usually typecast as unpleasantly hard but misunderstood) and he would prove it in this film. The 1937 original film, which starred Fredric March in the Mason role, had been reviewed as the best movie ever made about Hollywood. Critics said much the same thing about the 1954 version. The eminent British critic Dilys Powell wrote in *The Sunday Times*: 'By far, the best of all the films about life behind the cameras, the lights, the wind machines and the cocktail bars of Hollywood.'

This was a picture that would prove to be almost auto-biographical. It was close to being Judy's own story – the young performer plucked out of nowhere who becomes a huge star, only to ruin it all with too much booze. Except that, to all intents and purposes, her role was played by James Mason. Unfortunately for Judy, when so much of this happened to her later on, there was no one to provide the shoulder she needed to cry on – no one like the woman she played in the movie. In the picture, Norman Maine (Mason) sees his wife Vicki Lester (Judy) triumph while his career goes down the toilet. Her performance as the wife who suffers while she achieves undreamed of success herself was nothing less than magnificent.

Neither Janet Gaynor, who had been widely praised in the non-musical version, nor Barbra Streisand, who played the role in a terrible 1976 remake (*Village Voice* dubbed it, 'a bore is starred') that transferred the scene from Tinseltown to the world of pop, could compete with the emotions that Judy wrung out of that picture. It is impossible to think of anyone doing it better. No one but she could have managed the 'Born in a Trunk' song – a sequence lasting a quarter of an hour that had been written by Roger Edens and Leonard Gershe, and not by Arlen and Gershwin – a number that symbolised so much about her. The verve and the energy had to be seen to be believed, another of those clichés attached to the name Judy Garland that was so right for her. The finale to that number, in which she performed her own distinctive interpretation of 'Swanee', has become an iconic classic in the Judy story.

The ballyhoo of the Hollywood world premiere at the Pantages Theatre, screaming cars, searchlights, interviews for television and radio, was repeated for the film's New York openings, at two theatres, the Victoria and the Paramount. Judy was interviewed herself and asked about her prospects for an Oscar. 'Oh,' she said, 'don't let's even think about that yet, just keeping my fingers crossed.' The interviewer gave her the usual shmooze, although this time it was thoroughly justified. He said that he thought the newly released LP of the soundtrack was 'one of the greatest things ever'. And he added that a New York premiere had never gone on television before and this one more than justified all the attention it was receiving. 'This little girl is a combination of Nora Bayes, Danny Kaye and Al Jolson,' he declared. The broadcaster might well have read what George Jessel had said a generation before.

Few would doubt that. Jessel was actually there, too. To him, Judy's appearance in the film represented 'one of the greatest performances seen in my life and all Broadway, all television, all Hollywood are here tonight'. And to emphasise just how big a night it was for him, he added: 'It's not because I have any monetary interest in the picture or the Paramount Theatre, but because I named Judy Garland and have been something of a father confessor to her.'

Judy might have 'confessed' to him that she was unhappy with the way the film was released. Days after its opening, the picture went back to the Burbank Warner Bros. studios to be recut. Exhibitors complained that, at 181 minutes, it was too long, and without an interval to allow for popcorn and the other necessities of movie going to be sold, to say nothing of giving audiences the chance to have a toilet break was bad for business. But what happened after the abortion of an edit was bad for *A Star Is Born*.

Perhaps because of that, the film didn't achieve the box office it deserved – but that is not always a definition of artistic achievement. No one doubted Judy's own brilliance. When she and Mason – along with the musical director Warner's Ray Heindorf and Arlen and Gershwin for 'The Man Who Got Away' – were nominated for Academy Awards, the big money was on them all. The $4.8m that the picture had cost – expensive for the times, now a drop in the ocean of film economics – was perceived as being worth every cent.

Judy's stock had risen so much as a result of the publicity for the film that she was now being courted by the great and the good – and the bad and not so good. There was an invitation to dine with the Duke and Duchess of Windsor, who were doing their best to fill their days and nights with things to do and not appear to be the nonentities they had become since the 1936 abdication – despite their wartime experiences when the Duke was shunted off to the non-job of Governor of the Bahamas, which was practically an insult to a former King of Great Britain and its dominions overseas (as the title had it). It was not an invitation she could accept. She said she wasn't feeling well and reluctantly said no. Nevertheless, it was a pointer to things getting better.

Yes, a lot was getting better. Better both in terms of looking good privately, as well as professionally. In March 1955, the brightest event was the birth of her youngest child and only son, Joseph Wiley, known forever after as Joey. Things were difficult at first. One of the baby's lungs failed to inflate and there were serious doubts about whether he could survive. Both she and Sid were anxiously trying to console each other while the doctors at first shook their heads and then announced that a miracle had happened – he was going to live.

So everything was all right, then? Not quite. For a woman whose career was so often seen as paramount, it didn't mean that nothing else was important.

That was the view of most of the critics who were certain that she was going to have reason to smile after the Oscars ceremony, soon after Joey's birth. Judy was still in hospital, recovering from the Caesarean-section delivery, so she wouldn't be able to accept it in person, but everybody just *knew* she would get the Academy Award for best actress. Her nomination was seemingly a shoo-in for the little bronze statuette. As it happened, what occurred on the day would, in retrospect, have been worthy of inclusion in the picture itself.

On the day of the ceremony, the hospital had been turned into a TV station and Judy relegated to the role of a stand-in – for herself. The TV companies were so sure she would win the Oscar that they had brought a mass of equipment, cameras, lights and editing kits to her hospital room. Wires were placed under her bed as Judy sat up, in a pretty new bed jacket and her best nightgown, with make-up people and hairdressers doing their work while technicians fumbled around her, showing little respect for the lady's body. The lights were on. The producer was standing where her doctors and nurses normally stood, the cameraman and the rest of the crew were watching the ceremony on the monitor. Other workers were standing on ladders outside, looking at the monitor through the windows of her room. The envelope was opened – and the winner was announced live in Hollywood. The Oscar for best actress had gone to . . . Grace Kelly for *The Country Girl*. At that moment, virtually saying nothing else, the producer cried: 'OK, that's it'. There wasn't even an apology for all the havoc and lost hopes. The wires and cables were removed, the cameraman packed up his gear. Judy's bed was disturbed along with the patient and she was left to sob alone.

The pity was that when, in 1983, *A Star Is Born* was re-edited and re-released with much of the material that had ended up on the cutting-room floor being swept up and stuck together again (although some scenes had been lost and had to be replaced by stills placed under the soundtrack) no one thought of somehow adding a scene just like that. It would have fitted in beautifully with this story of the inhumanity of Hollywood.

The songwriter Sammy Cahn told me on my radio programme how wrong he thought Judy's failure to win the Oscar was. Sammy carried replicas of his own numerous awards around with him on his key ring. The year that Judy lost, he added a tiny Oscar to that collection – for his title song for the movie *Three Coins in a Fountain*. 'The Oscars are frequently very unfair,' he said, sitting at the piano in a BBC studio. 'In that year, they were more unfair to Judy than I think they had ever been before – or perhaps since. Grace Kelly was OK, but nothing she did could match the verve of Judy Garland in *A Star Is Born*. Who now remembers *The Country Girl* – or what Kelly did in that?

'I guarantee that for every thousand people who recall *A Star Is Born* and the Garland performance, you won't even find one who remembers the other film.'

If they did remember it, it was more likely to be for Bing Crosby in an unusual straight role. He didn't get further than an Academy Award nomination either.

Nevertheless, it was difficult for Judy to go back to anything like a 'normal' life after that, although she tried. And how she did try!

Judy in one of her first performances. Three years old and already needing to perform.

The Gumm Sisters. Plainly, the little Frances Ethel (soon to be known as Judy Garland) was the star in the family. But Virginia (centre) and Mary Jane (right) didn't appear to mind when all three Gumm sisters appeared in the 1929 movie, *The Big Revue*.

Judy, (on the left) and Mickey Rooney (with Jane Withers sharing the limelight). All were proving that MGM loved its child stars.

Two 'In-between'. They plainly loved each other – but not romantically. Louis B. Mayer would never have approved.

Judy in the film everyone knows – even those who never saw it: *The Wizard of Oz* – with Toto her dog.

Judy and Ethel, the archetypal stage mother.

She's grown up and at 19, married – to composer David Rose.

Husband number two, ace director Vincente Minnelli. The marriage didn't work, and their best production together was a little girl called Liza. HE WAS GAY, SAID THIS BOOK'S AUTHOR

Judy's best film – the 1954 *A Star Is Born*. It was virtually her own story – with her part played by James Mason!

With Sid Luft, third husband and Svengali.

It was a tiny part, but she had never acted better than when she played a German woman in *Judgement at Nuremberg* with the much-admired Spencer Tracy. Both received Oscar nominations – but neither got an award.

The Judy Garland Show was a sensation – but came off the air after just 25 performances. She knew what she was doing when asking Mickey Rooney to be her first star guest. It was a chance to recall old times, although this edition was put back till later in the series.

With her fourth husband Mark Herron. Unsuited was an understatement.

Seeing Judy here at her wedding celebration in March 1969 with her fifth and last husband, Mickey Deans (centre) and 'crying' star Johnnie Ray, it is not too difficult to believe she was just months away from death.

She kept old friendships, Marc Rabwin and his wife Marcella remaining loyal to her and she to them. She still loved visiting Dorothy Ponedel as she had in the years before. And if she couldn't visit, she phoned a great deal.

Because of her multiple sclerosis, 'Dot', confined to a wheelchair, was unable to work. She remained proud of Judy and her friendship for her. As her niece Meredith told me: 'Even more than her make-up, Dot was very proud of Judy. After Dot got sick and could no longer work or socialise, Judy, among others, would come, bring her gifts and go shopping for her. I remember Judy bringing sandwiches from Cantors [a big New York-style deli on Hollywood's Fairfax Avenue, in the heart of the city's Jewish district]. They would party like one big happy family.'

That, of course, was what Judy thought of her relationship with her fans. It was a family affair.

CHAPTER TEN

More Triumphs, More Troubles

The fans wanted Judy to have her own TV series, but again Sid held back. He wanted something truly exciting for her. It appeared to come when he signed her for a CBS show for Ford motors, *The Ford Star Jubilee*. This was planned as a 'special' that was really going to be very *special*. It went out and received so-so notices, although some were as ecstatic as Judy reviews usually were.

The broadcaster was happy enough with a not particularly marvellous Garland performance and signed her for an annual appearance on their network as a result. For the fans, it was never really going to be enough.

As for Judy herself, she was not totally comfortable in those early TV appearances. The shows were all broadcast live and the pressures of having to sing when it appeared her voice was straining – and having to make changes of dresses between numbers – was even more of a discomfort than it was during a stage show. In those concert appearances, she could afford to keep the people out front waiting if necessary; a live TV show had to start and finish on time with everything in between worked to a precise schedule. It all made those MGM stresses seem as nothing. It would still be some time before the idea of a regular Judy TV show would come to fruition. But there were other things on the horizon.

For one thing, she had her first fan club. Her very first fan club. Fans had for years been bombarding the movie magazines asking for details of a club they could join. Incredibly, they were always told that such an organisation did not exist. Most just sat back, unhappily, and waited for the next Garland film or television programme to come along.

However, that was not what one 14-year-old boy did.

Al Poland, now a retired Broadway producer, told me how it happened – and why it had never occurred before. As far as he was concerned, it was another one of those love tales in the Judy Garland story. 'When I saw *A Star Is Born,* I thought Judy was the most talented person I had ever seen,' Poland told me. 'I also strongly thought that she needed my help.' He thought that as perhaps only a confident young teenager would think. Had he known of the difficulties, he might not have been quite so sure. As he said: 'I set about joining a fan club. Since there weren't any, I set about founding one. To use modern vernacular, I took on Judy as my first co-dependent relationship.'

It was with the assurance of extreme youth, combined with a necessary dose of chutzpah, that he made the first move. At first, his idea of setting up the club attracted only two other members. When he wrote to the movie magazines asking them to help him fill the gap that he knew existed, they turned him down. They would only announce the existence of a new fan club with the written consent of the star being so 'honoured'. That seemed to put an end to the hopes of putative club founders – and probably would have done in this case had they been more than 14 years old. But not Al Poland and his pals.

'We had a summit meeting, my two pals and I. My parents were not at home. One of the girls said, "Why don't we call her at her home?" The idea immediately caught fire.' But what were they to say – in the unlikely event that they got through and Judy Garland agreed to take the call from three teenagers? The summit meeting came to order and decided the next step: 'I wrote a script of what I would say. We got the operator on the phone – and in 1955, a long-distance call was an event. One a year in a family was spectacular. I think the operator was as excited as we were. We called all over Hollywood trying to get the number.' Unlikely as it seems today in these times of high security, they eventually struck gold – or at least gilt. 'We finally got [the number] from Warner

Bros. Even with them, a long-distance call carried a great deal of weight. The nature of a long-distance call was that this was important. So it was not questioned.' Amazing, but true; the Warner Bros. operator gave them a phone number. Even in 1955, it could have been a firing offence, but the girl on the Warner switchboard was perhaps new and inexperienced and did not know what she was doing and what she was not supposed to do.

Al booked the call and at the appointed time – you couldn't dial from New York to Hollywood in those days – a woman answered as the operator said, 'Long Distance is calling for Judy Garland.' He had in the meantime written the word 'Help' on his script, which he said he was now waving around like a white flag.

The woman at the other end said, 'Wait a minute.'

'Then this unmistakable voice came on the phone. I nervously began reading my script. I said, "I am Al Poland and I'm president of a fan club for you." And she said: "A fan club for ME!"' To Al's surprise and to that of his two friends, it seemed that she meant it and added the magic words: 'How wonderful!'

Al continued: 'I said, "Oh Judy, I love you so much." I said that I wanted to go into show business. The minute she said yes, I said we needed a letter from her so that the movie magazines could publish our address. She asked me for my address, which amazed me. We chatted for a bit longer. "Al," she said. "Yes?" I asked. "Happy New Year."'

Two weeks later, the letter arrived. It was the perfect proof of how much Judy valued the help of her fans and the relationship she had with them. The letter was shown to the movie magazines, they published Al's address and virtually overnight her new club had 3,000 members.

The surprising thing was that Judy actually didn't realise she still had fans. The old insecurity was manifesting itself in ways that only the people close to her could have understood. 'She was in a career low at that point. *A Star Is Born* had been a year earlier. She had done her special for CBS. This was the end of 1955 and there was nothing on tap.'

But the mystery remained why there had never been a fan club for one of the world's leading entertainers. A club usually went hand in hand with the success of a performer reaching stardom. The idea that Judy Garland didn't have one was barely worth thinking about. 'As far as I know,' Poland says now, 'there were no official fan clubs that generated her co-operation. It is possible that MGM might have generated something, but this was the first member-orientated club. Fan clubs were political organisations.' And political organisations needed good public relations or, to put it less kindly, propaganda. 'We targeted three movie magazines with each issue of our journal, *The Garland Gazette*. There were letter campaigns to get her on the covers, to get stories about her published.'

What was also political was the way the kids organised those campaigns. They could have been preparing for a presidential election, the way they worked. 'We changed our handwriting, sent them to relatives so that they would have postmarks in different cities. The members sent carbon copies – there was no Xerox in those days – of the letters. The one who sent the most letters to Judy was sent a letter congratulating them with a little prize, which we bought out of our meagre dues. I sent her (Judy) the note and she copied it on her own stationery in her own handwriting and signed it.'

If one wants an analysis of what this all meant to her, it is more than likely that with this club she had found a group of people who wanted her for herself, who wanted nothing more than a signature on a piece of paper and had no ulterior motives. Said Poland: 'The fan club, I think, gave her a great deal of pleasure. It certainly brought the membership enormous pleasure any time she was doing a concert performance.'

And that membership delighted in the perks that came with their dues. 'If you showed your membership card, you were given special treatment.' And that special treatment came from Sid Luft as well as from Judy. 'Sid welcomed us and we sat in her dressing room as she picked the black off her tooth and removed her fright wig [both from the "Couple of Swells" routine] and the next day we had a picture taken backstage with her. There had been no one to take a picture, so she yelled out, "Sid!" Sid Luft took the picture.'

It was all so untypical for a big star to be genuinely so pleasant to her fans, although, as we shall see, it was very much in character for Judy and would become even more evident in London. Al Poland agreed. Most stars tolerate fans as necessities and get the hard work, like writing letters and signing photographs, to be done by secretaries or other hangers-on. As far as anyone knows, Judy did all that herself.

Of course, it was all very good for business. But that wasn't the true motive. 'I think that her need to be loved was very genuine. That was what she experienced with the members. She was incredibly loving. She was very witty. Lucille Ball said Judy was the funniest in Hollywood. She shared her humour with us and was at ease with us. I don't think it was a function of business at all. And I think in her day stars played the role of *being* stars. Really enjoyed it. I think her relationship with club members was part of that. She lifted me up as nobody else ever has. I made my career in the theatre. It's not because I love the theatre, I worship talent. I still feel at sixty-nine years old, that Judy was the most major talent I have ever experienced in my life and she is my measuring stick for talent.'

He demonstrated that by putting his money where it counted. 'I saw Judy's show at the Palace thirty times. The first time was in Detroit. When you saw her out of town, you would go to see three performances, not just one, because she varied each one slightly. Very spontaneous.'

There would be more tours of the United States that Al Poland attended and many more that he did not and there were other special personal appearances, too. In 1956, Judy was in Las Vegas, then only beginning to bask in its reputation as the place where every successful entertainer had to hear the applause of people newly released from the one-armed bandits and crap tables. She was there for five weeks. One night, she was suffering so badly from laryngitis that she couldn't go on. (At least, that was what she said – except that Jerry Lewis took her place and insisted that she stayed on stage with him, acting as his 'second banana', a role she hadn't played since joining the family act in Lancaster.) She was told by a doctor that her throat was so bad, it was possible she would never sing again. She would be told that on other occasions. Sometimes, it was a good excuse for deciding, on a whim, not to go on stage. But she would always come back, to another engagement, another spot.

When the tour took her to Long Beach, California, Frank Sinatra chartered a Greyhound bus from Los Angeles to take a bunch of his buddies, all showbiz icons like Humphrey Bogart and Sammy Davis Jr, to the show. Of course, it was fully equipped with a bar. The guests were reported to be happy but reasonably sober by the time they reached the venue.

When one's own contemporaries wanted to see an entertainer as much as did 'ordinary' people, it spoke a lot for status.

Al Jolson had been the first big star to initiate a series of Sunday concerts – purely so that other show people could hear how great he was. It sounded, at first, like considerable conceit, a commodity of which 'The World's Greatest Entertainer' had his full ration, but the fact was that professionals dearly did want to see him at work and were not sorry to be able to do so on nights when their own shows were closed. When Judy returned to the Palace in 1956, show business was now offering the same kind of tribute to Judy. It was the only theatre open on Sundays. Alan King, who was now a staple attraction on the Judy live shows, recalled (in John Fricke's book *Judy Garland: A Portrait in Art & Anecdote*) how George Jessel comforted her with the immortal words, 'Judy, when you're good, you're the greatest entertainer I ever saw. You're like sex. Even when you're bad, it's not too bad.'

Jessel was kinder about Judy than he ever was about Jolson, whom he always felt had cheated him out of the lead in the first talkie, *The Jazz Singer* (Jessel had starred in the stage version). But when I met him, he put Judy just behind Jolson, 'who was better in the film than I would have been. Judy was lovely. A wonderful, sad woman, the best *female* entertainer ever. Everybody loved her, although she had her problems. Al never did anything good for anybody, never mailed a letter for anyone – a no-good son of a bitch – but he was the greatest entertainer I ever saw.' With that statement, a man who was regarded as a true aficionado of what was good and not so good in his business put Judy Garland into perspective. When we had lunch at the showman's club, the Hillcrest in Hollywood, he saw no reason to gush. Judy Garland was number two, which in the eyes of most people of that generation was praise enough. Again, it emphasised her status.

She was also interviewed on this Palace opening night by Jinx Falkenburg, sometime model, singer and now radio talk show hostess – one of the first in that business in America. In her dressing room Falkenberg noted that she had just changed from her clown make-up ('Be a Clown' given a stage interpretation) and terry-cloth robe into a black lacy gown – 'with a mink stole, pearls and diamonds in your hair and stars in your eyes'.

'I do think there are stars in my eyes tonight, really,' she declared.

Jinx told her she had spoken to a number of people who had all agreed, 'Judy Garland had never been greater than she was tonight.'

'Oh, it's because it's my home. The Palace is my home. I don't think I've ever felt so free. I'm glad they say I was good because I wasn't too scared.' In that, she was confirming something about her stage appearances that intimates had known but which she had never revealed before. Usually, she *was* scared. But when she sang 'Shine on Harvest Moon' at the Palace at that 1956 show, she had the courage of an infantryman on the battlefield (which theatres and other venues had so often seemed to be for her).

The interview was broadcast live, which audiences on both sides of the continent had come to expect. Judy now appeared on the radio whenever there was something to say and broadcasters like Joe Franklin always found excuses for her to say *something*. And, once again, she was making as many records as she had broken in concert appearances. A spin-off she might not have thought much about was the fact that Judy's material was ideal for long-playing albums. The vinyl discs had been around for seven years when *A*

156

Star Is Born was released and, as we have seen, the soundtrack was a big hit – especially since it contained tracks that had been excised at the time of the original butchering of the movie. But now her live performances – unlike so many by other artists – were ideal for the 33⅓rpm turntables. What is more, the simple, tasteful artwork on the sleeves made them collectors' items. Discs like the *Miss Show Business* album and *Judy* needed no further explanation. They were sophisticated recordings for people who thought themselves sophisticated too. They didn't appeal to teenagers, but they weren't intended to.

One of Judy's records was called *Judy In Love*. But not, it seemed, with Sid Luft. Again and again, she initiated divorce proceedings against him – and again and again he talked her out of them. When I met Luft in 2000, he told me: 'You know, Judy was not easy to live with, but I knew that if I wasn't with her, her life would be in peril. I think that turned out to be true. Sadly.'

That might well have been so. Peri Fleischman is convinced they were good for each other. 'I loved Sid. I was crazy about him. We were very close and I liked him for the same reason other people did – because he was charming and nice and seductive.' However, she is not in the least surprised that eventually divorce would be unavoidable. 'I wouldn't be shocked about anything about him or her.'

Divorce would take a few years. But that did not mean they didn't try. They were constantly at war. There was a whole year when they didn't see each other, but the separations didn't last. They really needed each other at the end of the 1950s. She needed him because she still had to have a man in her life – besides which, he was keeping her reasonably straight if not entirely on the narrow road. He needed a project and a meal ticket.

Sid was exceedingly hard on her, forcing Judy to work when she didn't feel ready for it. On the other hand, he had to put up with a lot and there are countless stories of how he helped her and perhaps saved her life.

Peri Fleischman revelled in having him in her family. 'Sure, I was proud of him. Anyone in our family who did something wonderful, I'd be proud of that.' But there were no family occasions when Judy would get together with her husband's relatives, particularly his sister. 'I was not part of their gang,' Peri told me. 'They mixed with people in their business. But I felt important – because *she* was important and so was he.'

Judy's love for her children never diminished. She took them on the stage with her. As John Fricke recalled, Lorna enjoyed 'Dixie Melody', Liza joined her for the now trademark performance of 'Swanee', and Joey appeared – in her arms – as she sang 'Happiness Is a Thing Called Joe'. It helped to cement her sometimes apparently crumbling marriage.

She was making a great deal of money and yet was always broke. Everything she made, Sid spent. Lorna once told me: 'We used to sneak out of hotel rooms in the middle of the night, wearing several layers of all our clothes, to avoid paying the bills.' Judy told them she was doing that for the fun of it. It certainly helped give the Garland kids a very unusual childhood.

Several people became beneficiaries of this very unusual life that Judy was leading. At good moments, she was the most generous entertainer in the business. In 1957, she was back in London, appearing at the giant Dominion Theatre, which had been converted from a cinema for the occasion. That was a time when the up-and-down roller coaster of the Judy Garland life was on show more than ever before. But generous? She insisted that the giant billing outside the theatre should proclaim: 'Judy Garland and Alan King'. The comic, who wondered if his New York Jewish humour would go down well in London, was overwhelmed.

So were the critics. The two of them had a sensational first night. The fans who came that evening never forgot it.

I wasn't so sure. I remember the evening I went to the theatre in the middle of the run for the fact that it was the first time I sold a story to a British national newspaper. Judy was embarrassingly bad, so upsetting her audience that it made a piece in the *Daily Express*. As I reported for them, Judy's voice was frequently off-key, she forgot her lines, was constantly taking glasses of what she said was water and at times she seemed to stagger. It was not the show that people expected and not, it has to be admitted, what they got at other times during the run. The orchestra leader, Gordon Jenkins, one of the great popular maestros of the day, was so moved by her performance that he frequently burst into tears as he conducted his musicians from the theatre's pit.

If what I experienced was an off-night at the Dominion, there were enough 'on' nights to compensate for the disappointments. The Dominion management showed their appreciation by naming a green room after her. It is still, more than half a century later, called the Judy Garland Room, with pictures of her to remind visitors of what the Dominion maintain was a triumph. The theatre to this day collects memorabilia to add to their collection.

Dennis Sykes enjoyed the Dominion show immensely, although even he, a committed fan, has reservations. Standing outside the theatre on Tottenham Court Road, now the centre of Britain's hi-fi retail business, he told me: 'I was here on two evenings at the Dominion and she was very good indeed. There was no comparison with some of the other occasions I saw her here in London. But it was a very exciting event. She did not come over as a great artist. She was, nevertheless, a high-voltage performer even when she was less than absolutely wonderful.' But, he conceded (and as I had discovered for myself), 'when she wasn't on form, you noticed. It was very, very noticeable.'

Yet he could add: 'With Judy, there was personality, humour, showbiz know-how, together with warmth and that wonderful ability to communicate with an audience. She had a friendliness that was irresistible. She certainly communicated with me.'

His fellow fan Ken Sefton, who was at the first night, was less equivocal. 'I went on the first night and the last night,' he told me. 'I wasn't a fanatical fan like some of them are. I didn't have to be there every night, but I saw she was wonderful.

'On the last night at the Dominion, Judy came out of the theatre almost as the show ended. They had a backstage party, but Judy was sent home because she was going to be on the Royal Variety Performance the following Monday. Sid said she needed to rest, so the star never went to the party.'

The fact that she had been at the show itself was something of a miracle. Following the laryngitis attack, she had been told to take a year's rest. But, of course, she didn't. She needed to bask in the spotlight and the sound of applause and Sid needed the money.

So did the people working with her. Ken Sefton knew that from personal experience. 'The Dominion is a huge theatre. She had ten dancing boys with her. She put them up at the Cumberland, which is quite an expensive hotel, not some bed-and-breakfast place. She gave each of them an embossed cigarette lighter bearing her signature.'

The relationship with her London fans was never clearer than when Brian Glanvill finally caught up with her during her Dominion tour. It was the first of several face-to-face meetings they were to have. 'She was never anything but unfailingly kind to me. Ken [Sefton] and I met her on the steps of Londonderry House in Mayfair.' The date was – he remembers the precise date and probably the time of every meeting with her – Thursday 10 October 1957. 'I had this huge bunch of chrysanthemums, which I presented to her and they dwarfed her. I hadn't realised she was so tiny. Eve Perrick, a columnist on the *Daily Express*, wrote about me the next day.' She had been riding with Judy. She wrote: 'As we got out of the taxi, a shy, solicitous member of the Judy Garland fan club stepped forward with a bunch of flowers, anxiously inquiring after her health.'

Glanvill's meetings with her did not come without a degree of sacrifice, although he would never see it that way. 'I used to buy a Mars bar for my supper so that I had the money to go every performance. My mother complained that I needed new clothes and so on. I said, "I'll always be able to buy new clothes. I won't always be able to see Judy Garland sing."'

The Royal Variety Performance at the London Palladium in 1957 was without a doubt a triumph – if only because she managed to calm her nervousness and be spectacularly good in the process. Along with people like Mario Lanza, Gracie Fields, Frankie Vaughan and a dozen or so other guest stars, she stood on the Palladium stage and bowed to the Royal Box after wowing the well-heeled audience with most of their favourite Garland numbers.

If it seemed that everything was all right in her world, there was that little matter about money – and the lack of it. Sid told her as the London tour wound to its end, 'You know we haven't made a penny.' She said, 'Well, we played London and had a good time.'

A good time that was exceptionally expensive – as all her concert appearances would prove to be, since she had to pay all the bills herself, while Sid pocketed the cheques and hoped the books would balance. On a later tour of America, Sid revealed how much he was spending – which was little different from the costs in London. Producing a show would cost $150,000, made up of things like $12,000 on sets, orchestrations for Gordon Jenkins (who was earning $1,125 a week, a huge sum which was no reason for his bursting into tears in the pit) cost $16,000. He also had to pay the 50 people in the band and fork out for lawyers, PR people and choreographers. Quite a bill, which he always hoped would be recouped but never really was.

There would be other evenings, and much more serious problems for Judy and her producers back home in New York.

In 1958 the difficulties turned into a tragedy. So tragic, in fact, that it made her problems at MGM fall into insignificance by comparison. It was the first occasion an event occurred which was to be repeated time and again and become all too familiar to the people involved in her life.

Everything had looked wonderful when a small moustachioed man called Ben Maksik announced that Judy would open at his Town and Country Club in Brooklyn. It wasn't a fashionable venue; it was popular with people who didn't want to dress up when they went there for the food and, principally, the talent. People didn't usually go to Brooklyn if they didn't have to, but everybody in show business knew about the Town and Country, because Maksik always had the best performers entertaining there.

When he announced that Judy was coming, he believed he had the very best. Certainly, the rush to book tables had rarely been as strong. The feelings of great expectation before the show opened in March 1958 seemed to tell him he had scored a big triumph. The press were particularly excited and after seeing Judy on the first night, looking her best and sounding even better than she had done recently, were not to be disappointed. Robert Dana in the *New York World-Telegram* wrote: 'Nor sleet, nor snow nor a flooded Belt Parkway that sent Manhattan tourists scurrying to Brooklyn gas stations for directions could dampen the enthusiasm of the multitude that showed up last night at Ben Maksik's Town and Country Club for Judy Garland's long-awaited opening. After it was over, the Cadillacs were nodding to the Volkswagens as their masters glowed in a kindred aftermath of exhilaration.'

Exhilaration it certainly was. Just as in London, the really serious fans – and at times one wondered if there were any other kind – would try to go night after night, even to a club where the prices were roughly half what the head waiter expected to receive in exchange for a good table. 'The notes pulsate,' wrote Dana, whose own blood pressure had obviously been sent sky high, 'through her throat as if from a meadow lark as she gets her bearings.'

It was, in a way, an unfortunate simile. Judy's trouble was that she actually did lose her bearings on this trip, lost what she was supposed to do, lost a sense of the appreciation of the people who respected her talent above all. It was a demonstration of just how far and how speedily she was racing downhill. A star who had mesmerised audiences for most of her life, and who was doing it in Brooklyn for much of that engagement, was about to go into reverse and, in the process, to virtually destroy the faith of her lovers – for that was what her fans had become.

The first big problem was that Judy insisted she would do only one show a night, instead of the two Maksik had expected and had paid for – $15,000 in cash in advance of the $25,000 per week the contract specified, signed on the back of an envelope, while Judy and Sid were on the liner *United States* on their way to England. That had been Sid's demand. But Ben Maksik still thought he had got a great deal. If, as they did, some people looked down on the idea of a Brooklyn nightclub, Judy Garland would put them right.

The Town and Country was a remarkable place. It could serve 7,200 covers in three sittings – as it did when performers like Tony Bennett played there. But even during Judy's stay, before she came on, there were 600 people dancing on the floor at one time – in a hall 400 feet by 140 feet with no poles or pillars to interrupt the view. As Ian Maksik, Ben's son, told me: 'Imagine those 2,500 people who came to see Judy Garland parking their cars, checking their coats, having dinner, dancing and seeing the show. Then, when the second show began, as it normally would, we had professional pushers who pushed them out again. The lights went on and these twenty-five muscle men came in, in their red jackets, as the people paid their checks. Imagine, 2,500 people paying their checks at one time. Imagine what kind of facility this was. We had seventeen checkers just making out the checks. This was an amazing operation. Just imagine that – and then another 2,500 people would come in. It was like Radio City Music Hall.'

But Radio City hadn't had the problems that the Town and Country were about to have with Judy Garland.

Even though some big stars did do three shows a night, for Judy they had sold tables in advance for just two, which the contract on the back of that envelope stipulated. But then, after it was all signed and the show about to open, she told Ben Maksik it wouldn't be possible. She would only do one show per night. She wasn't well enough to do more. It was more than just a blow. Nevertheless, Ben was sure that, even with just that one show a night, he would turn in a profit of sorts. And it would be great publicity for his 'joint'. If she had performed for three months, as planned, they surely would have made that profit. Indeed if, by any chance, she had fulfilled her original contract, they could all have packed up and bought themselves new Cadillacs. As it was, after nine days, Judy was out. Fired, she claimed. There would be no profits at all.

'In this case,' said Ian Maksik, 'we didn't make any money. We had paid her in advance. So we took a loss.'

And so did the fans, many of whom had booked weeks before and were ready to go there to celebrate weddings, bar mitzvahs and anniversaries. More customers had no idea about the changed schedule than those who did know. They expected, those who planned to go to this Radio City of Brooklyn, to have the choice of two shows. The Maksiks were not happy to disappoint them. 'We had to chase 2,500 people away because of her,' said Ian. 'Not just because the news hadn't got out that she was doing only one show. We had to chase those people who had made pre-bookings for the second show and demanded to come in. We had to tell them they couldn't come. We had no choice but to cancel the second show and had our salesmen call everybody who had booked for it.'

That was easier said than done. Judy Garland enthusiasts do not readily take no for an answer. 'That didn't stop all the people who didn't know there was no show and were already lining up to get in. They thought they could get in by giving the maitre d' a few dollars.'

If they had given Judy more than just a *few* extra dollars, she still wouldn't have come. The maitre d' was incensed. After all, he had seen the first show and knew he could have made a killing – passing the word along that a good table for Judy Garland would be an investment that would involve a lifetime of memories. Actually, he needed to be able to do that. As Ian recalled for me: 'It was very difficult for the maitre d' to make any money at our place because we had no poles [pillars]. So my dad put up one pole at the back – so that he could bring people from behind the pole, get a tip and then bring them in. One night, we happened to open up the maitre d's table and there was $7,000 there, in cash. His tips. I don't know if he declared it to the IRS or not.' People were so keen on getting in his good books, they would paste $100 bills to their foreheads and walk in – with instructions to the head waiter to take them.

Now he was being denied these opportunities to fool the Internal Revenue Service. Fashionable and posh or not, this was a money-making enterprise for the waiters as well as for the Maksik family. And, as things turned out, the man who had ordered his architects to build his club without pillars, so that everyone had a ringside seat, would be out of pocket to the tune of hundreds of thousands of dollars. It turned out to be just one of the most disastrous events in Judy's career.

But not, as we have seen, when it began. As the critic noted, things could not have been better at the start – for those who were lucky enough to book for the usually less popular first show. Ian Maksik, who now trains people in the catering industry – no doubt taking his father's Garland experience into account – recalled for me just how great it all looked.

The *World-Telegram* writer was not the only one who was ecstatic that Friday opening night. As Ian Maksik told me: 'She was the greatest entertainer in the world. She had her manic state, but when the spotlight hit her, she was Miss Judy Garland. She was great. My mom said you could hear a pin drop.'

In fact, on that opening night, when there just was an inkling, if only backstage, of how bad things could be – but which no one believed would happen – it was as fascinating to see those 2,500 people in the audience as it was to study Judy herself. For that was what they did. They didn't just watch and listen, they were so attentive, they wouldn't blink if they had the chance.

'My dad said he was watching a man who had a piece of filet mignon – and our filet mignon was delicious – held on a fork. He didn't put it in his mouth. My dad was watching him and he said that the man, for the entire performance, held that filet mignon on his fork and didn't put it in his mouth. His mouth was open – marvelling at the Judy Garland show. My mom said something like that happened almost every night. People were mesmerised by her. When she was good, she was absolutely the best. It was all something else.' The show was costing millions, but Ben Maksik had no serious doubt he had made a good investment.

Actually, in hindsight, even without the fiasco of the limited number of shows she would do, there had been signs from the beginning that there were likely to be problems. Before she would even get out on to the stage on that first seemingly glorious night, she had to be pushed on by Ernie, her hairdresser. People in the front might well have heard the man whispering, 'Go on, Judy. You're on.'

The performances were mostly good if not as brilliant as some people might have hoped. But after nine nights, the engagement was cancelled. It had never happened before.

Ian Maksik still recoils as he thinks of how painful that trip was for his family. It wasn't so good for Judy herself, either, when the misadventure started to unravel.

It was an appalling situation. Ben Maksik had been warned that Judy had been behaving erratically. The one-show-a-night rule was symbolic. But he was taking out an insurance policy to make certain that she would be OK – in the form of a kind of pampering that had never been known before. Not just the best dressing room, a Cadillac to take her to and from the venue and every facility an artist could possibly want, but also a house by the ocean, at Sheepshead Bay, the lovely area of coast between mainland Brooklyn and the eastern part of Coney Island. There, for the run of the show, it would be home for Judy, her children, their nurse and a chauffeur, with other essential personnel living there, too. Needless to say, it was furnished in exquisite style.

Maksik agreed to all this to smooth the way for his star, who was in the midst of not just one, but at least two crises. She had separated from Sid, charging him with trying to choke her. At the same time, she was at war with the Internal Revenue Service, which she said was trying to squeeze her non-existent bank balance. She owed $8,000 in unpaid tax on the money she had earned from her show at the Palace. Maksik said he would deduct $3,000 for two weeks and $2,000 for the third week from her salary to clear the debt. Sid may not have been living with Judy, but he was still running her business affairs, such as he could. He was virtually broke, but still spending money on first-class hotels (and the first-class suite on the *United States*) and other fripperies he regarded as necessities. At one stage he had only been saved when a racehorse he owned broke a leg and had to be destroyed – he pocketed $30,000 in an insurance payout.

Maksik didn't think, once the business of the number of performances was cleared up, that he could go wrong. But he did. Very wrong. They could have sued her, but it would have cost more in legal fees than they could hope to recoup in damages. As Ian Maksik said, it was all so unpredictable, no matter what they had been told. 'We had taken losses before – great acts, expensive acts who didn't draw anybody. And there were some others who were just sleepers and the place filled up. That was show business.' But with Judy Garland, star of stars, he didn't think it could be anything but a triumph. 'She was absolutely the best.'

Nine days after opening night, it happened. That Sunday night her behaviour was indeed something else. It might have been easier had Judy said from the beginning that she wasn't going to be able to go on that night. People in the audience who were not aware of the way shows operated and did manage to see her – and possibly eat their filet mignon at the same time – had no idea there was trouble afoot. But backstage, they understood before the opening number that there was going to be hell on earth in that spot of Brooklyn. As Ian explained: 'That Sunday, I was there. The dancers came on and did their short performance. They played the Judy Garland overture. Nobody came out. The orchestra played again. Finally, our stage manager helped Judy Garland on to the stage.' She began singing 'Life Is Just a Bowl of Cherries'. Distinctly over-ripe cherries, it turned out.

'I was sitting ringside,' recalled Ian, 'and I could see that the back of her dress was open. You could see it. She just made it to the microphone. You couldn't see the pupils in her eyes – like the pupils had gone into her head. You could just see the whites. She hit her head against the microphone. And she started cursing and talking about my dad to the audience. From the back, my dad said to our maitre d', "She's sick. Get her off the stage. Get Bobby. You go on."'

Bobby Van was her dancing partner as well as acting as her MC, and was then on the threshold of an exciting career himself and about to become even better known as a choreographer. Together, all week, Van and Judy had done the Irving Berlin tramps number, one of the dozen or so partners who replicated Fred Astaire's *Easter Parade* performance of 'A Couple of Swells'. 'They were great together. He came on and he danced without Judy and, of course, the audience was aghast. Some people asked for their money back. Other people just regarded it as a show-business event they had never seen before. They were spellbound.' Spellbound and understanding in a way Judy Garland audiences – and probably *only* Judy Garland audiences – frequently were. 'I heard people say, "Help her. She's sick."'

A few were less charitable. There were boos among the cheers, isolated voices in a sea of bewildered and disappointed men and women in their best clothes who dearly wanted to demonstrate their loyalty and go home thinking what a wonderful time they had had.

'More people were saying, "Ooh, ooh" rather than booed,' said Ian Maksik. 'They didn't applaud either. But they realised there was a sick woman up there on the stage. The sympathy went out to her. They wanted her to be better. They wanted her to be the Judy Garland they knew. I can tell you there were tears in the audience that night. I don't remember one person complaining to me. They were just wanting someone to help her. It hadn't happened before. She was just physically unable to do this performance.'

Later, Judy would claim that she wanted to go on and was fired unfairly. She told the audience she couldn't go on but it didn't matter – 'because I have been fired'. She was suffering, it appeared, not just from laryngitis, which continued to plague her, but also from a bad attack of colitis. There was one other 'suffering', her antipathy to Maksik and his club. She pleaded for Sid, as usual, to come to her aid and get her 'out of this joint'. Maksik was ready to throw her out, but Sid was not so pliable. For safety, Judy had handed her jewellery to the club owner to keep for her in his safe. Now, Maksik was saying that he intended to keep it in lieu of all he had lost on the deal. He was a much smaller man than Sid, and older. He knew he was no match for 'Mr Garland', as some people called Luft – or for the bodyguards he said he had standing by. The safe was opened and the gems handed over. As Judy stumbled out of his office, Ben Maksik could only hope that he would never see her again. He was not disappointed.

The Maksiks were not the only ones who were suffering because of Judy's behaviour.

She came to the Town and Country with her own orchestra, led by Buddy Bregman, who was not just a band leader and producer of the show, but one of the most important music men in America at the time, soon to go to London to be heading music at BBC2 and become head of entertainment at the ITV company Rediffusion. At 28, he was one of the youngest in the business, but he was already head of Verve Records as well as playing and recording with some of the most significant players in show business – including being behind Ella Fitzgerald's famous Cole Porter and Rodgers and Hart Songbooks. His album with Bing Crosby, *Bing Sings Whilst Bregman Swings*, was a universal bestseller. He also wrote the hit song, 'I Need Your Lovin' with Jerry Leiber and Mike Stoller. In addition to all that, NBC had hired him for his own show and he was conducting for Eddie Fisher's sell-out programme at Las Vegas.

He was Judy's choice as her musical director but it took some time before he realised what was in store. It looked good, not least when he moved in with her and the rest of her entourage to the house at Sheepshead Bay, 'a gorgeous home'. From the moment they arrived in the New York area, everyone knew about the show and the anticipation was magical. 'It had got so much adulation in New York the week before we arrived,' he told me. His own reputation had gone before him, too, so he himself was a beneficiary of that adulation.

Since his career to date had all been a wonderful experience, working with Judy looked like being a marvellous opportunity. This was going to be something of a staging post on the journey to what was likely to be the most exciting show in his career – and hardly insignificant in Judy's own life. She, with Bregman, was about to open at Carnegie Hall, arguably the most prestigious concert hall in the world.

It would be virtually the same show as the one at the Town and Country.

Bregman's relationship with Judy had begun, he admitted to me, with the crush he had on Eydie Gormé, the popular American singer who was herself on the threshold of an exciting career. 'I arranged and conducted her shows at Las Vegas,' he said. 'Now she was opening at the Coconut Grove [which was about as fashionable a nightclub as you could find in Hollywood]. As I walked in, I noticed Bobby Van and he was sitting with a woman who was not his wife.' Van didn't have to tell him it was Judy Garland and added, 'We're doing something together.'

It turned out that after Gormé's performance Judy turned to Van and said, 'Hire him'. In other words, tell Bregman she wants him to be in charge of the music for her shows. She didn't want to do the 'hiring' herself. Bregman agreed to be hired.

'It was while I was working with Verve Records so I could only work for her at night. Well, it's when she's up. It kinda worked out.'

And she told him about his first assignment for her. 'She said, "We open at Ben Maksik's, where we're all sold out for five million dollars in sales." ' That put the whole engagement into perspective. Five million dollars is a lot of money today. In 1958, it was a fortune beyond avarice.

Bregman was prepared for the show and, he thought, for the star. He was not quite ready for what would happen along the way. 'I knew her reputation. How could you not? But I did not know what it was going to be to work with her.'

Before they started rehearsing at Judy's home in Mapleton Drive, one of the better roads in the best part of Beverly Hills, he decided to pay her a visit to see how she was getting on. That reputation indicated that she would be a bundle of nerves. Anyone venturing into her lair was likely to find himself in trouble. Many people working with her, whose own jobs depended on her being in a good mood, did so with trepidation.

'I said, "Hi, it's Buddy." She said, "Come in, I'm making breakfast." Oh, I thought. It's eight o'clock at night. That's a good start.'

But a start that might have begun with a threat. 'Two statuesque men, six feet eleven, were standing outside. I thought they were [made of] stone or were trees. They were bouncers.' Soon, he could have been forgiven for wishing that he himself was going to be bounced out of the Town and Country Club show.

He went on to explain the indictment for his side of the Judy Garland trial. It began with a rehearsal for the show in her home. 'One night, I'll never forget it. We were doing "I've Got It Bad and That Ain't Good". This was a good description of the way Judy was performing. 'She goes to the door. I was playing loud and I hear someone outside was saying, "You bitch! I'll kill you." And I hear slapping. The next thing I see is her on her bum, sliding across the floor. It was Sid. He had hit her on the jaw. She slipped on the black and white floor. I always wondered why the "trees" didn't do anything about it. But she went on her bum and she slides on the floor and I'm playing the music to what she's doing.'

What happened next turned out to be a typical evening of private Judy Garland entertaining, if one would want to call it that. 'So she said, "It's OK, honey" – while she's sliding. She listened to everything I said. "I think you should do this . . ." I was into producing, orchestrating, putting this whole thing together – it's my métier. Consequently, I was playing and someone said, "Well, she's never sung 'I've Got It Bad and That Ain't Good'." I said, "I was there and I played it."'

At the club itself, he recalled, 'We started in a funny way.' The public out front, those who were lucky enough to get tables, were not aware at this stage that things weren't all hunky-dory. At that stage, Bregman had to make the best of it, rewarded by her talent on stage, suffering because of the way she behaved off the boards. 'But every night was a nightmare.'

Despite the obvious problems, he was excited about the Town and Country Club. 'Ben Maksik's place was the biggest between New York and Chicago. It was like a huge garage, like one of those maintenance places where they put in twenty or thirty cars. This was nice. Round tables, seating ten. When Danny Thomas was there, they sort of sold out. When Jack E. Leonard was there, they were *really* sold out. But when Judy came in, you couldn't get in the place and they were screaming for her – and she held them.

I watched her [on the first couple of shows]. They were OK. She didn't go overboard. But the people were just looking at her, thinking, "Oh my God, it's Judy. It's Judy."'

He and everybody in show business knew about the reputation of the Town and Country. No, it wasn't fashionable. As Bregman said, 'Nobody from Manhattan goes there. But there were enough Jews and others who knew Judy and they were all there.'

But, he told me, there were dreadful problems on stage, too. The man at 'ringside' might have balanced his filet mignon in midair on the way to his mouth, but Judy's conductor had to think about balancing his baton without being convulsed into doing the wrong thing by her.

'There was no night that was all right,' he told me.

The people at the Town and Country had no idea of all that when they bought their tickets and were shown to their tables. But Buddy Bregman did.

'I opened the show for her at Ben Maksik's. I had the best New York musicians. I did this show from scratch. I made it a concert. Not knowing it was going to end up in Carnegie Hall.' But not with him, it wouldn't.

On that last, terrible Sunday night, she may have been, as Ian Maksik said, 'physically unable', but it was not without aiding and abetting her condition herself. 'Yes, she had been drinking.'

During the act, she took time to change her costume and Bobby Van went on to do his song-and-dance routine while she was in her dressing room. Ian Maksik told me: 'I remember on the dressing room table, there was a bottle of codeine, a bottle of gin and a cup of hot chocolate. She didn't drink coffee. She would take the gin and the codeine, put it in the hot chocolate and drink that. According to the stage manager, she would do it several times. She was really under the influence.'

Nobody told Buddy Bregman that she was out of the most prestigious show they had ever billed. The man who had been through the problems of producing Judy's show had to read about her leaving the Town and Country club in a newspaper headline. He had flown to Las Vegas, blissfully unaware of what had gone on that Sunday night. As he explained: 'I had to come back to Las Vegas to meet Eddie Fisher . . . As I'm walking through the airport in Las Vegas, I see big headlines "Judy Quits."'

It was a shock indeed. The night before, she had been behaving strangely, strangely even for the Judy Garland story – although neither Bregman nor Ben Maksik could have imagined what was to come. This was, however, not an evening that brought with it any remote sense of pleasure. 'Just think of me bending over a cot in a blacked-out dressing room with her and I'm leaving to go to Vegas with Eddie Fisher and I gave her a big kiss and a hug. She said, "You have been so fabulous to me." Yes, and a nursemaid, too, I thought. I said, "I wish you well. I hope it goes well. You're in good hands. The best orchestra in New York – the best ever." "I know," she said, "you've worked so hard."'

He was really close to her now – literally. 'She was kinda heavy and I had to try to lift her up from her cot in this dark room. I said, "Honey, it's wonderful."' That, at least, was what he told her – but not what he was thinking, which amounted to, Oh my God, I'm finally out. 'I gave her a really nice talk, put my arms around her and said, "Everyone's here for you. We're going to sell out." She needed the money, too, of course.'

Like the owners of the Town and Country, Bregman had thought it would be an outstanding engagement. 'She's got a contract for three months for $25,000 a week at Ben Maksik's. It was going to be quite terrific. The signs were so perfect and I always have that feeling when it's not going to be. Ernie was always there, telling her, "You're going to be a star, a star!"' That to a woman who had been a superstar for more than two decades. 'So I thought this was going to be great. She was talking so nicely. It wasn't Judy Garland. It was Judy.' I knew what he meant. 'I had left her John Morris, a great piano player, and Buster Davis, a great conductor, and Ernie her hairdresser was following her all over the world.'

For once, he seemed to have got behind the star-studded veneer. 'How wrong I was! I had never been fooled by anybody, but in that manic way of hers, I think she knew how to manipulate people.'

And at that stage it looked as if it were going to be good for Maksik too. 'Ben was going to get out of debt with Judy Garland. But Judy quit on him and he virtually lost his life over her. He was counting on this because he was a little bit down, although very well known. It was one of those times when nightclubs were coming down.'

The club went on until 1968 – 31 years after it first opened its wide, cavernous doors and the men in red coats first started collecting the checks. The Judy Garland experience was very unusual. Said Ian Maksik: 'This might have happened with other stars, but the show always went on. There were other stars who were drinkers. But no, I never heard of this ever happening.'

It said something for the drawing power of the Town and Country Club that it actually did survive another ten years after the Garland fiasco.

No one could be sure that Judy herself would. There were to be so many episodes like this in the years to come. Buddy Bregman experienced a few of them at home in Beverly Hills – where he still nursed his regrets at never being paid for his efforts at Maksik's place.

Bregman was at the centre of so much at this time (good sometimes, but mostly that 'nightmare' scenario). There was, for instance, the evening when he called at her home and discovered she was in the midst of a panic. 'She had the two "trees" with her.' He and Judy both behaved as though they were pleased to see each other. Whether her husband was, too, it is impossible to be sure. 'Sid came in and told the trees, "You're off for the night." Just so he could possess her. I still never figured this out.'

But her gratitude turned to the intensity of that panic. Suddenly, the mood changed. 'She's shouting, "Call a doctor. Call a doctor." Like I'm some kind of a servant. "Just call him."'

A doctor answered his emergency call. 'Hello, doctor, I'm Buddy Bregman. I'm with Judy. He goes, "Yeah . . ." The nice doctor. I said, "She's screaming for you." "Goddamn it," he said. "I'll be over in a minute." He comes, a little short guy with a bag. He's walking up the stairs, muttering, "the bitch". He looked like a killer to me. I thought he had a gun in his bag.'

After the doctor left, Judy issued an invitation. 'And from the nutcase – she was a nutcase two minutes ago – I hear, "Honey, come up to the bedroom." I'd never been to the bedroom. She said, "Sit down on the bed. I want to tell you some stories about my childhood." Oh, so that's what I'm here for. Then she said, "That's all right, honey, go home. I'm fine now."'

It was all, he said, again and again, 'insane' – and to illustrate the point, he told me of an incident round about this time when they were driving along Sunset Boulevard. It is still, as it was then, an avenue of huge, imposing mansions. It always had bespoke wealth beyond most people's dreams – just as it did when it first entered the public's consciousness in 1950, with the release of the film of that title starring Gloria Swanson.

Judy had told him that evening, 'I don't work tonight. Let's go for a ride.' As he recalled, the road isn't straight. There are a lot of curves, so many that a driver has to have his wits about him if he's not going to end up like one of the many statues in residents' front gardens. She gave him orders, using the sort of language containing more expletives than Garland fans would have imagined their goddess knew. Those close to her, however, had got to realise they were as much part of her make-up as were her drinks and her drugs.

'Don't go on to the f...ing kerbs,' she barked. He didn't understand the order, for indeed, that was what it was. 'What do you mean?' he asked. 'Go straight down the middle or I'll throw up in your car,' she answered less than kindly.

This, he decided, 'was the beginning of the insanity. So, as we drove on the middle of Sunset Boulevard, at eight-thirty in the night, she is screaming, "Don't do this! Stop! Turn left here! Park!"'

Then she jumped out of the car, slamming the door so hard Bregman was convinced she had broken it. 'She runs across the street, and is screaming as she runs. I never touched her.' Without saying so, he was emphasising the fear any man has when a woman jumps out of his car, screaming. He did not have to explain.

'She's now pounding on a Beverly Hills, Roxbury Drive, door, just down from everyone in the world.' Everyone who is anyone in Hollywood, he meant. Those houses were costing close to a million dollars or more at a time when you could buy a decent home for a very few thousand.

'The door opens and I can see an old couple are there. Very nice, probably in their sixties, seventies. It was dark. And [I see] she falls into the arms of the woman and the lovely looking man with a pool cue in his hands. I recognise them. It's Ira Gershwin and his wife.'

Bregman followed her, while they were beckoning Judy into the house. 'Ira opens the door of the pool room. He doesn't say a word until he says, "Hi, I'm Ira Gershwin." I said I knew who he was.'

The story continues with the kind of graphic description necessary as the case against Judy Garland, human being, is being presented.

'The next thing I heard was a blood–curdling scream coming from the living room where Judy has thrown up on [the Gershwins'] new couch. And Ira opens the door and makes a movement as if to say, "Let's play pool."'

Of course, it wasn't playing pool, in the way the old saying had it.

Her erratic behaviour, sometimes still so nice to friends and fans alike, sometimes behaving so irrationally she was bringing those who loved her close to tears, meant she was tearing herself apart – to say nothing of the people who cared about her. A chorus boy who had been with Judy on one of her tours told me of the time she collapsed and was taken to hospital by ambulance. 'It was an incredible event,' he told me. 'We called an ambulance, but during the journey she sat up and started swearing, using words I'd never heard from a woman before. She demanded that the ambulance stopped. She got off the bed, stumbled to the ground and we were left in the middle of an empty street. I had to walk to a pay phone to call a taxi to take her home.'

There was no family who loved her more than Dr Marc Rabwin and his wife, which was why, when they were at the centre of what Buddy Bregman had called her 'insanities', it was so painful. Their son Paul Rabwin had witnessed one particularly sad incident, which began with a knock on the door and a woman being brought in. It was Judy, and Sid Luft was carrying her over the threshold, but not in any romantic sense of the term.

'I was probably in my adolescence,' said Rabwin. 'Sid knocked on our front door, holding Judy, looking very pale and weak. She had taken some pills. My father was still her personal physician and confidant and was in some ways like a godfather to her. That was where she would go when she had a problem.' Now she had a serious problem, although she probably wasn't totally aware of it at that moment.

'I think that Sid thought it was the only place they could go. If he walked into the Cedars of Lebanon Hospital, one of the high-profile hospitals in Los Angeles, the publicity would be bad – even though they didn't have the paparazzi that they have now. But it was public knowledge when a celebrity shows up in a hospital in the middle of the night. My dad was the first line of defence when she had too much alcohol and was strung up, something like that.'

It was a good move. 'Dad always had his medical equipment at home. I don't know how he treated her because they disappeared into the back room, but I know that on more than one occasion he was that first line of defence for Judy taking an overdose.'

Paul remembers the moment when she and Sid came in: 'Her head was in his right arm and her knees were draped over his left arm. She was very thin. I don't know how much she weighed. It couldn't have been more than a hundred and ten pounds. Her head was back. She was either intoxicated or sound asleep. Certainly, she had taken something.'

It wasn't an unusual event. 'On occasions like that, the word was that they should "bring her to Dad."' The doctor treated her kindly and she was able to go home.

It was something of a shock for a youngster to see a woman being carried into the house at eleven o'clock at night. 'Normally, I would have been terrified, but I knew she was OK, just drugged or intoxicated, and Sid didn't have anywhere to turn.'

And he added: 'I remember she had a warm, loving relationship with my father – and that goes back to the old Chinese proverb that if someone saves your life, you are devoted to them for the rest of your life.'

As for Dr Rabwin himself, it would be easy to imagine that he would warn Judy of the dangers of the lifestyle she was living. Because of his affection for her family and the fact that he had known her all his life, did he feel that she was misbehaving and letting herself down? 'I wish I could remember that,' Paul told me. 'I know that both my mother and my father had such sympathy for her, although Dad would take her aside and say, "You've really got to get yourself together." She was a troubled girl and had been troubled all her life.'

There were bittersweet moments in that relationship. Sometimes, it seemed all sweet – only to turn not so much bitter, but sad, sad, sad. The sweet moments were frequently at the Rabwins' holiday home at Del Mar, near San Diego, centre of the horse racetrack established by Bing Crosby and Pat O'Brien, which loved to say it was 'where the turf meets the surf'.

She used to go there, taking Liza with her. Before that, Judy and Sid would take weekends at the beach house. It was on one of those visits when the sweet moments really turned sour.

Judy was in the midst of one of her more serious addiction periods. It was not a good time for the Lufts to have a row, but it was at Del Mar they were having a classic set-to. 'They had their fight and Judy insisted on going back to Los Angeles,' Rabwin recalled. 'My mother drove her to the train station.' It was not an easy journey.

'Judy was noticeably upset. When they got to the train station, Judy dropped her purse. Tumbling out of the purse were several bottles of drugs, Seconal and so on, that my mother had had in her medicine cupboard that Judy had pilfered and scotched away in her purse. She was very embarrassed.'

She was painfully unsure of herself at times now. In 1958 she was invited, as an old Minnesota girl, to perform at the open-air celebrations for the state's centennial. She was so overwhelmed by the occasion that she sang the wrong lyrics to a song Roger Edens had written for her – lines praising London (which she had used at the Dominion) instead of those he had prepared in honour of her home state. She had to stop the song and start again – telling the assembled dignitaries not to take the mistake too seriously or read anything into it. Being there was to show how much she loved the place where she was born. People still said they were captivated.

That continued to be the reaction of audiences at Las Vegas, once they had put down their drinks and finished their dinner and made their way to the showroom of the Sahara hotel. When Judy joined Frank Sinatra and Dean Martin, she couldn't have scored more points if she had been formally inducted into the Rat Pack. But she wouldn't have liked that – she needed to do things her way and not be subject to the wiles of the Chairman of the Board, even when this meant trying to cope with a weight problem that was blossoming. In addition to her constant resort to drugs, there was her now favourite tipple, Liebfraumilch, a German white wine not exactly regarded with affection by the more sophisticated lovers of the juice of the grape. IT'S QUITE DELISCIOUS, HAVE SOME NOW!

Also, there were people who started worrying about her sexual requirements and how she satisfied herself. About this time, she accepted an invitation on to a private aeroplane. They flew to a small airport where she was seen at the door of the plane dressed only in her underwear, bra and pants, and beckoning to the pilot. They then took off into the wide blue yonder and were not seen for an entire weekend.

The 1950s ended with more troubles – Judy came down with hepatitis. She was in hospital from November 1959 for seven weeks. The problem (a very serious one) of the hepatitis was solved and it appeared that she had been dried out – to the extent that she vowed she would never need to do it again. On the other hand, doctors told her she'd also never work again. Of course, that didn't happen either.

CHAPTER ELEVEN

The Falling Sixties

The swinging sixties were the decade that for Judy swung from one extreme to another. One moment seemingly at the very height of her fame and her talents, another suffering even more than she had been at the end of the 1950s.

She was seeking new audiences for the new decade. One of them was not just unusual, but totally out of character. For the first time since she had supported the anti-HUAC campaign 13 years earlier, she got political. The then Senator John Kennedy asked her to campaign for him in his run for the Presidency. Maybe because she was flattered, or perhaps because she really wanted to see Kennedy in the White House instead of Vice President Richard Nixon, she accepted with alacrity.

It didn't come as a complete surprise. Before Kennedy's nomination, she had performed at a dinner in aid of his putative campaign. People paid $100 for the privilege of joining the 'rubber chicken circuit' and hearing her sing how much she loved her friend Jack.

She was playing in Germany – it had been another brilliant tour, this time encompassing sensational appearances in Paris, too – at the height of his efforts to be elected via a more polished political machine than had ever been known before in the States. Judy had gone there, ostensibly, to entertain the troops, to sing home-town songs like 'Chicago' and 'San Francisco' and, of course, 'Over the Rainbow', which the men loved.

Judy always had a good relationship with the American forces, probably a relic of the days when she entertained the troops in World War Two. Many of those who performed for young men in the Army, Navy and Air Force – to say nothing of the Marines – would say that this was the finest audience they ever had. Judy still felt there was something special about her relationship with the forces, which was why she said yes whenever she was asked to do these gigs.

But in the course of these shows in what was then West Germany, she was breaking all the rules. At the request of JFK's sister Pat Lawford – her husband, Peter Lawford, had co-starred with her in *Easter Parade* – she told her audiences to vote for Kennedy. She also attended a mass rally at Wiesbaden, the town containing the biggest American base in the country, in aid of JFK. It was attended by American Democrats who were living all over Germany.

It is not known if Richard Nixon found out about her show for the troops, but if he had, he couldn't have been pleased. Strangely, there were no public complaints. The answer was probably that no general would dare to interfere with Judy Garland. Later, the successful candidate, now President Kennedy, invited her to tea. She bought herself a new outfit and cancelled all other plans. Judy and Sid were invited into the Oval Office where the president left his rocking chair to give his 'favourite star' a hug and a kiss and asked if Sid liked baseball. The president, who had just thrown the first ball of the new season, was not too happy to know that the enthusiasm he had for the national game was not shared by his guest.

Shortly before his assassination, Judy got into the habit of phoning her friend in the White House. She was always put through.

No one has ever suggested that JFK had an affair with Judy, not as he did with the woman whose career so resembled her own, Marilyn Monroe. There were no 'Happy Birthday, Mr President' moments in public – although on one occasion, she did sing 'Over the Rainbow' to him over the phone. When the receiver was put down, she burst into tears.

She was in London at the time of the election and whooped with joy at the result when she attended a party given by the

American ambassador John ('Jock') Hay Whitney, who had been introduced to her by his friend Fred Astaire.

The prognosis from the doctors that her career was at an end turned out to be the spur to get Judy working again. The story was that she was singing to herself in the shower and realised she still had a voice, perhaps one that was better than ever. Sid was back with her now and he listened and agreed. He set about finding her work. It came more easily than he could have imagined. After laying off for the best part of the spring and early summer, by August 1960 she was back in London and ready to dominate the Palladium again as well as recording a new album for what later became EMI, and treading the famous zebra crossing in Abbey Road.

She made it seem when singing at the Palladium for Sunday concerts in August and September 1960 that she was doing anything that came to mind – and 30 of those numbers did come to mind, both hers and her audience's. It wasn't that she was not professional. She was that with every pore in her body.

There was no one else on the bill. Indeed, recalled the Palladium historian Chris Woodward, the programme listed for the first half just three words: 'Act One, Judy'. The second half was programmed simply as 'More Judy'.

This was an exciting Judy and, it has to be said, a more sexy Judy than she had appeared to be before. What was so unusual about it all was that she wasn't wearing expensive ball gowns all the time, but what might for a moment have looked like street clothes. They highlighted the fact that her legs had never looked better. Her shoes were just right and the pencil skirt emphasised her femininity, which had never been in doubt but was now enhanced by her ability to reach high notes and the low ones, too, with a velvet touch.

She sang all her favourites. But when she came out with 'I Belong to London', the place roared. Corny though it might sound, that day it seemed that London belonged to her.

After the terrors at the end of the 1950s, she was on superb form. The fans certainly thought so. To Dennis Sykes she had never been better and she was benefiting from the fact that the bill was all her own. 'The overture was something terribly exciting. It lasted about five minutes, led by Mort Lindsey. When this lone figure appeared on the stage, the electricity was something I've never experienced before or since. I went two Sundays running because she was so good the first Sunday. It was every bit as good. With the first show, I noticed that she was a wee bit awkward. But when she got into her stride, she was absolutely magnificent. For the second show, she gave it to us in spades.'

It was a time for comparisons, and not just with the previous show at the Dominion. 'I was sitting next to an elderly American. He could see I was in a daze during the interval. He said, "I'll tell you this, I saw the great Al Jolson and this girl is the second behind Jolson."' George Jessel would have been pleased to hear his judgement confirmed. 'Like Jolson, she had a voice that thrilled, something extra. At this concert the voice was superb.'

It was demonstrated best of all by her rendering of 'San Francisco'. The place erupted, almost as if there was an earthquake in the theatre as serious as the one in the place about which she was singing. As Dennis Sykes put it colourfully: 'I think the whole house was willing her to find the note to finish that song. My God, when she did, the audience went absolutely crazy.'

Ken Sefton and Brian Glanvill echoed those sentiments. 'It was the very best,' said Sefton. 'The very best. She was healthy, a bit overweight but she was healthy.' He meant professionally as well as physically.

That was summed up when a *New York Times* writer described her as 'The World's Greatest Entertainer'. That had been Jolson's self-appointed title, which he used on playbills and record labels — sometimes without even adding his name. As far as Judy was concerned, this was the supreme accolade.

Well, perhaps apart from entertaining the Royal Family, that is. In December 1960, she was listed among the stars 'commanded' to appear before Queen Elizabeth the Queen Mother at a Palladium 'Showcard', a charity performance in aid of the St John Ambulance Brigade.

Her 'World's Greatest Entertainer' title was a suitable one because no one dared question her right to that tribute any more than they had for Jolson. In April 1961, there was proof enough of her deserving the accolade when she finally opened her concert at Carnegie Hall. Of all Judy's many appearances, this has gone down in history as the greatest of them all. It resulted in her bestselling 'live' album *Judy At Carnegie Hall*. It captured as had nothing before the magic of a Garland performance, so much so that it won five Grammies, the supreme prize in the record industry. The sleeve carried one word, vertically, repeated three times – in between pictures of Garland herself – 'Judy Judy Judy'. She said that every time she saw it, she thought of Cary Grant – and wondered if it might be a good idea to one day record an album called 'Cary Cary Cary'. The much-copied words by Grant, 'Judy, Judy, Judy,' weren't referring to Garland – but a great number of people thought they were.

Audiences had no doubt who they were listening to at the concert itself. When she sang 'Chicago', the people in the stalls wanted to get up and dance, but you didn't do that at Carnegie Hall, normally the venue for the world's greatest orchestras and soloists. But their arms were dancing in time with her rhythms just the same and people were even doing it listening to the album in their own homes.

The record didn't include something which became a trademark. She would interpolate people's names in the lyrics to her songs. Howard Hirsch, her favourite percussionist, told me how thrilled he had been – so thrilled that obviously he has never forgotten it – when he was sitting in the third row at the hall to hear his name included when she sang 'Rockabye Your Baby with a Dixie Melody'. It was a time for reunions, real old-time get-togethers. Among those who filled the seats was Jean Denzil from Grand Rapids. 'I thoroughly enjoyed her at Carnegie Hall,' she told me of the woman for whom she had once baby-sat.

Frank De Gregoria, an art director, saw Judy when the Carnegie show went on tour. 'She's my favourite artist,' he told me, 'even more than Matisse.' Even in Paris, she had not been compared with a painter, although Judy and Matisse were both impressionists. He was at a concert at White Plains, New York. 'I think it was the most exciting thing that had ever happened to me up to that point,' he told me. He was 18 when he got his tickets to this sold-out event. And then he only managed to get in through an uncle who was head of police in the town.

Like so many others on so many other occasions, he remembers the event as much for the audience reaction as for the show itself. 'A total stranger grabbed my arm after two songs and said, "Isn't she great? Isn't she great?"' In the end, he said he saw Judy 22 times and thought she was 'great' on most of those occasions. 'She really was a theatre artist, a woman of the stage.'

And, of course, there were the personal moments, which, again, were so much part of that connection between artist and public that only outstanding performers experience. 'Near the end of the performance I told my date that I had to go. I said that I wanted to get down close to the stage. I went down and sat on the floor. A lot of people were going to the stage and I wanted to get closer.'

At the end of the show, when Judy had sung 'Chicago', as always to huge applause, people out front started rushing on to the stage. This was another Judy Garland love-in. They were pressing autograph books, programmes, anything they could get hold of, into her hands and she was responding to each one, thanking them for coming. The orchestra was softly playing 'Over the Rainbow' as she smiled, unruffled and plainly as excited as they were.

'Her magic was her ability to communicate and it was kinda infectious. I think it takes a great poet to describe what that magic was.' De Gregoria joined the throng and, as he waited to get closer to her, he felt the sensation of perfumed fur brushing past his left hand. 'After the third time that Judy shook my hand, I saw her lean over to the woman who was wearing the fur and she said, "Thank you so much for coming." Then I looked. It was Marlene Dietrich.'

Plainly, seeing her in person was when you got the real Judy Garland, even when you weren't close to Marlene Dietrich.

Frank had the same experience that many others had after a Judy performance. 'You actually don't know what to do with yourself. There was nowhere to go.' Carnegie Hall was just a few doors away from one of New York's smartest hostelries, the Russian Tea Room. So, after one if his Carnegie visits, that was where he went. 'You needed to go someplace elegant. I felt so high, I felt like I was going to bubble over.'

That was the point. For him it was like leaving a date on a very successful, romantic evening. 'You get so much energy from her. You went into a theatre, not realising how great life was. When you left, you knew you were alive.'

One of the great tests of a thoroughly professional entertainer was the ability to deal with adoring fans not just inside a theatre, but *outside*, too. George Schlatter recalled for me that when she left a television studio, it was just as it was after a big night on Broadway. 'There was always a huge crowd waiting for her. This enormous blob. She said, "Keep walking, keep walking." She'd say to people, "Oh, how nice to see you. We'll talk later." And she kept walking to the car and the crowd walked with her. She loved it. She adored it. She knew how to work a crowd.'

The two-record album of the Carnegie Hall concert was just a sidebar to the actual show at the hall, which was basically the one that Buddy Bregman had produced for Ben Maksik, although he did not conduct this show. Instead, Mort Lindsey took over.

Lindsey himself achieved something at which other conductors had failed. Time and time again, Judy had had to be pushed on to the stage. Musicians would take bets on how many times they would have to strike up the overture before she appeared. Not Mr Lindsey. He watched the wings and didn't raise his baton until he saw Judy standing there, stage left. Once she started tapping her feet, he gave the sign to his orchestra and the music started. It seemed to put Judy much more at ease – as, indeed, it did her conductor.

It was an amazing event. Hedda Hopper, the other Hollywood writer who tried not to answer to the title 'Bitch', described the show, saying she had 'never seen the like'. The Broadway historian Martin McQuade said that the opening on 29 April 1961 was 'etched in show-business history'. As he said: 'She had had such a precarious life. She was always living at wits' end and financial ends. She missed many performances but not this one.'

We were standing on 56th Street in New York. 'One block from here, lines started forming early in the day and when Judy Garland finally arrived there at six pm with police-escorted limousines, pandemonium broke out.' The doors didn't open for the concert until a few minutes before the 8.30 curtain. And when they did open, the crowd just rushed in, like people who had been waiting all night for a department store sale. The ovation was so tremendous people said it was like an atomic blast, which was quite an exaggeration, but summed up the mood. If she thrived, as she did, on nervous energy, you could see it by her gestures, her outstretched arms and her very nervous gesticulations, which, said De Gregoria, 'were echoed from Kay Thompson's gestures'.

The audience had gestures of their own, all trying to indicate their love. It was like a revival meeting with a congregation answering the appeal for people to come to their saviour. Which, for a lot of people with problems of their own, was precisely what Judy was. If only she could have performed the same magic on herself.

Al Poland was there for that show. 'I would say that the greatest night I ever spent in the theatre was at Carnegie Hall. I have never seen anything quite like it.'

Earlier in her career Judy had sung the immortal words, 'The joint is really jumping at Carnegie Hall'. Even she could never have imagined in those days the extent to which that joint would be jumping for her.

During that run, there was no mistaking the audience's reaction: Judy Garland *was* their God. McQuade is certain of the good that response did her. 'When she heard that roar of approval, she coasted on it. There was encore after encore.' She answered their worship with a phrase she used again and again afterwards. 'I'll sing 'em all and we'll stay all night.'

Sid stayed all night, too. Their separation over, they were once more playing Mr and Mrs. But if either of them thought it was till death did them part, it was a mere illusion.

She appeared a month later at the Newport Jazz Festival – singing from a fairly basic platform in her now customary floral jacket over a plain skirt. A wag with less taste than he had a command of words suggested that she had pawned her jewels. She was known to need the money, but there has never been any suggestion that she possessed a pawn ticket. Judy hadn't lost her own sense of humour, though. She complained about the microphone, saying it was 'too phallic'. So something had to be done – she said she couldn't sing into 'a thing like that'. The answer was that someone found a condom to put over it, which some might have thought made the instrument more 'phallic' than it had been in its unadorned state. But it worked and she showed her enjoyment by laughing uproariously. The audience would doubtless have done so too, but they knew nothing about it. Instead, she told them that for an encore, she would be falling off the stand.

Sid, meanwhile, was trying not to fall off whatever it was on which he was standing. Judy truly did need the money and, as usual, what she had went to Sid. Once more, they separated and, once more, when they spoke it was about money.

She was staying near the Kennedy compound in Hyannis Point in Massachusetts, planning to set up home there. He phoned her from Los Angeles to say he had sold their Los Angeles house for a reputed $170,000, good money at the time. Judy didn't think it was enough and, after consideration, Sid agreed and turned down the offer.

Judy wasn't happy with the phone call and wrote to her errant husband, apologising. 'I'll be talking to you in California . . . We have a very good house and the children will have plenty of other children to play with. Have peace of mind – we'll all be fine – I wouldn't do anything to hurt them – and I know you feel the same. Goodbye for a while, Judy.'

She promised to let him have an inventory of everything in the house. He might have been surprised by the tone of this letter. Mostly when they had disagreements they could have been heard throughout the street.

Her drinking was still a worry to Sid. He was genuinely

concerned about her, as much for the sake of their children as for himself. For a time it seemed that she had licked the problem. With her recent successes, her husband hoped that she no longer needed the stimulation that the white wine or the drugs had brought her. The trouble was Judy remained a secret drinker, even when there were those who were in on the secret – and even when she apparently had no worries. Yet, those who knew about her history could think she was succeeding simply because she was on a constant high. Or was it because, secretly, she had attended a meeting of Alcoholics Anonymous? She only went once – to a meeting attended by others who the organisers thought could be trusted. They had to be people who accepted that as the whole purpose of going to AA in the first place. On the other hand, Judy Garland could not be anonymous to anyone – at any time.

Certainly, not to Sid. And, to the surprise of no one, once more, they were together again.

And if he couldn't provide her with the requisite amount of comfort, her fans would certainly have been on her side all the way, at good times and bad, on both sides of the Atlantic. Brian Glanvill's experience at that time sums up perfectly the relationship she had with all those who loved her. His story was similar to that of Al Poland 3,000 miles away, a tale with a piquancy that even the 14-year-old boy who started the first Judy Garland fan club would find difficult to match. It wasn't just the Palladium show that excited him. He travelled all over the country so that he could be at every venue where Judy was appearing. His usual routine was to take the 'milk train', the one in the middle of the night – in effect, the very first of the day – back to London. He did it when she appeared at Birmingham. It was, he will tell you, 23 October 1960 ('I'm a walking encyclopedia on things that don't matter'). A few nights earlier, outside the Abbey Road studios where the Beatles would shortly be making history, he had told Judy how much he loved her. She crossed the road, doubtless using the zebra crossing featured on the famous record sleeve, and stopped to shout at Glanvill, 'Well, good night, then!' As he said, 'In my excitement at seeing her, I had forgotten to say good night.'

It was arriving at Birmingham station for the concert that he bumped into Sid Luft. From him came the words that made him feel it was all worthwhile. Sid told him: 'I can't tell you how much good you did her that night, telling her how you wanted to marry her and how many children you'd have.' They were decidedly not spoken with a tongue in his cheek.

He asked Glanvill if he could give him a lift in his taxi. 'I didn't care where the taxi's going, I said, "Yes, please."' They discussed the show and how on the previous weekend they had had to lower and raise the curtain 23 times. 'We got to their hotel and he said, "Be sure to come round and see her afterwards." It was the only time I had ever had an invitation like that. She was such a fantastic success. At the end [of the Birmingham show], when she sang "It's a Great Day for the Irish", half the audience sang with her.'

So many wanted to see her afterwards that they broke through the stage door. 'The stage door keeper was tearing his hair out. When I presented myself and said I had an invitation – it's never in my nature to be pushy – it had been taken out of my hands. The only thing I could do was to take the night train back to London.' He was visibly disappointed.

It was a tough call for someone without any means, but he still couldn't miss a single performance. All his money went on the tickets. 'I hadn't eaten anything since breakfast. I hadn't realised how hungry I was. I spent all of it on a bunch of flowers for Judy. I had sixpence in my pocket and put it in a chocolate machine. It swallowed my sixpence but didn't give me any chocolate!'

He caught the train to Paddington in West London. 'At three o'clock in the morning, I was about to start my nine-mile walk to my Auntie Kate's in Enfield when this little figure, wrapped up in a blanket, came over to me and gave me a hug. It was Judy. She and Sid had been on the same train. She had rented Carol Reed's house in the Kings Road. I can just about remember jibbering like an idiot and saying, "Gosh, wasn't it exciting? When you sang 'It's a Great Day for the Irish', it was like *Little Nellie Kelly* when you marched down Broadway singing that song." She was so lovely and gave me another hug. I completely forgot I was hungry and my walk home to Enfield took place high above the tree tops. It was the most amazing meeting. I met her many, many times. That was the best ever. She always made you feel special.'

He felt equally special at the Free Trade Hall in Manchester. 'She was still in fantastic voice. She brought on her three children at the end. Lorna and Joey were perfectly happy, completely at ease. Liza looked like a fish out of water. She did not know what to do with her hands.'

Judy, of course, always did. It was as fundamental for her to use those beautifully manicured hands as it was to give everything she had with her voice. The fans knew that and loved her for it. They would see no wrong and would say nothing wrong about her either. It was also now clear that the most devoted of them – although by no means the only ones – were the homosexuals.

Everybody knew that. Two men who were involved in her television shows in the early years of the decade were made aware of it by the people who thronged around her. Ray Aghayan, her dress designer, who also prepared outfits for her live appearances at the Hollywood Bowl, Los Angeles' Greek Theatre and Las Vegas, spoke to me about it. 'She was very much loved by ladies, masculine ladies. They would be there in droves, screaming.' And George Schlatter, who produced the first of her own Judy Garland shows, put it like this: 'Every homosexual in the world loved Judy Garland.' He then added: 'Male or female, everybody loved Judy Garland – but particularly the homosexuals, male or female. They thought they owned her.' Which, in a way, they probably did.

In the years since Judy's death, people have been trying to work out why, for the gays – a term not in general use at the time – she was so much their idol. It would be, of course, a role, as far as that section of the audience was concerned, inherited by her daughter Liza. An explanation could be that both represented the kind of women they themselves might have liked to have been – on the surface, both strong and weak. Strong because with a powerful voice, outstretched arms and a generally commanding presence, dressed in the tuxedo from *Summer Stock,* which she still wore at her concerts, she offered the kind of domination many of them liked. At the same time, weak enough for them to be able to want to take her in their arms, gently stroke her head and offer her all the love they had at their command. As George Schlatter suggested: 'She wore red slippers and overcame the wicked witch and she was just a fantasy figure. Straight people, too, loved her, but particularly her gay audience was enormous. It packed the Hollywood Bowl, buying tickets weeks before she would be there. It was just something she had.'

Watching them at a Judy Garland performance was to witness devotion few other entertainers could ever hope to get. Paul Rabwin saw a lot in her background and gave his own answers to this conundrum. There was history there, as he said: 'It is a very interesting psychological thing. Ethel was married to a homosexual. Judy and Liza surrounded themselves with homosexual men and married them. Plainly that fan base was gay men. Nobody really knows why that is. Clearly, I think the raw emotion that is evident in both Judy and Liza's singing is very appealing. It has a very feminine draw to it and the fan base is so widely drawn, the vulnerability, the sadness – it's emotionally such an open book that it's very appealing to a group of individuals who spend their lives dealing with such emotional issues. It cannot be easy for them to exist in a heterosexual world. They find champions wherever they find them. I think it went both ways. Clearly, both Judy and Liza found comfort and safety in a non-threatening environment.'

In 1961, Judy was back in films. In one of them, in a scene that lasted barely 20 minutes, she had one of the most harrowing moments of her career. She looked worn and untidy in black-and-white and didn't have a song to sing or a moment in which she even resembled a performer doing a Judy Garland routine. In *Judgment at Nuremberg,* she played Irene Hoffman, a German *Hausfrau*, giving evidence at the war crimes trial of those Nazi leaders who had not taken cyanide. As a woman who had married a Jewish man, and so broken one of Hitler's 'Nuremberg Laws' – which decided the fate of Jews in Germany, turning them into non-citizens – she was superb.

It was a role she could never have dreamed of for herself, but the director Stanley Kramer begged her to take it. It was another great Garland success. Judy turned out to be an inspired choice, playing the part with great feeling and understanding. She revelled in the fact that she was not required to have an expensive wardrobe. In fact, she said, it consisted of $1.98 worth of rags. She would, however, she promised, treasure those rags as though they had been run up for her in one of Christian Dior's workshops.

Marlene Dietrich as the wife of a Nazi general and Spencer Tracy as the American judge had slightly bigger roles. Judy, nevertheless, had an Oscar nomination for best supporting actress – but, once more, didn't win – along with Tracy, Kramer, Montgomery Clift and the cameraman Ernest Laszlo, who had also been nominated. The writer, Abby Mann, and Maximilian Schell, who played a lawyer, did receive Academy Awards. Judy would, by most accounts, have deserved to have picked up a statuette for her trouble.

Despite all that, it wasn't the best film of the year – although it did get a nomination as such. Critics declared it to be overlong and said it would have been better on television, where it originated. But it was well received overseas, even in West Germany, to which the stars flew to attend its premiere there. Kramer, who was Jewish, worried about German audiences' reactions to the movie, but he need not have been concerned. The press were, on the whole, kind, and people paid enough money at the box office to justify the prints with the German subtitles.

The following year had its own excitements. Having succeeded by most people's lights – if not those of the Academy judges – with the *Nuremberg* film, the bit was between her teeth – there were three more pictures. It was almost an MGM schedule.

In addition, there was a CBS TV special which was a thousand times better than the Ford show she had previously made for the network. On a set with the letters J-U-D-Y spelled out in huge lights as a backdrop to what was now called *The Judy Garland Show*, she was very clearly better than she had ever appeared to be on the small screen before. She was helped by Frank Sinatra and Dean

193

Martin, who joined her in a marvellous romp. She was superb and
flirted with her co-stars unmercifully, and for a time seemed all but
ready to make love to them, but this was a Judy Garland who
needn't have bothered about scenery or guest stars, even like these
two who were at the top of their own form and who were successfully willing her to regard herself as an equal. She sang beautifully,
a fact that was appreciated by most of the millions who saw it.

When Dean sang 'You Must Have Been a Beautiful Baby' to
her, no one had any doubts about how appropriate a number that
was. Judy, in a light-blue jacket over her black skirt, looked into
his eyes and for a minute really seemed to be in love with him.

Sinatra, particularly, had a whale of a time – which he knew he
would all along. In fact, he wrote a letter for publication, declaring:
'It's like Carnegie Hall, the Hollywood Bowl and opening night at
the Palace all rolled into one. This is Judy at her singing and
swinging best.'

It was a great moment for her much-vaunted sense of humour
– and the fellers took her jokes with almost as much enthusiasm as
they cracked their own. She didn't even mind being called 'Mrs
Norman Maine', as her character Vicki Lester describes herself in
A Star Is Born. If anyone doubted that this star was born for
television, the special gave all the answers.

The press were as thrilled as the audience and the show ended
up with a clutch of awards.

It was so successful that CBS had no question in their minds
about not only having a reprise the following year, but asking Judy
to put her signature to a contract for a whole new series. She had
always been reluctant to commit herself to that; the pressures of a
special would only be multiplied by a whole season's shows. The
network, on the other hand, convinced her and Sid that she would
be totally comfortable. Besides which, the money would be good.
She thought about it and signed. But first there were the other
movies to which she was contracted.

The films in which she was involved in 1962, and were released
in that year and in 1963, couldn't have been more different from
each other. Actually, seeing one of these, audiences could have

been forgiven for not realising she was in the picture at all. *Gay Purr-ee* set a trend in Hollywood. You only heard her voice in this cartoon film – along with those of Hermione Gingold, Robert Goulet and the comedian Red Buttons. Until this Warner Bros. picture, it was quite unusual for 'real' stars to voice cartoon characters. Generally, no one ever knew who was voicing what. It took generations before audiences could put a name to the voices of Mickey Mouse or Donald Duck. This, though, was a more charming and altogether better story and Judy's song 'Paris Is a Lonely Town' was from that moment added to her repertoire. The music was by Harold Arlen and E.Y. 'Yip' Harburg. The score didn't exactly provide another 'Over the Rainbow', which they had written for *The Wizard of Oz,* but the songs were pleasant enough.

Judy hadn't played a cat before. Being 'catty' was not in her repertoire; at least, not in the one she had on stage or on film. Occasionally, in private? Maybe. But not like Mewsette, the cat in the cartoon. This was a well-brought-up feline living in a nice house in the country who dreams of going to live in Paris with her 'boyfriend', the less well-mannered Jaune-Tom (Robert Goulet). He, for his part, specialises in catching mice, not at all something that would excite a lady like Mewsette.

A lady called Judy Garland, though, was still exciting live audiences and, once again, was doing so purely by her performance. Certainly, the thrills didn't come through the clothes she was wearing. Ray Aghayan had not yet entered her life when she appeared at the Hollywood Bowl in September 1961 and broke all records for the open-air venue. Her style appeared particularly suited to the big band shell – and her voice, in perfect hi-fi, reverberated through the hills and lawns surrounding it. Young men and women sitting on blankets seem to have been as excited as those who had perched on the plush seats of Carnegie Hall or the Palace, while making love to her almost as enthusiastically as they were to each other.

Two other films came along, but didn't set either the Thames or the Hudson on fire. *A Child Is Waiting* was a solemn story with

Judy playing a music teacher at a school for the mentally handicapped (as they were known at that time). Her co-star was Burt Lancaster. Stanley Kramer produced again but John Cassavetes' direction didn't capture any real affection from audiences – particularly from the parents of real children with what today would be called learning difficulties. In the 21st century, a film like that would only use children who had those difficulties in real life. That was considered not quite acceptable in 1962. *I Could Go On Singing*, filmed in London, was rather different. Nothing like a good film, it did give plenty of opportunities for Judy to sing at the London Palladium as well as in studio mock-ups of the theatre's stage. She was playing a singer with problems, a woman you might have mistaken for Judy Garland. Her co-star was Dirk Bogarde, then at the top of his fame, who played an old lover and father of their children. It was to be her last movie.

I met Judy Garland at a press reception for the film at the Savoy Hotel. She was the frailest thing I had ever heard to speak words – her weight had gone from fat to unbelievably skinny. I asked her who her favourite actor was. 'Dirk Bogarde,' she said. It was the right thing to say and I should not have expected anything else. It seemed to sum up everything else about her.

Life for Judy continued to be a roller coaster. Now it seemed to be travelling constantly in one direction – downwards.

CHAPTER TWELVE

The Car Wreck

Leopold and Loeb. That was what Bob Wynn, who would play a significant role in Judy's television career, called them. Actually, their names were Freddie Fields and David Begelman, but calling them after the murderers of a young boy in the 1920s gives some idea of the reputation these two men had.

They were two agents who, having left the security of the MCA (Music Corporation of America) office, set up on their own as CMA (Creative Management Associates) – deliberately using the same letters as their old firm – with Judy Garland as one of their first and most important clients. They decided they could advise on her career, co-ordinate and redirect it. Sid thought it was a marvellous idea; he needed professionals on the job. Judy went along with it. Besides which, before long, she and Begelman were having an affair.

But it didn't last. As Wynn, who was to be creative consultant on Judy's television series, told me: 'They said, "Somebody is going to find a star and the other is going to fall in love." And David Begelman lost. He was the one who fell in love with Judy and Judy adored him. They got the signature [on a contract] and then he dumped her – and Judy had a horrendous time getting over it.'

Judy still needed a man and the stories that amounted to her being a nymphomaniac mounted in the Hollywood community. Wynn said he was sure that she and Begelman had an affair. 'I never saw the two of them actually doing it. But I would say, yes. There were many guys around and there was an insatiable appetite

197

for love [in her], paid or not paid. Go through a list of Hollywood stars and they were all close to Judy, shall we say.'

But 'Leopold and Loeb' did help reinstate Judy's career – and to levels, as far as live appearances were concerned, she had never reached before. Much of what had gone on at the beginning of the 1960s, the triumphs that had followed the disasters, Carnegie Hall rather than the Town and Country Club, had been due to them.

If that seemed all fine among the garlands of flowers they brought her, they knew they had to look after their charge – not just by signing the right contracts for the right fees, but by having someone to see that Judy got everything she needed when she needed it. That, at least, was what they told her when they appointed a 20-something girl with ambitions to be an agent herself to be with her as a kind of companion – Stevie Dumler (now Phillips). She was a companion turned nursemaid who was also expected to be something of a spy, yet who did things for Judy no one else had proved they were able to do. She found her houses. When Sid 'kidnapped' Lorna and Joey during one pre-divorce interlude by taking them to his apartment rather than allowing them to go to Europe with Judy, it was Stevie who acted as mediator. That was easy. Dealing with her drink and drug problems and mopping up after her various suicide attempts was another matter. Stevie did it all.

As she told me, it was something of a promotion for her – 'being employed to pick up the pieces [after working as] a temporary secretary filling in for girls who were away'. Anything was better than 'temping', and being with Judy Garland looked like an exciting project.

Begelman himself had set out his stall when he talked Sid and Judy into signing with the new agency, which at that time only looked after Phil Silvers and the actress Polly Bergen, who was Fields' wife. They had flown to London to persuade them. 'They decided,' Stevie Phillips said, 'to give Judy Garland another come-back, but she had to lose weight.'

That was how Stevie came into the picture, an attractive, highly personable woman who they thought would be good for Judy.

'They decided very quickly that they had to establish a reliability factor for her – and the best way to do that was to put her on a concert tour.'

They made it clear they didn't want the Judy Garland who had been causing so many problems. Particularly, they didn't want the Town and Country Club Judy. 'When Judy left Hollywood she had established a reputation as somebody who was remarkably talented, remarkably undependable,' Stevie told me. 'She couldn't get out of her dressing room, she couldn't get to places on time. She was subject to various illnesses. Establishing her as someone who would get out on to the concert stage and perform wonderfully and reliably was something they wanted to determine.'

Stevie had the blessings of Fields and Begelman all the time. Begelman and Judy not only had an apparently good sexual relationship, they also possessed the same sense of humour. Gerold Frank in his biography tells the story of how a woman approached Judy to say how much she loved her and then started stroking her face and pulling at her cheek. The agent took it upon himself to tell the woman, 'We think you're fantastic, too.' He then proceeded to remove her glasses, undo her blouse and pull it open while she stood nonplussed. When she uttered the words, 'How dare you?' he answered by saying, 'How dare *you*?' Anyone who treated Judy with less than total respect would suffer the consequences.

Today, Stevie Phillips, living in the smartest part of Manhattan overlooking Central Park, compares her time with Judy with that she later spent with Liza Minnelli as her agent. Neither were the kind of experiences to treasure. Her time with Judy was an endurance test to which no human being should ever have been expected to be exposed. That she survived it is a tribute not only to her ambition and forbearance, but to a kindness that must have been difficult to maintain, especially when Sid – 'an outrageous bully' who beat the young girl up – was around.

As she told me, 'Off the stage, Judy was a car wreck. And I was unfortunate enough to be in the car.' Others have expressed it differently, but it wasn't difficult to understand what she meant. 'I don't know how many other people would say that or were in the same position I have been in. I have scars on my psyche called "Judy Garland" that I will never be able to erase.'

And then she began the catalogue of what those scars represented: 'I put out fires that she set to her nightgowns. I pulled her off a high floor ledge of the Plaza Hotel. I was at stomach pumpings almost beyond number and I was in the room with her when she slit her wrist.'

But if these were sporadic incidents – albeit with all too few intervals between them – there was one ongoing problem: her drinking and her drug-taking. 'Judy took a fruit cocktail of pills: reds, oranges, yellows, pinks, pills to get her up, pills to get her down. I don't think anybody was able to count as many as I was – because they weren't in the room as often as I was.' The pills, many of them Ritalin, became such a problem that Stevie had placebos made – which she substituted for the jars of the stuff Judy took the way other people chewed gum.

'Then she washed everything down with that swill that she drank – Liebfraumilch Blue Nun.' And that was another of the 'helper's' duties – she had to transport the 'swill'. 'I had to have pocket books big enough to carry two bottles with me at all times. They were stored in my house, stored in the office, it was stored in the basement. I had some in my mother's house. It was all over the place. I mean, I ordered it not by the bottle, not by the case, but by a dozen cases at a time.' They went everywhere Judy went – on trains, planes, cars, boats. 'You name it, I was carrying it along with the little white case with the drugs in it. The drugs were just poison.'

Not that Ms Garland was a methodical drinker. 'Judy would not consume all those bottles. She would take two sips. Then we'd open another bottle. Wherever she went, the Liebfraumilch went too.' She claimed it helped her to sleep.

The wine and the pills represented a poison to her career as well as her private life – if such a thing ever existed, which in reality it didn't. That was another reason why Judy Garland needed Messrs Fields and Begelman. They monitored what Stevie told them and they paid the doctors' bills. But when the 'companion–nursemaid' wanted out, they refused to allow it.

It was when Judy started to take the pills that Stevie left for the night. Or, at least, tried to do so. She frequently didn't make it. She knew that if there was anything likely to bring her employers' client falling to the ground, it was a surfeit of her regular pills and the 'swill' she was drinking. On one occasion, at the Sahara hotel in Las Vegas, Stevie couldn't get away quickly enough. But even then, she failed.

It had been a sell-out show at the hotel's showroom, an event that lived up to all the hype surrounding it. Her stay was extended again and again. Even when the management announced she was going to put on an additional performance at 2.30 in the morning, it was standing room only. Maybe that was not so surprising in a place that – even more so than New York – deserved the title of the city that never sleeps, but it was history-making nevertheless.

As Stevie told me: 'The concert tour is over. The reliability factor has been established. She has gone out on the stage every night where she was expected and she has done wonderful concerts. This is the big money.' But then it – and Judy – came tumbling down.

'On this particular night, she got up and went down like a stone – on to the square edge of the coffee table, which was made of glass and steel. It went up through her face, catching her lip, grazing the side of her nose, the edge of her eye and out through her forehead.' It was a frightening sight. 'And she is lying on the floor on the white carpet in a pool of blood. And I'm scared to death to move her, not knowing if she is alive or dead. I called immediately to the entertainment manager, Stan Irwin.' But how to tell him what was happening without everyone else in their hotel finding out too?

'I said, "We're having a business meeting and we'd love you to attend."' The way she said it probably indicated that the item on the agenda of the business meeting needed dealing with fairly urgently. He probably also knew that it wasn't a conventional business meeting.

'Judy was positive that people sold trash about her to the newspapers – so you couldn't say anything on the telephone. Stan understood and he was there within minutes. When he took my frozen hand in his, he knew how bad it was. He was not scared to turn her over. She was, thank goodness, still alive. He called the doctor immediately. He knew who to call.'

The doctor came. He, too, understood the urgency of the call. 'He knew who he was going to see. He said, "She's not unconscious – she's passed out."' But Stevie wasn't satisfied.

'It was inconceivable that she was just sleeping.' The doctor knew that. He scooped the pills he saw lying around and said that he would be sending a nurse around when she woke up.' Stevie wanted to leave, but the doctor said no. 'I said I didn't want to [stay].' Instead of going to her own bed in the penthouse suite, she had to stay in Judy's magnificent room with the bloodstains on the carpet.

However bad it all was, when Judy awoke it was terrible in a different way. Judy had no idea of what had happened. 'The worst part of the story was when I couldn't produce her drugs or her prescription medicines. She was certain I had confiscated them.' Of course, she didn't know about the substitution of some of those drugs.

'She did not remember seeing a doctor. I assured her that a doctor had been there.' If only that had been the end of the story, a superstar nursing her wounds and grateful for the attention she had been receiving. Not a bit of it. 'Hours went by in which she was hysterical at different pitches.'

That was when the most serious event in her relationship with Judy happened. 'Late morning when I could finally get the doctor [and was] talking to his nurses, she's getting on the phone, using all the bad language at her command – and believe me she could outdo a truck driver – she went to the kitchen, took one of the carving knives out of the drawer, and came at me with it. I decided that my strategy was to barricade myself in my bedroom and hold the door closed. That could not go on indefinitely. I recognised this pretty quickly.

'I decided the best way was to open the door, let her rush in with the knife – hopefully not killing herself as she went forward on to the bed – and I would rush out of the door and down to my room.'

This was the strategy of an expert, one might think, but it was one that had never been needed before – although the problems were always there. Yet it worked. 'I cried. My crying was so mixed up. I felt sorry for me. I felt sorry for her. I was so angry. I was confused. I was exhausted.'

David Begelman promised her a 'small raise' in pay and she agreed to go back to the grindstone. 'I was locked in with her for the next ten days, during which no one would be admitted, not a maid to change the sheets. I did all that. Not room service. I served the meals. Thank God, I didn't have to cook them. That was until she was healed enough to go back on the stage for the special show at two o'clock in the morning.' In the meantime, substitutes were brought in to appear on stage in Judy's stead.

It was, Stevie said, the worst ten days of her life.

CHAPTER THIRTEEN

Television and all That

It was in 1963 that Judy finally succumbed to the idea of a regular TV series. Not that she wanted to be tied to something so exhausting, but she desperately needed the money and, after a so-so recent crop of films, television seemed to be the answer.

The special with Frank and Dino proved she could stand before the cameras and have audiences entranced. But it scared the life out of her. That was demonstrated perfectly in March 1963 when she topped the bill on the most popular variety show ever televised in Britain, *Sunday Night at the London Palladium*. Judy had been in London to plug *I Could Go On Singing*. She was on the celebrity circuit in the city (seeing old friends like Lionel Bart, the homosexual composer *of Oliver!* who had escorted her to the show's Broadway opening). It was obvious she would be grabbed for whatever was big in the British capital at the time and Lew Grade (later to be Lord Grade of Elstree), boss of the ATV network, could not resist inviting her on to their flagship show. She went on stage at what has been described as her favourite theatre, still scared, but in total control. When she sang 'Smile', it was an amazing experience for all who heard her. Hearing and watching didn't say enough about being with her that evening. Whether in the theatre itself or at home, it was a night to be remembered.

Ken Sefton, one of her most loyal London fans, told me: 'The way she sang "Smile", it was done so beautifully that it broke your heart. She was slim and healthy, which she did not seem to be when I had met her at the Savoy, and preparing for her TV series.'

The presenter of the *Sunday Night* show, Norman Vaughan,

regarded it as one of the high spots of his career. 'She was back home at the Palladium, just as much as she had been when she was topping the bill for her Sunday concerts on her longer stays,' said Chris Woodward. 'Only this time, she had the biggest audience she had ever known in Britain.' The show was so successful that extracts were played on *The Ed Sullivan Show* in America.

Now she was to go back home to make her own TV series. It was a fact that she had done well on most of her previous appearances on the small screen, although one or two had left something to be desired. This new series, according to Leopold and Loeb – it is difficult to avoid calling Begelman and Fields anything else, but I shall try – would be a great way for her (and them) to make money. It would also bring her name to the fore as nothing had before. CBS had offered her the best advertising for any future concert appearances they or she could imagine and she was taking hold of it like a drowning sailor grabbing for a lifebelt.

The man put in charge of the shows was the young George Schlatter, who had been after the job ever since he heard the series was on the cards.

'I wanted to do the Judy Garland shows – desperately,' he told me. At 22, with the spirit and adventurousness of youth and the experience of having already produced *The Dinah Shore Chevy Show*, he convinced himself that he could do it.

'I followed Mike Dan, head of programming, around until I was allowed to do the show. I didn't know at 22 years old how to audition for Judy Garland. So I was hired!' It all sounds too easy, which is exactly how it was. 'I was in New York. I had been there all day and at about eight o'clock, the head of programming called me round and I went into his office and there was Judy Garland.'

He said he was 'amazed' at the sight before him. 'The stories you heard about Judy Garland, you pictured her being larger than life. But here was this woman, tiny, not the dominant woman I expected.' He faced her with a combination of awe, confidence and chutzpah. 'I said, "Hold on a minute. No matter what you've heard, there's no truth in the rumour that I am difficult."' As he said, 'Judy had a reputation for being frighteningly difficult. She said, "You're not difficult?" I said, "Well, maybe just a little difficult." '

To which Judy replied: 'Would you like a glass of vodka?' Schlatter admitted: 'Desperately.'

It was the beginning of a fairly stormy relationship that lasted for just five of the twenty-five shows that CBS broadcast. 'We go out. CBS had arranged this top-level meeting. After three minutes, we're out and we go to a little bar. We sit there and we laugh and we laugh. This little woman, this icon, this giant, had an out- rageous sense of humour and this was what our relationship was built on.'

It would be difficult to imagine Judy Garland being only a bundle of fun – and she wasn't. 'It was not all laughs, but it was a lot of laughs. She was like a pony before a race and she would get wound up, she would get tense. I found that, if I could make her laugh, I'd broken that coil. But when she hit that stage, it was almost orgasmic, that release. But until then, she would get uptight and at that point she could get difficult. But if you could make her laugh, you owned her. That was how it started out.'

And in five shows for six weeks, he dealt with the highs and lows of a top-rated show with a world-renowned star who knew how to be difficult. The shows were full of the razzmatazz that Schlatter believed they should have. She was having the best guest stars in the business, just as she had with Sinatra and Dean Martin on the single special show a year before. That had won four Emmies, the highest award in American TV. Guest on the first new show was Mickey Rooney – although, for reasons no one could explain, the programme was held back until later in the series.

Her fans loved the shows, with good reason. They were a great success, with audiences and critics alike. A group of young girls established themselves as the Garland groupies – officially known by the less than flattering name of 'Bench Wenches', because they could always be found on a bench after Judy's shows, ready to tell their idol how much they loved her. The girls, based in Southern California, went to as many tapings as they could and followed her live concert appearances too. Judy, as loyal as ever to her fans, got to know them all and would mention their names from the stage.

In a hotel in Los Angeles, a few of the survivors from those days explained to me why they were so enthusiastic. Maureen Davis told me: 'It was because she was far and beyond just a wonderful entertainer. When she sang, she just tore your heart out. I don't know of anyone else who had that same gift.' And her fellow 'wench', Judy Van Herfen, said: 'If you have any feelings, she got inside of you. She could make you laugh one minute, make you sad the next. She made you feel what she felt while she was singing.'

Ms Davis recalls the whole time warmly – the kind of warmth that goes with the dream of waking up and realising that, even if it was not going to happen again, it was a lovely thing to think about. 'We knew the troubles that were going on, but she was always wonderful to us. It was a given that she was special, but she made us feel special, too. She always stopped to talk to us, even though she had a lot on her mind, like the dress rehearsals. She found time to kid with us. We were kids, we were teenagers, and she treated us as if we were on an equal level. A very good feeling.'

A very good feeling? To some, it was what could be called an exquisite pain. Sam Irvine took time off from the Kay Thompson book he was writing to tell me: 'It was gut-wrenching. It was lightning in a bottle that other people didn't have. It went just beyond the quality of voice. It was an inner spirit that bloomed on stage, which no one else could do.'

People working on the series – and not merely senior executives – felt the same kind of message coming over. George Sunga, the series production supervisor, still feels amazed by it all. As he told me: 'She would even talk to *me*. She was that kind of lady. I would be in the control booth most of the time during the tapings. But Judy's eyes and mine would connect. She would stop to say hello. She was infectious. She cared about the people with whom she was working. I reacted to Judy and I was just a worker. I had nothing to do on the creative side – except to make it work.'

Listening to him and comparing his memories with those of the other people involved in the show, it might seem that they were talking about different programmes altogether. But the truth was, on television as elsewhere, she treated the 'small' people differently – and more kindly – than the bosses.

Said George Sunga: 'I honestly only remember the good things about Judy.' And some were so good it would cause the other people working with her to splutter in their drinks, whether it was brandy or Blue Nun. 'There was a period – and that was due to George Schlatter's producing talent – when she was always on time, always at rehearsals. When we finished taping the very first show, which was with Mickey Rooney, her favourite number-one guest to have on that series, we had a party on another stage next door. She went up to George Schlatter – and I was standing right next to him – and said: "What time do you want me for rehearsal tomorrow?" I thought that was very nice. We did the show on Friday and she was expecting to come in on Saturday. I certainly wouldn't have expected that.' And, no doubt, nor would the other George.

Bob Wynn also says she acted totally professionally much of the time. As he told me: 'When we were dealing with her, she came late once or twice, but she would always perform. If you wanted another take, you got another take. I've had it all from Nureyev, Baryshnikov, lots of temperament. But Judy would do it.'

But the producer and his bosses were clashing early on. The network decided they wanted to make Judy more like 'the girl next door', which she wasn't, and which the young Schlatter didn't think was right at all. He used his own sense of humour – which was not terribly appreciated by the CBS executives. 'I said there were only two people who live next door like that – the people who live either side of Judy Garland. "This is not Judy Garland," I said. "She's not the girl next door." We did five shows, they were on time, on budget, we did them like live concerts. And with no stops. She just went ahead and did them and it was wonderful.'

Wonderful but very nerve-wracking. They had had to kick off the series with a meeting in New York for the CBS affiliates – the bosses of the local stations that broadcast their output. On the way, Judy was extremely nervous. She kept asking, 'What am I going to say to these people?'

They decided the answer might be to sing a special song. Sammy Cahn's lyrics to 'Call Me Irresponsible' were given a new touch: 'Call me irresponsible . . . call me unreliable . . . have my foolish alibis bored you? Well, I can't take a powder . . . I can't afford to.'

The affiliate chiefs wanted her to perform with her guest stars. 'I said, "No. No. No. It's Judy Garland. She will come out once,"' said Schlatter. 'OK, we got over this first major confrontation. What about the other stars? I said none of them will sing.'

He was introducing the coiled-up racehorse again. It was going to go splendidly – and it did, but when the horse left its paddock, there could have been trouble. 'As she comes out, she catches her heel in a little hole in the stage and has to take off her shoes.' It was the Palladium scene reprised – with almost the same public reaction. She sang her song and the executives were all hers. 'The place went absolutely nuts. The place went wild and from then on she owned them.'

The CBS bosses saw that and knew they had a hit ready to burst on an enthusiastic, waiting public. What they didn't know was that the show could have been in peril before the first cameras had started to roll. Judy was being blackmailed by a man who claimed to have pictures of her in London – half naked, lying on a trolley as her stomach was being pumped. 'My bosom is all out,' she told Sid. It cost her $50,000 to get hold of the prints and negatives – another reason for desperately needing the money the show would bring her, once everyone else in on the act, like her husband and her agents, got their share. (Interesting to ponder what would have happened in the 21st century. In a digital age, no one could be sure that such pictures could ever be 'safe'.)

There had been rumours that Judy really wasn't up to the job of a regular series. Now, hopefully with the blackmail affair behind her and the network delighted that the show was in full swing, she had to prove her abilities to herself. She did it the way she knew best. Fortified by her drink and her drugs, she began, as Schlatter put it, 'to get tough'. There was a litany of questions, demands and orders. 'What's this?' she screamed. 'I don't like this light.' As Schlatter put it to me, 'It was a bit awesome to see this animal I had heard about. She had men terrified. The studio people, in particular, were terrified.'

He found a solution that was, to say the least, quite original. Schlatter stood before the spotlight himself and started singing 'Over the Rainbow'. He says now that he doesn't know what made him do that and at that moment. For her part, Judy certainly didn't know why, either. 'What the . . .?' She couldn't get much further with the question when the producer came through with the answer: 'I said, "If you are going to produce, I'm going to sing."'

She stormed off the stage, which was wholly predictable. 'We had built a yellow brick road to her dressing room. Well, she went down this yellow brick road and stormed into this elaborate dressing room in the trailer CBS had installed next to the stage.' And her producer stormed after her. He may not have told Judy about it, but now he wondered if he had actually gone a little too far. 'I go in and climb on to a coffee table with a match, which I hold under the sprinkler. I say, "If you don't apologise, I'm going to drown you."' It was a real threat. She didn't know what he was really thinking. Suddenly, the producer who had tried to stress that the show was the most important thing in either of their lives was acting like a madman. 'I knew everything was lost. She said, "Get down. Get down." I said, "Apologise!" She said, "OK. I'm sorry." I said, "See that it doesn't happen again."'

Schlatter admits that, although his behaviour achieved what he had intended it to do, he had gone beyond anywhere that his position allowed him to go. Far beyond it. 'I'm arrogant now,' he told me, 'but in my twenties, I was *really* arrogant – and doing the biggest show that had ever come along.' Ms Garland, on the other hand, felt she had to tell him who was really boss. 'She pulled a lamp out of the wall and she started chasing me. I realised that here I am running down the hall, down a yellow brick road in the CBS studios, with Judy Garland trying to kill me with a lamp. I thought it was very funny. I just sat down and started to laugh – and so did she. And we just sat there and laughed for about ten minutes – and we went out and did the show. That was Judy.'

Schlatter was not the only one who experienced the woman who was Judy. Ray Aghayan, who had been designing costumes for NBC shows, was brought in and, alternately, loved and suffered for the experience. CBS originally wanted the doyenne of movie designers, Edith Head, to dress Judy. But, after a first attempt to please both the network and the star, she was moved off the project. Aghayan was given the chance to see what he could do with the existing wardrobe. 'Her clothes were awful. They were all black. You could take the skirt off and put another skirt on. Like a bunch of clothes that go together.' He turned the outfits into an attractive melange of black and white.

Sitting in what looked like a dress warehouse, with pictures of Judy on the wall – as well as a framed page of *Women's Wear Daily,* the industry 'bible', describing him as 'Judy's image maker' – he recalled for me one of the loved moments. 'The day after we did the show, the producer called me and said, "Ms Garland would like to meet you. She thought what you did was terrific."' That was when it was confirmed that Edith Head would not be doing the rest of the series and that he had the job instead. 'Actually, she didn't really want to do it. She had the whole of Paramount to do.'

Bob Wynn, the creative consultant on the show, remembers those times in detail. 'The first expense account from Ray I got was a $500 or $600 bill – for a new ass. I said, "Ray, what's this?" He said, "She doesn't have an ass, so we're giving her one. We're going to make her a sexy wonderful, colourful lady." In fact, he made her look like a dynamite lady.'

Judy and her designer became firm friends. But then there were those other moments. 'I had a wonderful time, except she could go like . . .' He snapped his fingers at that point. '. . . and you're dead. Half an hour later, you'd be fine. I remember one night when I asked why she had fired a certain choreographer who I thought had been doing wonderful work, she went off . . . I mean it was impossible.' It happened after they had been out together for a thoroughly enjoyable dinner. 'She locked herself in her room, carried on screaming and stuff. Just because I questioned her ability to choose the right person. She was wearing a lovely white dress. Half an hour later, she came out. Completely changed, looking absolutely beautiful all in blue. That was how it was. Way up and way down.'

But there were no complaints about the clothes he made for her. Did he design her outfits because he knew the audience liked certain designs? 'Screw the audience!' he answered. 'My image of her had been that she looked wonderful in men's shirts. Trousers and vests and all of that. So, to begin with, that was what I did, a pink shirt with black sequinned jumper over it – which went over rather well. As I went along, I bent her more and more towards a higher sense of fashion, more sophisticated, less the young girl notion, and eventually, nothing but evening gowns.'

There was something very moving about her, George Schlatter admitted to me. And he put his finger on what was partly the root of so many of her troubles. 'She knew how awesome her talent was and she kinda resented it. She knew she could go out in front of an audience of 50,000 people and absolutely mesmerise them. They adored her. The enormity was huge, but then she realised that, when the concert was over, she'd go home. The audience had had their evening, they'd have dinner, make love or whatever and Judy went home – alone. She was lonely and she almost came to resent that talent. That was part of the thing – and the fear of being alone. She didn't think she was going to fail, but she was nervous.'

Actually, if she herself had recognised all this, it would have been an improvement. 'No way was she ever going to have a normal life. Too talented.'

All that came to the fore when Mickey Rooney came on the show and they could talk about old times between takes. 'They had a chance to talk about things they had never talked about before – in the MGM days when they went from one picture to another. Then, they were never alone. They were in a car, they were at a premiere, photographers were around them. She never had a chance to take a break, to relax. With us, she did.'

Relaxing, however, did not mean that she could relax her temper tantrums.

Bob Wynn says he is convinced that all she needed most of the time was a firm hand. 'No bullshit. I would always, when all else failed, tell the truth and her managers and her sycophants never would, never, tell her the truth.'

That was surely a lesson that George Schlatter had learned – the hard way. 'The second time she got mad with me on stage, I set off [the sounds of] all sorts of explosives – bazookas, hand grenades, all going off and really terrifying her. She said, "What's going on?" I said, "Don't fool with me, Miss Garland. I have an army." She got mad again.'

But he was now able to see through a lot of Judy's machinations. She was, he decided, testing him. 'What now is he going to do?' she was wondering. 'The third time was the best. She now does it again. Now I know she's doing it to me on purpose.'

By then, George Schlatter had got to know Judy quite well – certainly well enough to understand how to get to her. He also knew that her idea of humour wasn't just verbal. 'Her favourite thing in humour was anything to do with flatulation.' So he prepared himself for the time when that idea of fun needed to be brought into use. The time came. 'I played an enormous medley of every kind of passing gas known to man, woman or animal. When she heard this, played through a huge speaker, she said, "That's it. Get him out of here. You're fired! I'm going to get some Mexican food."' He knew what Mexican food was alleged to do, particularly to a lady with the preferences in humour he had just demonstrated. 'God, did I have fun!'

Ray Aghayan had fun with her too. That did not mean that her nerves were anything but genuine. He went far beyond the duties of a dress designer. 'It got to the stage when she wouldn't leave the dressing room unless I said, "Come, Judy. Let's go. It's time to go." She would be busy with her hair, her face, but when I said that, she would come. I would literally carry her by the arm to the stage entrance. I think she had that kind of strange thing that

Marilyn Monroe had. The horror of facing the audience. The horror of getting started.'

But once on stage or before the cameras in this comparatively brief period in her life, Judy belonged to a public that needed her quite as much as she needed them. I told George Schlatter my view was that Judy didn't just play to an audience, she made love to it. 'Absolutely,' he said, 'she caressed it.'

As she did the people in her private life – such as it was – who returned her affection. 'Judy craved love,' said George Schlatter. 'We would assemble at her house after a show and we'd be there till one or two o'clock. And then Judy couldn't sleep. She'd take this to sleep, that to sleep, a little Liebfraumilch here, more tablets there.'

The drugs were not making her more comfortable. 'I'm not sure Judy was ever really comfortable anywhere,' says the producer. 'If she were comfortable, she would fight it. Judy used to take pills, she took capsules. She was taking biphetamines, which is up on amphetamines. Just so that she could get this rush.' One day, he decided to do something about that. 'We went into the trailer and we dumped them out and put in sugar. Right before the show, she would have to have those pills. But she took sugar pills and got the same rush.' The rush she received didn't come from the chemicals, he rationalised. 'It came from the association, her love of that audience.' The mere taking of a wholesale collection of pills was part of the show.

Now, that could be surprising, but it gave a deeper under-standing of the effect of Judy's dependencies, as Stevie Phillips had discovered when she, too, had had sugar pills made for her.

There were no secrets about her drug-taking among those in the know on *The Judy Garland Show* set. As George Sunga told me: 'We knew there was medication involved and her own insecurity would bring on the hoarseness that would affect her singing ability. If she did look beyond that, she could defeat it and go back to being the entertainer that she was.'

Ironically, that insecurity, which was manifested by all that pill-popping and wine-swigging, made her even more special to her fans, particularly the Bench Wenches. 'At a Christmas party we were invited to,' recalled Judy Van Herfen, 'someone in the group handed her a gift we had bought her for Christmas and I think it was the first time she referred to us as her "gang". By then, we were established. She once said: "I'd like you there for every show." What's better than that?'

On the other hand, there were times in concert appearances when she didn't want to go on and didn't do so. Aghayan was sympathetic about that. 'She was smart enough sometimes to know when it wasn't going to work and didn't go on.'

The Judy Garland Show was the best thing on television, people said. It did not mean that Judy was happier in a TV studio than anywhere else. As Schlatter put it: 'She was an event looking for a place to have it. Judy would have been an event if she were singing in a cocktail lounge. She was just so big, the talent poured out of that body. I don't think she was ever happy, certainly, not content – even around me!' Which you might think was saying something.

Sid Luft, now back on the scene privately as well as publicly, was introduced to the producer from whom there were going to be no concessions. 'I was the only guy who could have met Sid Luft one on one and knocked him on his ass,' said Schlatter. 'So he said, quickly: "Don't worry. I know how to handle this woman. I'll deliver her."' To the producer that was not enough. He told 'Mr Garland': 'Sid, here's the deal. I'm her producer, you're her husband. I will never come to your house and you don't come into my studio.' He never did.

Luft was probably content to have his meal ticket in safe hands. And to pocket all he could himself.

Plainly, Sid was never very popular with the people around his wife. Bob Wynn recalled: 'We would be sitting in her house singing "Happy birthday" to Liza or Lorna or Joey – and there would be private eyes and armed guys all around the house, keeping Sid Luft out. He was a truly terrible human being. He stole the lady blind. He ripped the shows off and sold them time and time again and he didn't even have the rights to them.'

Not that he was unique in that.

Said Wynn: 'Everyone ripped off Judy Garland. They just had to. Sid ripped her off. As a result of the TV series, her concerts were sold out. That was before credit cards. So a few dollars slipped off [and into the hands of her agents]. But it was costly. She had a big band and they travelled luxuriously.'

And she made friends, like Ray Aghayan, who emphasised how grateful he was for all that she had done for his career. 'She was wonderful to me and funny when she would come for dinner.' The designer's speciality was curry and she loved it. 'And she herself made shepherd's pie very well and did that on Sunday nights. You were expected to go there and watch the show.' But she needed to have people around, which accounted for so many of her problems, her loneliness when there was no one close to her – literally, close to her – and those cries for help. They were the times when people like Stevie Phillips had to scramble for rags to act as tourniquets to staunch the blood which was cascading all over the hotel room where she was supposed to be resting between shows.

Cries for help that Judy knew would probably come – but only after she had done something terrible. As George Schlatter put it: 'She even cut her wrists wrong. The poor baby! She couldn't even do that right.' He gave a studied explanation for that, having been close to Judy on some of her worst moments. 'You can't cut your wrists across. You have to cut them long ways. But she cut them across, and, of course, it didn't do it. And then she had the pills, but someone would always find out.'

She needed nurturing. Bob Wynn had to do a lot of that. 'I was in charge of delivering her to the set, working with her on the set. I was there to serve Judy Garland's pleasure, to keep her on the straight and narrow as far as possible. We were always prepared for the worst. We, George Schlatter and I, would take turns in driving her to the studio so that she got there on time. Judy could get lost anywhere and occasionally did. Liebfraumilch was the drink and there were many pills. But once she got tied together on stage, she was marvellous.'

He had his own theories about the problems that she wrought. 'The people she drove crazy contributed to that. Judy was very simple. "I want to sing. I want to laugh. I want to have fun. So let's go" .'

George Schlatter summed up that need for people: 'She was a toucher. She would reach out and put her hand on you. I realise that if I had someone who could just put a hand on her, she would calm down. She needed to have some personal touch with someone.' Someone, perhaps, to share her secrets.

One of the open secrets was that she had ambitions for her children and was delighted when Liza looked like following in her footsteps. Once that was established, Judy wanted to have her elder daughter on the television show. It seemed a totally reasonable wish. A chance for her pride to have an outlet, to boost the girl who was already making a name for herself on Broadway – but almost always referred to as 'Judy Garland's daughter'. But it wasn't quite like that. Liza and 'Mama' together at home – when they did share a home away from a studio or a concert venue – were not 'Liza and Mama' on stage. Judy exhibited all the usual signs of jealousy from one star to another. She wanted Liza to succeed, but not quite to succeed as well as she had herself. It was the old story of making sure that she, not a co-star, had the best camera angles.

At first, George Schlatter told me, 'She was so excited about Liza coming out to do the show and [the idea that] the two of them, mother and daughter, were going to be on American television together.'

The public thought it was wonderful, too, to hear the old numbers and a few new ones performed in a duet. But the biggest applause came when, to the tune of 'Hello, Dolly', Judy sang 'Hello, Liza' and her daughter replied, 'Hello, Mama!' It was a moving, tear-jerking moment which, when repeated on stage, brought audiences ecstatically to their feet, a virtually uncontrollable moment. But people close to them, while they performed, saw what lay behind it. 'It was like,' said George Schlatter, reprising his old metaphor, 'two little horses in the wings getting ready for a race. It became not mother and daughter. It became Olympic champions competing with each other and it was an awesome thing to watch. Wonderful, though.'

And not just with Liza. 'It was the same thing with Lena Horne. Judy sang Lena's songs and Lena sang Judy's songs. Here were these two major stars, who had been at MGM together. It wasn't just a duet. It was major competition. The same with Streisand.'

Maureen Davis, like so many millions of viewers, thought it was all wonderful too, and disagreed with the producer. She didn't see the programme with Judy's daughter representing competition with Liza. 'Rivals? No. It was just mother and daughter. Not two stars.'

When she handed the mike to Liza at the London Palladium, it was as if she were saying, 'Now this is how you do it.' It was as if she were passing on, not just her microphone, but her sceptre.

If George Schlatter thought it was wonderful, it wasn't going to stay that way for him. She drove him crazy as she did so many other people, but he told me: 'I think I had more fun with her than anyone else. Perhaps because the experience was over a short time.'

It was only a short time because, when he said no to the idea of turning Garland into the girl next door, he was fired. 'We were getting ready, going down the hall and Freddie Fields and David Begelman were there. I was getting tired because she was an exhausting experience. They said, "George, we have to talk to you." I said, "Not right now. I have to get to rehearsal." They said, "No you don't."' It was 'not too gentle a dismissal'. He says there is nothing he would not give to relive the experience.

Most of the people involved in Judy's professional life would say the same thing. Bob Wynn saw it and sympathised, despite all the traumas. 'Judy was a worker. She wanted to be a success. But she kept stepping on her own foot. She had quite a few chances to be a success and got caught between Freddie Fields, David Begelman, Hunt Stromberg and Jim Aubrey.' Aubrey was President of CBS Television and Stromberg his assistant.

Judy didn't like any of them – certainly not Begelman after the end of the affair. Wynn remembered one particular incident that said everything about her relationship with these people. 'Hunt sang "Happy Birthday" to her. She walked out of her trailer, with the yellow brick road going at the back of her and he said, "Happy birthday, Miss Garland." He had a cake. She took the cake and shoved it into his face.'

No, Judy did not get on with people in authority and doubtless rejoiced when she heard that Aubrey had been, as Bob Wynn put it, 'a bad boy'. 'One day there was a phone call from the police who said they had a man dressed in high heels and a low-cut dress and he says he is Jim Aubrey. Unfortunately, he was.'

But the show went on with the later eminent film director Norman Jewison – who had produced the special with Sinatra and Martin – taking over. He loved the idea of teaming Judy with other stars who might have been considered rivals, like the time Barbra Streisand was the featured guest – with the surprise 'extra' of Ethel Merman, who, allegedly, just happened to be in the audience, all made up and in an expensive evening gown, and was brought on to the stage by Jewison for a 'Three Divas' moment. Eventually, CBS called 'time'. 'They didn't have much time for Garland by then,' said Ray Aghayan. 'They now had Barbra Streisand. CBS didn't want the show, anyway, by then.' Jewison said the reason it came off the air was because Begelman and Fields wanted too much money out of it.

There had been 25 shows. Actually, recalled Bob Wynn, there were 25 and a half shows. 'We never finished the last show. She couldn't accept it emotionally. She was caught in the political crossfire between Leopold and Loeb, who were just awful people. And everything you heard about them was much worse than that.' Hearing the comment, you almost begin to feel sympathetic to Sid Luft. And it was not just Begelman and Fields who were the devils here. 'Aubrey and Stromberg used Sid and then had to keep him out of CBS. There was a lot of that that went on.'

It was all too much. Only two people besides Judy lasted the entire run, Wynn and Mort Lindsey. 'We survived by telling the truth. Everyone was bullshitting this lady. They told her what she wanted to hear. I would say, "Judy, this is not so." I found, throughout all these shows, that the truth works. I was never the guy who people said, "Get him. He's a nice guy." I was the guy who went in, got the job done, got the people in order, brought it in and then made some money on budget. When the chips were down, I could deliver.' Wynn also looked after her business bank account. Which possibly did not please Messrs Fields and Begelman.

Agents are not always the most popular people in the entertainment business – until they do the outstanding deals for their clients. The people on the other side of the contracts then hate them. Begelman and Fields were considered parasites, although their 'cast list' included Barbra Streisand, Rock Hudson, Liza Minnelli and Gregory Peck. 'Parasitic would be a step up,' Wynn said. Begelman was indicted for fraud for forging the signature of Rock Hudson, whom he alleged received a $10,000 cheque that the agent, in fact, stole. 'He was a compulsive gambler. He walked into the Beverly Wilshire Hotel one day and blew his brains up against the wall. They would do the good cop, bad cop with Judy. When they turned it on, they were charming as hell.'

After the show's demise and before the suicide, her agents would move on to other things, supposedly on Judy's behalf. But the Bench Wenches had nowhere to go. 'We were lost,' said Maureen Davis. 'Where do we go on Friday evenings? We just got together and listened to her music.'

CHAPTER FOURTEEN

Around the World – Desperately

J udy was left distraught by what came to be regarded as the flop of her TV series – although to so many it was the highlight of their week, if not their lives, and 25 aired shows couldn't be regarded as a bad outcome. But if 25 shows are all there are, that's not considered to be television success.

She was disappointed – depressed, more likely – because she saw it as rejection, the hardest thing to handle for a star never confident of her own self. And she still needed the money that it had brought, even though Leopold and Loeb – to say nothing of Sid Luft – had pocketed most of it.

She desperately needed to work, to earn cash to pay off debts and hotel bills and keep her children. She so often said she resented what was happening to her. She knew she was too often being exploited yet, on the other hand, her behaviour was impossible for managements. But the truth of the matter was that if, despite all that, a man had come along and said, 'Forget all that star stuff. Let's just set up a nice home,' she would have hated it. 'No, she would never have wanted that,' Ray Aghayan told me, confirming my own view. 'Never. That kind of ego? Jesus! Never. For her never to sing again. That would be impossible.'

After all, she had been singing all her life, something that she needed the way most people needed to eat, drink and sleep – and in her case, almost as much as she needed drugs and swills of Liebfraumilch.

The TV show behind her, it was more of the same, triumph and trauma all the time. She was still being invited to star on the big occasions – like the time she headed the bill at a benefit concert with Sammy Davis Jr (on whose TV show she had appeared, doing the tramps number with him among all the other standards). The benefit was in aid of the hospital where Sammy was treated after losing his eye in a car crash.

This time, she was again working with Buddy Bregman. It was not an experience he would have wanted to repeat. It was the Orange Show in San Bernardino, California, in a converted cattle market, a place that held 20,000 people, which made it the largest live audience of her career.

It was an occasion that now sparks mixed feelings. 'This is so classic that I can hardly tell it without laughing,' said Bregman. 'But it's true. Nightmare! Nightmare!' The scene takes some imagining. Bregman was conducting the 35-piece orchestra through the chorus of 'When You're Smiling' – and there are, as people who know something about the tune and about music will recognise, six 'empty' beats after the first recital of the title and – in this case, while Judy was out front at the exact spot from where the cattle auctions are conducted, waiting to complete the phrase. If people bought cows and bulls there, Bregman was not about to buy Judy Garland's demands at this moment after the band had been playing and she had started singing.

'She is like down the block. That's how big it is. She was like a mile away. You know how you can feel when someone's coming behind you? She says, "Cut to Rainbow."' He was expecting her to do what they had planned and rehearsed, but she decided she wanted to sing 'Over the Rainbow' while the band was playing 'When You're Smiling'.

'She is doing dialogue in between the fills. I say, "What are you talking about?" I'm looking at the band. She's saying, "Cut to Rainbow, Goddam it!" No, ma'am, I'm not going to do that. "Do it! Cut to Rainbow!" No, go back there and sing. We had time to talk. We do "When You're Smiling". And she says, "I hate your guts!" She wants to be away in five minutes. That's what it's all about.'

Looking back, you could almost see the shudder as he said: 'This is more of a nightmare than you can think of. She can't win with me, because I am not giving up in front of these 20,000 people. She knows I'm not going to let her get off. In the end, she sang the song and the applause as she walked down the stage was incredible. We did seven or eight numbers and that was OK.'

But then came the other side of what are obviously his mixed feelings. "I will tell you one thing – when I turn my face to her and she's got her legs crossed with one leg hanging over the stage, she's like a little waif. It was fabulous. She had a moment there with 20,000 people that was the first time I was ever interested in her as a performer. It was magic. When I turned, just a little spot on her . . . wow! I got chills. That was the seminal moment when I understood why the populace loved her. I was so close to her, it was insane.'

Sid was also close to her. 'He used to drop in. [Eventually, the concert] raised tons of money for Sammy's hospital. But I think she got scared. She was never in control. I think that was it. She was nervous. It was just one event in a year of working with her constantly.'

Later, they met at a party given by Dirk Bogarde. She either didn't recognise him or was deliberately trying to ignore him. 'I was telling this story to a couple of people. Judy opened the door and I said, "Hello, Judy honey, how's it going?"' She didn't know who was talking to her. 'Oh, err . . .' was as far as she got in the recognition exercise. 'Buddy?' he said, prompting her. 'Oh, yes,' she answered. 'And no one could have been closer to her than I,' added Bregman.

Her past now was constantly cropping up into her life. There was always something to remind her. It came flooding back to her in May 1964 when her sister Mary Jane – Suzie – died. They hadn't seen each other all that much and when they spoke, it had usually been when there was something to argue about. But the passing of one of the Gumm Sisters was not just very piquant, it served as yet another blow to her.

There was soon to be another even bigger change in her life. Finally, in that same year, she and Sid Luft were divorced. Sid had visitation rights to his children and, as he was to tell me, Liza was still very close to him. But Judy was very much on her own and very much in the hands of Begelman and Fields.

Before the divorce became final, her agents and Sid had arranged more concerts for her, few of which matched what she had done before. But they were all in the business of making money for themselves and creating exhaustion for Judy. She went to Australia and was a sensation in Sydney, but nothing like. as good in Melbourne (where, if anyone had bothered to do a graph of her career it would see the line so low it would have been off the page). *Time* magazine wrote of it: 'At 41, Judy Garland may have gone over the rainbow for the last time'. The consolation for her was that 'Down Under' she was accompanied by a young sometime actor called Mark Herron. They had been introduced at a Halloween party by Ray Aghayan, who later regretted doing so.

They were a distinct 'item' now with Herron accompanying her on the virtually obligatory trips to the nearest hospital ward or drying-out unit. On more than one occasion, when they had reached Hong Kong, he was convinced she had died. From Hong Kong, they had three weeks in Japan – and ended up in London, a city that was playing an ever bigger part in her life. There were more concerts at the Palladium, which her British fans were now regarding – and hoping she believed it to be so too – as her true home. The highlight was not so much her various paeans to the city, but her duets with Liza, who was looking stunning. As Chris Woodward put it: 'As usual, there was electricity in the audience.'

Ken Sefton was invited backstage. 'The press had her back against the wall, firing questions at this frail little thing. I remember saying, "Let the lady sit down". So she was put on a chair. I was introduced as the new editor of her fan club magazine. She said, "I hope you'll write something nice about me".' She needn't have worried about that. She could rely on nothing but unalloyed adoration. And it would be accompanied by a sketch by Sefton, the dress designer, featuring her as she was at that moment in a beaded trouser suit.

'I sketched her in action. She got her spectacles out of her handbag, looked at the sketch and said, "Do I really look like a Chinaman?" '

Judy was invited to the National Film Theatre on London's South Bank, which specialised in celebrity interviews, and answered questions from the audience, wearing very much the London look in a miniskirt. That was prescient of her. Carnaby Street and the Kings Road had not yet come completely into focus. She was asked about Barbra Streisand, who so often was being described as the new Garland. 'Oh,' she replied, 'Liza Minnelli? Oh, I think she's marvellous.' The audience collapsed. They knew the question had been about Streisand, and not her daughter.

It was on this trip that she managed to sign more autographs in one session than probably ever before. For on 8 November, the same day she appeared at the Palladium, she accepted an invitation and amazed the members of her British fan club when she turned up. She went to their meeting at the Great Russell Hotel in London's Russell Square – and stayed five hours. No other performer anyone can remember would have done that. The dancer Ann Miller heard about it and couldn't quite believe it. 'Nobody would stay at a fans' meeting for five hours,' she said.

It was only the year before that Judy had agreed the fan club should be formed, as enthusiastic about the idea as she had been when she received the calls from Al Poland. She was in London, so the club couldn't resist the opportunity to invite her to their meeting. Ken Sefton said that they didn't for a minute expect her to accept. 'There were seventy-five of us there. We did not expect her to come because she had the reputation for being so unreliable. Suddenly, she appeared at the door with Mark Herron, her maid and the Allen Brothers, one of whom was Peter Allen who married Liza. They all sat at the front row, passing scrapbooks to each other, which Judy looked at and said, "You've got pictures here that I've never seen." '

The entertainment that day would have left a lot to be desired, had there not been this surprise item on the 'bill'. 'We saw a very bad print of *The Harvey Girls*. She sent it up all the way through, making funny remarks – and said she wasn't very keen on that film. We had a break. We went into another room. I heard her say, "Another room! We are doing well!"'

All that delighted the membership. 'She was so funny, a funny, warm, witty woman, very intelligent on many subjects.' But it wasn't all sweetness and light from her. She pulled the film to pieces and was not beyond making comments about her fellow actors. She said of one star, 'Here comes old sour puss.' But there was nothing sour about Garland herself that day.

Sefton said he was sure that she enjoyed herself. But suddenly he thought there was a threat to that enjoyment and to that of the members. He could not have been more wrong. 'Some fool of a member, when it was all over, said, "Aren't you going to sing for us, Judy?" And we had been told in advance, don't pester her for autographs, don't take flash photos, let her have an afternoon free.' But she was pleased to oblige – to the sound of shock radiating from one member to another. 'She looked across the room where there was an upright piano and she said, "Does this thing work?" Peter Allen tried a few notes and pulled a face and she said, "Well, if you don't play for me, I won't let you marry my daughter!" The Allen Brothers harmonised while Peter played "I Wish You Love."'

The piano needed tuning and, to be fair, her voice was slightly off key. But what did it matter? Not at all to her hosts that day who couldn't believe their luck and couldn't do enough to show their appreciation. 'I Wish You Love'? To quote a Garland standard, they were returning it 'More Than You Know.' What they themselves, those members of the British Judy Garland fan club, wished her didn't need to be sung. It was etched on 75 faces.

Then, just before leaving, she sang 'Make Someone Happy'. That afternoon she made 75 people ecstatically happy. And she herself was delighted.

Brian Glanvill remembered just how delighted he was as he sat on the floor of the Woburn Suite: 'Hearing her sing without a microphone was one of the most magical memories of all.' Of course, Glanvill is more than just a fan. As he said, if he ever wrote a book about Garland himself, people said he would have to call it

'Saint Judy'. That day she was particularly saintly to her British fans and it has to be admitted they had plenty of reasons to think so.

As she left, she said: 'Thank you so much. I cannot imagine a nicer, sweeter thing than what you did today.'

'It was a magical day,' remembered Ken Sefton.

In 1965, Judy experienced what she hoped would be a really magical day in her own life. She and Herron were married in Las Vegas. 'It should never have happened,' Ray Aghayan told me. 'She was a very strong woman. She would need someone like Sid Luft as a partner. Mark was very soft, very kind and all that. He was getting the wrong end of the stick, to say the least.'

It was obvious that it wouldn't last and, indeed, it didn't. Judy was back at work and Herron was frequently with her, although she hardly noticed. Above all, she still needed to be loved, and Herron did love her – but not in the way she needed. He fulfilled none of her sexual needs.

Aghayan, still regarded today with great respect and admiration in the television and film business, spent a lot of time with her, looking after her costume requirements for a whole string of concerts. 'A lot of people did love her,' he told me behind the clouds of cigarette fumes as he chain-smoked through his take on the Judy Garland story, 'but not in the way she needed to be loved, to really belong. Her opinion was that they really liked her, wanted her because of the sound she was able to make. But it had nothing to do with her.'

When she was late for a concert, as she so frequently was, the audience would start clapping for her. 'Clap their hearts out,' as the designer put it. But she would comment: 'That audience, they haven't come in here to see me sing, they have come in here to see me fall on the floor or break my leg or see something terrible happen to me. They're sycophants, all psychos.'

Ray saw much of that himself as they went from one concert venue to another. His experience was very much like that of George Schlatter who, like Aghayan, had to battle crowds with her. As the man who was plainly Judy's favourite designer told me:

'Once it worked – even when she was an hour late – she would start kissing people, holding their hands, and all of that. I was with her in a car when we went to see Albert Finney in *Luther*. We came out of the theatre to get in her car to go and it was absolutely covered with people. There was no way you could drive. They were on the windows, on the roof, the radiator. It was the most frightening thing I had ever seen. She said the trick was to never stop, to touch them and keep walking – never stop walking. Then, you'll be OK, but the moment you stop, you're going to be torn to pieces.'

If she *were* torn, it would have played havoc with Aghayan's clothes. 'She could not be easier with choosing dresses,' he told me. 'Half the time, she didn't even see them until we fitted. She trusted me, people said how wonderful it was what I had done for her. They forgot that when I got her, she had lost a great deal of weight and she was much easier and much more comfortable to dress than she had been before. When we were on television, she rarely got fat. She first started to get fat when she went to San Francisco just to have a good time. But eventually she lost so much weight, she was like a pencil. Very sad. I am sure doctors, psychiatrists, can find reasons why. But I for one, having been there almost every day for a year and a half, can't imagine that anyone else could be able to offer what she could offer – and sit down, literally, and just automatically destroy it.'

Bob Wynn was one of the 'gang' who spent time with Judy off the set as well as on. Even today, he is mesmerised by her talent, so much so that sometimes he still talks of her in the present tense. 'She needs laughter, music, song and dance,' he told me. 'She can do a sketch better than ninety-nine per cent of comics around.'

He also loved what he called 'the earthy side of Judy'. And that was obvious one evening after the show had been locked up until the next one the following week. 'Judy, Martha Raye, Peter Lawford and a couple of others, we all went to dinner at a Mexican restaurant. I had just bought the place [where I live now] and we had an old station wagon I used to use to haul manure. This was the vehicle that all five or six of us used.'

The complications of using that car telegraph themselves in advance. Just imagine up to half a dozen highly paid celebrities travelling in a car more used to transporting the end products of cattle and other assorted farmyard stock. One night the restaurant valet brought 'this junk of a car' round for the party to drive home. He apologised for bringing the wrong vehicle. 'I'm sorry, Miss Garland,' he said, 'it's not your car they have brought.' 'Oh,' said Judy, 'it *is* my car.'

On the journey back, Judy decided that the manure was the perfect subject for discussion – and not a few laughs. Wynn was not feeling well. 'Oh, I'm sorry, Judy, this Mexican food is not doing too well with me.' At which point, the girl who sang so sweetly about what she believed was at the other end of a rainbow told him she knew precisely how to deal with his problem. 'The trouble with you, young man, is that you don't know how to fart.'

'And then Judy and Martha Raye proceeded to teach me to fart, passing one so that I could blame it on you, shaking a wet one down my pant leg. It would go on and on.'

Many others, like George Schlatter, have talked about her propensity for gas-passing exercises. It is entirely possible that this slightly disreputable behaviour, all those years later, was a reaction to the image of the goody-goody girl in the gingham dress into which Louis B. Mayer – to say nothing of her own mother – had forced her.

So there were none of those 'mixed feelings' moments for Wynn. Ray Aghayan, on the other hand, was with her for times that he cherished and for others he wished he had never experienced. Among them were the moments when he really did, as he had said, see her 'literally and just automatically' ruining herself.

'Yes, I saw it happen, right in front of me,' he said. But there were still the curry and shepherd's pie times. 'We used to sit at the bar. She really shouldn't have drunk at all.' So what he used to do – until she caught on – was give her a Tom Collins that wasn't. 'It would be all bubbly water and I let a tiny bit of liquor float on top. Well, she figured that out in about six or eight weeks. She would say, "What's this? Do you think I don't know what you're all doing?" She would sit there behind the bar at like midnight and entertain you till five in the morning. She would tell all the stories about this picture, about that picture, how it was working for Busby Berkeley, how she got fired, which, according to her, was always unnecessary.'

When it wasn't 'wonderful', it was 'hard'. 'She would cancel concerts. Those years of my life, if I hadn't been very young, which I was at the time – I was thirty – I don't think any normal four-square grown person would have put themselves through it. I thought she was wonderful. You couldn't help but think she was wonderful. She was disturbed. Period. But when she opened her mouth to sing, you didn't have to think about that.'

But there were times when it was hard to actually think at all about the good side of life with Judy. 'What became very difficult was that I was sharing a house with my assistant half the time, but often at four o'clock in the morning, it was like the end of the world. She was saying if I didn't get there, she would be dead in half an hour. That was the gist of it. She had taken sleeping tablets. I would have to get in my car and go all the way to Brentwood. All the doors were open. I would go to her bedroom. And there she was, lying in bed, asleep, comfortably. That was hard after a few times. Then what I would do would be to go into the kitchen, make a cup of tea and wait till the maid came. That went on. She did that to quite a lot of people on the show. I'm an idiot, but most of them were smart and just changed their phone numbers. They were mostly married and their wives weren't happy about it. I never [changed my number]. I was at the bottom of the list, the last one to be called.'

So many people watched that process that it could easily be used as a case study for budding analysts – and probably is.

CHAPTER FIFTEEN

They Saw It Coming

T he second half of the 1960s were probably the worst years of Judy Garland's life. Again it was a roller coaster. Again she was alternately happy and disastrously sad. Some clever people would diagnose this as typically manic-depressive, except in her case what is now known as a bi-polar disorder was brought on by her constant pressing of a self-destruct button – a button that had been in her hands ever since Louis B. Mayer decided the only way she could work would be with the help of pills. Strengthen those pills to an unimaginable degree and wash them all down with sweet white wine and you have Judy Garland circa 1965.

If this decade really was the swinging sixties, then so much of Judy's life was swinging the wrong way. Her marriage to Mark Herron was truly wrong from the start, just as Ray Aghayan had told me he knew it would be. From 1966 on, barely a year after they married, they were rarely seen in each other's company and when Judy had troubles, she did the unimaginable thing and called on Sid Luft to come back into her life – probably not sexually – to help sort matters out.

And yet she continued to work and, for much of the time, to succeed. In that year of 1966, she twice starred on the *Hollywood Palace* TV series. They were produced by Bill Harbach, son of the eminent lyricist and librettist Otto (*Desert Song*) Harbach. 'She was an absolute powerhouse,' he told me. 'To me, the unbelievable personality and power in her voice is still striking. She was unique. There was no one who could deliver a song like [she did].'

Roger Edens worked with her on the same show, adapting the

famous 'Judy at the Palace' routine. But, no matter how good she was, the powerhouse sometimes seemed to fuse. 'She started drinking,' Harbach told me. 'I asked her what number she wanted to open the show. She said the then new Burt Bacharach and Hal David song, "What the World Needs Now". But she really didn't do it so well. It was a jazz waltz. She got by, but wasn't happy with it.'

But even in that down moment, she was conscious that something had to be done to keep her reputation alive.

'When the show was done, the night watchman came by around midnight. She was having a fun time in her dressing room with friends. He heard a door slam and then saw she had gone into the empty theatre. He could still hear people laughing. She went out alone and grabbed the light in this empty theatre [the one that is always kept burning as both a security measure and a sign that a theatre must never be allowed to go 'dark'] and sang "What the World Needs Now" to herself. She knew she hadn't done it right and it bugged her through the night at her party. And this man saw her alone in this empty theatre, holding on to this huge light stand, singing a capella. That's a scene in a movie to me.'

For Edens, that confirmed that 'nobody got past her either on stage or in the movies'.

If Judy didn't think she did well enough with a single song, it was nothing in comparison with other disappointments that were on the way – concerning her stage and her film careers and, much more significantly, her private life.

Professionally, there was a dreadful concert appearance with Tony Bennett at the Baltimore Civic Centre. Bennett, whom Judy admired – it was very much a mutual admiration society – did a wonderful first house. But when Judy went on in the second, she didn't. In fact, had the second half been an audition for an amateur dramatic and choral society show, she would have failed. No producer would even have gone to the trouble of saying, 'Don't call us, we'll call you.' Nobody was going to make any calls after a show in which she could barely stand up unaided and had no voice.

That sort of thing, even more than all that had gone on before, disturbed those for whom she represented so much. Al Poland, the schoolboy who founded her first fan club and told Judy he loved her when he was 14 years old, thought he could achieve his lifelong ambition and produce a show starring Judy. It was 1967 and he had just taken a 90-day option on producing *The Threepenny Opera*, which he thought would be right up Judy's stretch of Broadway. Lotte Lenya had helped him get that option. She was the widow of Kurt Weill, the creator of the *Opera*, and had starred in its early productions (both Louis Armstrong and Bobby Darin added her name to their lyrics of the show's best-known 'aria' 'Mack the Knife'). She was a great fan and was particularly keen to have Judy play in her own role.

Nobody could have been more keen than Poland himself. It would be the fulfilment of a dream. 'It was my idea to have Judy play Jennie in a tour of the opera. And I would give her the "Mack the Knife" song and "You Can't Let a Man Walk Over You."'

The trouble was he couldn't find Judy anywhere. But she turned up the same night that he was at Jilly's, the New York night-spot that was Frank Sinatra's favourite hideout. 'She came in with Tom Green, who was to produce her upcoming Palace engagement, and with Buddy Cole and Sid. She said, "Come and sit with us." So I sat with them and I [at that moment] determined it would not work. She was not in good health at the time. She was somewhat incoherent. I just felt I would be in a relationship with her that I did not want.' It was not to be the last disappointment he experienced with his idol.

George Schlatter also had something of a disappointment at that same venue. 'I was in New York, she was in New York,' he recalled for me. 'At about one o'clock in the morning I got a call from her and she said, "You've got to come over to Jilly's." I said, "Judy, it's one o'clock." She said, "You've got to come." She'd lean on you. You couldn't say no to her.'

Judy was living on New York time. Californians tend to go to bed at night – unless they were called Judy Garland. 'I get out of bed and go over to Jilly's and there's a guy playing the piano. She sat there, threatening, drinking Liebfraumilch. She said, "Well, what do you think of the piano player?" I said, "Judy, you can screw him. But don't let him play for you." She said, "They were right to fire you. You're no good. With your explosions!" I went home.'

Whether she did 'screw' the piano player isn't on record, but the notion fits in with her reputation in that regard. As Schlatter said of the pianist: 'He spent time with her and he was willing to stay up all night.' Mark Herron no longer had that privilege in any form. Later, in 1967, they were finally divorced.

Judy still thought about going back to the movies. But one that she wanted dearly first looked as if it were really going to happen, then became the film that never was. She had become very friendly with the author Jacqueline Susann, whose book *The Valley of the Dolls* was number-one in the current bestseller list. Susann had sold the book to Twentieth Century Fox and told them she had the ideal actress to play the lead part of a woman singer, down on her luck, addicted to pills that were ruining her career – Judy Garland. Liza advised her not to take the part if it were offered. People would see it as too autobiographical. But Judy was insistent. It was too good an opportunity to miss. And she saw it as a chance to get back into movie stardom, not with comparatively small films like *A Child Is Waiting* or *I Could Go on Singing*, but with a really big movie based on a book everybody was talking about. Besides, she needed the money. Desperately. Sid had admitted that he had gambled the money that should have gone to the Internal Revenue Service.

Darryl Zanuck, the last of the old-time Hollywood moguls, thought it was a great idea. The publicity value alone would be worth the investment. Scripts were written and approved. Judy was fitted for costumes and her make-up decided upon. For a week, she came to the studio but when the time arrived for her to go on the set, she had to be pushed on. She couldn't remember her lines. Sid, still playing his joint role of fairy godfather and Svengali, was called in and couldn't get much sense out of her – other than to beg Zanuck to forgive her for her problems. She was suffering from a virus, he said (on her instructions). She was actually drugged out of her mind. The next day, despite Sid's appeals and Jacqueline Susann taking up her case for her, Judy Garland was once more fired from a movie. When she tried to find a way of undoing the firing, nobody would take her calls.

Sid, and other people who cared about her, tried to tell Judy that she would get over this just as she had all her other problems. Besides, surely there was the pleasure she must feel in the fact that Liza was becoming a star on her own account and had just married Peter Allen? Judy was happier with the latter situation than with the former. She was so insecure that she wanted to be the only star in the family.

The fact that she opened again at the Palace on Broadway in July 1967 – to ecstatic reviews and audiences – proved she really was still a star. The show ran for four weeks and she followed it with the customary tour.

In 1968, she was back in New York at Madison Square Garden, a place more used to boxing matches than entertainment Judy Garland style. She needed to get near her audience, which wouldn't have been easy in that giant auditorium. So runways were installed from the stage into the audience, on to which she could prance and sing – just as Al Jolson had done 40 years before.

This was now called the Felt Forum – the president of 'The Garden', Irving Mitchell Felt, thought it was a just reward for all the money he had put into the place. As for Judy – and those so devoted fans – her appearance there was no reward at all. The roller coaster was travelling downwards. Very fast.

Al Poland was there on opening night. 'I left at intermission,' he told me. 'She had not rehearsed and she had chorus boys on the stage with her. I had a friend who was one of those chorus boys in the show and he told me she had not come in for rehearsal in the afternoon. So the chorus boys were dancing and she collided with them – because she did not know the staging. She was not in good voice and people were rushing the stage with teddy bears. I just did not find that of the level that you had come to expect from Judy Garland.' And that from a man who idolised her and who was so thrilled when he saw her at the last night of the Palace show the year before. He still maintains that the Carnegie Hall performance allowed him 'the greatest night I had ever spent in the theatre'.

It wasn't like that at the Felt Forum. 'By that time, the fans had reached a fanatical level. They were either hoping for a triumph for her or for her to fall on her face. They would have been happy with either.'

Judy was not oblivious to this or to the fact that falling on her face seemed the more likely outcome. 'She went back on to the stage and said, "I'm in trouble. But I've been in trouble *all my life*."' She was raising her voice at this part of the statement. Said Poland: 'I found it jarring and embarrassing that a bunch of little men rushed to the stage and presented her with teddy bears. I was just sickened and left.'

And yet, as almost always, most of the audience was still with her. Plainly, not everybody was so sickened. The 'little men' with the teddy bears were not – and not all the chorus boys were either. There was a sense of devotion to her with which it was impossible to argue. That was particularly so with her musicians. The percussionist Howard Hirsch is still so devoted to her that once a year he goes to visit her grave and plays his bongo drums to her. He was in the orchestra with her for 14 years 'and it was definitely love at first sight', he told me. 'There are two kinds of people, good and bad and she knew who was good and who was bad. She depended on how my honesty gave her the spirit to trust in somebody, because there were so many people who had stolen from her, had hurt her, had, business-wise, beaten her up. It was the tragedy of so many people who had done that, making a travesty of it. That's why I gave my life to her.'

On one occasion he thought Judy was about to lose her life. 'She was holding on to the curtain. Instead of letting the curtain go, the stage hands started lifting it into the air and she was holding on to it so tight that she was beginning to rise into the air four or five feet.' Understandably, he doesn't see the funny side of this, but of all the Garland stage adventures, this totally unreported event must have been something to see. 'Somebody finally said, "Stop raising the curtain. Go the other way." Finally, she got down and she said, "Here I am," and people started applauding her. Trumpets played the overture, "Rainbow". I became her musical support. That was the most important part.'

In fact, he says that whenever he plays the bongos, particularly with 'Come Rain or Shine', he hears her singing. 'Every number is made of rhythm, melody, form and harmony. I gave her rhythm. She always showed up for rehearsals. I gave her that injection of soul. She blew me a kiss.'

Kisses didn't cure the anxieties of her oldest and dearest friends. Paul Rabwin recalled an evening that is as engraved on his soul as it had been on those of his parents. It happened when his mother, Marcella, who was very active in local politics in Beverly Hills, was paid a particularly significant tribute. She and the local mayor were guests of honour at a dinner called 'The Top Two'. And to celebrate the occasion, the other people at the tables at this typically classy event − the men in evening dress, the women in their finest gowns and jewels − were to be entertained by two of the top entertainers living in their area − Rudy Vallee and Judy Garland.

It was a somewhat embarrassing experience, to say the least. 'Rudy Vallee was now old, but still a big star [even though Al Jolson had once said, "Rudy Vallee? Where's that?"] He lived in Beverly Hills and they had named a street after him. Judy Garland came as a personal favour to my mother and they invited her to entertain, too.' Unfortunately, they didn't know what that would involve. It was, as Paul Rabwin told me, 'one of those sad−happy things'.

It was a wonderful dinner. Judy was sitting with her dear friends the Rabwins and a young man. She was nervous. It had been some time since she had last performed on an occasion like that. She was given the honour of going on last, which Rudy Vallee might or might not have appreciated. What happened next, if one is unkind about the situation, could have been considered a kind of professional sabotage on the older man's part. 'He was an old vaudevillian and he was telling some old jokes, doing a little soft

237

shoe, singing a few songs – but not very well. And he was not getting off.'

Judy was not happy. After listening to the obvious torture of Vallee's performance that seemed never to finish, she politely excused herself and made for the ladies' room. When she came back, Vallee was still on and she was still unhappy – actually, she was getting less and less happy by the minute. She excused herself again, got up and returned to the ladies' room.

This time, she was gone for about ten minutes. Then it happened: 'Finally, Vallee got off and they went looking for Judy. They found her and told her it was time to go on. It was not a good moment. My mother told me she had befriended Jack Daniels for the last twenty minutes.' Presumably, the smart Beverly Hills venue was out of Liebfraumilch. 'She was basically plastered.' And it was while plastered that she wobbled on to the stage.

'She came on the stage for the big event and absolutely gave one of the worst performances of her career. She was practically falling off the stage and couldn't sing a note in tune. People said things to her from the audience. She swore back to them, having some verbal heckling going back and forwards. My mother had to make the "finger across the throat" symbol. People were heckling her with insults and she was just hurling them back.'

It was like a game of tennis, each 'player' managing a constant volley. 'When my mother made the cut sign, Judy knew she was just cooked,' said Rabwin. 'She got it and my mother went and brought her back to the table. The place was silent. It was just mortifying. And then someone yelled, "Sing Rainbow". That was all. Just "Sing Rainbow".

'My mother turned to Judy, just looked at her. And there, this drunken, pathetic woman who had just been booed off the stage, started to sing "Somewhere Over the Rainbow". It was perfect. It was fabulous and the room erupted in cheers I had never heard before. It was just an amazing turnaround. It hit to her emotional heart. It was symbolic of the great paradox of Judy Garland. A great symbol of the turmoil that was going on inside her.'

It did seem to sum up her whole life. Any movie of Judy

Garland's life would have to include that scene. Although, as Rabwin commented: 'It was *A Star Is Born* on steroids. Almost like a scene from that film – except it would have been laughed off the screen.'

CHAPTER SIXTEEN

The Wrong Side of the Rainbow

Now there was little that was going well. Judy began OK when her show opened at the Garden State Arts Center in New Jersey. But she got worse and worse on the next three evenings and finally, on the fifth, collapsed on stage.

In December 1968, she and a young man flew to London. Judy was to star at the Talk of the Town theatre restaurant, formerly known as the Hippodrome. The talk of even her most loyal friends in that town was that Judy flopped – badly.

Ken Sefton, among the most devoted of followers, was there on both the first and last nights of her Talk of the Town appearance. He was sadly disappointed. 'She clearly wasn't well. She was also broke and was glad to get the engagement.'

As Sefton walked into the restaurant on 30 December he came across the proprietor of the establishment, the showman Bernard Delfont. 'Thank you for bringing Judy over,' he told him. The response he received was surprising, none of the usual bravado. 'I hope it's going to be all right,' the bouffant-haired impresario replied. He knew something that had been hopefully hidden from the public. 'We're not expecting her to be on top form, I'm afraid.'

As Sefton remembers it, the first night was not *so* terrible. 'It wasn't that bad,' he told me. 'She was killing time and went over to a girl at a table and asked, "How old are you, my dear?" She said she was eighteen. Judy replied, "Nobody is eighteen any more."' Certainly, Judy wasn't, either mentally or physically. She was all of 46.

After the first couple of numbers she invited the female impersonator Danny La Rue to join her from the audience on to the stage. She needed his help, explained Sefton, 'because she didn't have the voice any more'.

The four-week season was interrupted a couple of times because of Judy's claim that she had laryngitis, which she probably did – accompanied by the effects of everything else she was still taking. As Sefton noted, knowingly, 'Anyone can have laryngitis, but not Judy.' Even so, there was still someone in the audience to call out 'Thank you, Judy'.

But there were also people to boo. One night, a rowdy group on a table close to the stage decided to dispose of the rolls that remained on the cloth in front of them by throwing them at Judy. She cried off the show for the next three nights. That sort of thing had never happened in Las Vegas. Could this really be a reaction to the woman who had driven audiences crazy at Carnegie Hall, the Palace and her 'home' barely a mile away, the Palladium?

Yet, despite it all, she appeared to get over it. The roller coaster might just have gone into an uphill mode. By the way she looked at Mickey Deans, a piano-player-cum-singer who ran a discotheque, the young man who was accompanying her everywhere she went like a pet dog, it seemed that she was content. She said: 'This is it. For the first time in my life, I am really happy. Finally, I am loved.'

There were not many people who believed that.

On 9 January 1969, they were married at a London Catholic church. Two months later, there was a civil ceremony at the Chelsea Register Office, while outside crowds were singing the Beatles hit 'Hey Jude'. It was no secret that the only man who could control her life, to really act as a husband, to say nothing of being father of her children, was Sid, who was always lurking in the shadows. But it was Deans who was with her when she appeared for the second time on the television show *Sunday Night at the London Palladium*.

The show on 19 January 1969 delighted her British fans. They would have been thrilled by whatever she did, but she deserved their cheers. She was their heroine who stepped into the breach when Lena Horne, the originally billed star, was ill. It was not easy. Coaxing her on to the wide Palladium stage resembled getting a baby in a high chair to take another spoonful of mush. She was introduced by the compere Jimmy Tarbuck, who had – in this live TV show – to say her name two or three times with no reaction forthcoming, and then, finally, to go to the wings and bring her out. There was tumultuous applause from the audience, not all members of which realised it was for real and not part of the act. By the time she started singing 'I Belong to London', none of that mattered.

As Chris Woodward told me: 'She was very nervous and was not as good as in previous years. But she had brought everything in her talent.'

When she said that she wasn't able to sing at one stage, someone called out from the stalls: 'Just be there, Judy.'

If only she had been like that at the Talk of the Town. It was another part of the Garland paradox.

It would be so nice to think that Judy had at last found contentment and was all set for living happily ever after with Mickey Deans. But, to no one's surprise, it didn't happen. In fact, it couldn't happen. There was to be no 'ever after'. And if there were few of the big rows and disturbances that had characterised her past four marriages, it was simply because there just wasn't enough time to have them.

The threatening clouds were obvious from the beginning. Mickey Deans scraped together enough money to pay for a celebration of their nuptials at the fashionable Quaglino's restaurant and sent invitations to other American stars like Bette Davis and Ginger Rogers, who were in London at the same time. Sir John Gielgud was sent one, too. None of them either acknowledged the invitations or turned up. There were three possible explanations for this: the cards failed to arrive; people did not want to be seen in the company of Deans, whom they considered to be beneath both the bride and themselves; or, most likely, Judy was a potential embarrassment and they were frightened of being part of what they believed would be the well-publicised inevitable scene.

The couple tried to laugh it off and caught a plane to Paris, spending money they did not have. 'Aren't I entitled to a honeymoon?' Judy asked a reporter, rhetorically.

Mr and Mrs Deans (an arrangement of names that Judy Garland would never have tolerated) stayed newlyweds and convinced people around them that they were as lovey-dovey as newspaper pictures seemed to show. Sharing a bill with Johnny Ray, a singer who sold a million records doing little more than crying into the microphone (his two big hits were 'Cry' and 'The Little White Cloud That Cried'), they took off for a tour of Sweden and then Denmark. If anyone had analysed the decision to go there, they would have been forced to one conclusion — she still desperately needed the money. Going to Sweden was like going back to the Town and Country Club in Brooklyn.

After a tour not notable for anything over-tragic — which was as much of a relief as anyone close to her could muster, although one show was called off — the couple flew to New York and then decided to go back to London. There was talk of more work for Judy there and she was now beginning to believe her song, 'I Belong To London'.

They took an apartment in Cadogan Square after their arrival in the capital on 17 June. Five days later, at ten o'clock on the Sunday morning, Mickey Deans knocked on the door of the bathroom. Judy had been in there, it seemed, for hours. There was no answer. She didn't call out to him. She wasn't singing about 'The Man That Got Away' in the shower. Finally, he forced his way into the room and found what he had always been dreading. Judy was lying there — dead.

It was New York on 27 June 1969, just 17 days after her 47th birthday, almost 45 years since she first appeared on a stage and showed people she could sing, dance and do all the other things that Judy Garland did. The service at the Frank E. Campbell funeral home, leading out on the traffic-clogged East 81st Street, was in its way the most successful Garland show for years. It was crowded with all her celebrity friends who had always come to her performances, until it became just too hard an experience. The ones who had failed to show up for her wedding party made sure they were seen to be there on this day.

They crowded into the pews as the white coffin – remember, this had to be to MGM specifications – was brought in and they wept as they wondered about so much that had filled a still-young life. To some, it was genuinely painful. Liza, Lorna and Joey, to say nothing of Sid, were clearly heartbroken. Nobody ever really knew what Mike Deans felt. Some recalled her childhood – like Mickey Rooney, who threw himself on to the casket and couldn't contain his weeping.

Howard Hirsch, Judy's favourite percussionist, told me: 'About halfway through the funeral, suddenly down the aisle came Mickey Rooney, yelling and shouting. He spread out his whole body on the casket and cried. I reached out and tried to touch the casket from my seat, but he was on top of it, crying for five or six minutes. It was quite an amazing spiritual outlet for him.'

Not everyone was so moved. Said Hirsch, 'I looked around to see who was here. A lot I couldn't see. Next to me was Lauren Bacall. Not one tear came out of her. Not one. I myself was like a bathtub.'

The casket remained in a vault for weeks. No one could find the money for a cemetery plot.

Since then, her friends have tried to analyse what made Judy Garland so special. Bob Wynn, still speaking about her in the present tense, told me: 'I think she's living better today than ever. I just went to a fan club meeting and she was alive and well at that meeting. The lady is a performer beyond belief. When she gets out there, whether it's the "Battle Hymn of the Republic" or "Somewhere Over the Rainbow", she gives 120 per cent. Whatever we had to do to get her on stage, it was worth it.'

George Schlatter certainly thought so. 'She went in like a

battalion of Green Berets,' he told me, wistfully remembering not just an important time in his own life, but the woman who was behind it.

The past caught up with her in so many ways. They mourned her in Grand Rapids, too, remembering the little girl who would still come out top of any poll to decide the identity of the town's favourite child. Lilah Crowe, back at the local museum, allowed herself to wonder what it would have been like had Frances Ethel Gumm not discovered show business. 'What would have been her life had she stayed here? Would she have been a grandmother? Would she have had kids raised in our schools? You must look and say "what if?" What if she had never been more than a member of a trio? And who knows how many other budding Judy Garlands there might have been?'

The broadcaster Joe Franklin put it like this to me: 'It was unbelievable and she will not be forgotten. She is getting more popular as the years go on. An exciting lady. There are so many women who do tributes to Judy, but none come near to her vocal prowess. She lives on in so many memories.'

Above all, there are the fans who remember precisely where they were when they heard of the death of 'Saint Judy'.

Brian Glanvill, a man as full of feelings as he is of memories, had tears in his eyes as he recalled weeping when he heard the news on the radio, while he was staying with friends at the English resort, Shoreham-by-Sea. He recalled the bouquet that never reached her and an opportunity that had never come. 'A friend of mine had thought I would be good for her and he spoke to Judy about it. She told him: "Tell Brian when I get back from New York to give me a phone call to see what we can do." I did make the call and it was agreed that I would see her the following week. But she died on the Sunday. Possibly, nothing would have come of it, but she knew I would give my life for her, followed her to the ends of the earth. This would have been my chance to prove it, but it never came true.'

Margaret Whiting, remembering her girl-to-girl chats in Ira Gershwin's bathroom, summed it all up: 'I can see why Judy has been compared with Al Jolson. They both had the greatest magic when they performed on the stage. He had a great magic, but she ran rings about him. Judy was an even greater performer. When people saw her, she was in their hearts. They will think about her till they die. She was immortal.'

Immortal enough for the American Film Institute to name her as one of the ten greatest female stars in the history of the cinema.

So with her death the jury came back and have now delivered for me their verdict in this trial. The unanimous decision was that she was indeed guilty of being one of the greatest entertainers of the 20th century. She was further pronounced guilty on two counts: 1) She achieved so much. 2) But she threw it all away.

And yet the questions remain. What was the truth of it all? Why did she die so young? Was she so worried about her career that she couldn't carry on living? Was money at the root of it? After all, as Bob Wynn said, 'She was like Sammy Davis Jr. They both made five dollars and spent ten.' Certainly, death came as the result of an overdose. But had it been taken deliberately? Was this another of those cries for help? Or had, this time, she just made too good a job of that crying? Officially, this was an accident. But no one has ever truly found the answer.

It's as much of a mystery as discovering exactly what *was* lying over that rainbow.

Index